# *The Bedside* 'GUARDIAN' 31

A selection from The 'Guardian' 1981–82

*Edited by*

W. L. WEBB

*With an introduction by*

Roy Hattersley

*Cartoons by Gibbard and Bryan McAllister*

COLLINS
St James's Place, London
1982

William Collins Sons & Co Ltd
London  Glasgow  Sydney  Auckland
Toronto  Johannesburg


British Library Cataloguing in Publication Data

The Bedside Guardian—31
1. English essays—Periodicals
082'.05    P6142

ISBN 0 00 216497/3


First published 1981 © Guardian Newspapers Ltd. 1982

Photoset in Imprint
Made and Printed in Great Britain by
William Collins Sons & Co Ltd Glasgow

# Introduction

I have been in awe of the *Guardian* for as long as I can remember. During my childhood it was delivered every morning by Ron Starling – a professional footballer turned jobbing newsagent who had, in his sporting prime, led the victorious Sheffield Wednesday team to Wembley. Each weekday I was humbled by the thought that I was holding in my hand a newspaper that had been handled by a man who once held the F.A. Cup aloft. Others may have chosen the *Guardian* for more intellectual reasons. But I doubt if their cerebral bonds are any tighter than those which Ron Starling tied round me.

Despite my passion for politics, I suspect that in those days I read little more than Neville Cardus. I certainly remember an infuriating afternoon in the second form of the Sheffield City Grammar School when we were told of the existence of the then still unashamedly northern institution, as if the words *Manchester Guardian* were wholly foreign to us. Our teacher (Mrs Potter by name) praised a cricket correspondent who was 'also a real writer'. The clear implication was that cricket enthusiasts like me might with encouragement break out of the chrysalis and fly away as music critics.

It was neither the flimsy logic nor the patronising approach to the greatest of games that provoked my undisguised wrath. The real offence was the assumption that I needed to be told about the *Manchester Guardian*. It was my paper. And with or without its provincial prefix, it has been my paper ever since.

That does not mean that I always approve of – even agree with – all that is printed on its pages. In their different, but essentially complementary ways, Jill Tweedie and Polly Toynbee infuriate me more than any other contemporary journalist – with the possible exception of Peter Jenkins. But the *Guardian* has never been one of those papers that defends its circulation by feeding its readers' established prejudices. The *Guardian*'s strength is that it is invariably controversial and almost always well written. Tweedie, Toynbee and Jenkins are all an easy read but a hard think. It is the combination of elegance and controversy which makes it worth buying. For most of Fleet Street's dailies (with the *Mirror*, since it has Keith Waterhouse, being the obvious exception) a collection of the year's best contributions would only be as interesting as the events which they describe. The *Guardian*'s pieces stand on their own merits. This anthology is filled with good journalism which is also good writing.

Of course the *Guardian* is not quite so daringly controversial as the television advertisements make out. It occupies the political spectrum from a position barely left of centre to a point where revolutionary socialists begin to infiltrate the Labour Party. And within that broad segment of political thought it often grievously neglects the instinctive working-class radicalism of the council estates and suburban saloon bars. It is, in fact, attracted to the new and the fashionable in a way which must disturb the peace of C. P. Scott.

One of its most distinguished contributors, Michael White, reported the outcome of a vote at an SDP Conference as 'Sports Page 146: Women's Page 89'. And although Feliks Topolski's painting of Tony Benn is not to hang in the National Portrait Gallery, the picture editor of the *Guardian* has done his best to redress the balance and counteract the bias. Tony Benn, like the SDP, is essentially a middle-class institution. And inevitably the *Guardian* leans, bends or wobbles in their direction. But that is the price one pays for Terry Coleman, James Cameron and Nancy Banks-Smith. Incurably prejudiced though I am, I pay the price willingly.

I would pay it for the editorials alone – both the thunderous calls to principle that sometimes reverberate all the way across the top of the page, and the little laughing lampoons that at first seem to be added on as a merry afterthought – but both turn out, on reflection, to be making a point as serious as anything included in the leaders of more ponderous papers.

Indeed it is in the leaders, as this anthology demonstrates, that the *Guardian* is at its pure distilled best. They are iconoclastic as well as irreverent (as *Guardian* readers know, the two things are not the same) but they rarely fail to make a serious point. The *Guardian* (not least because of the comments of Peter Jenkins, one of whose columns on this subject appears in this collection) was the one paper to keep its head during the Falklands crisis. Day after day, the leader writers got it right and wrote it well.

As is proper to a radical paper, the *Guardian* has on its staff one truly sentimental correspondent. His name is Frank Keating. If Mr Keating has a fault it is his inability to look at the sportsmen about whom he writes through anything except rose-tinted lenses. This error is not mirrored by Ian Aitken, Michael White, Colin Brown or Julia Langdon in their reports of politics and parliament. But it is not only envy which makes me feel that cricketers, in particular, are lucky that they are written about by gentle Frank. Cricket was created for good writing, and almost miraculously, the *Guardian* has been able to produce a cricket writer of outstanding quality throughout the last fifty years.

I do not pretend that Keating is either Arlott or Cardus. Or that Peter Preston is C. P. Scott, or that the cool approach to the war in the South Atlantic stands comparison with the all-out opposition to the invasion of Suez. In fact, I have no way of judging whether today's *Guardian* is better or worse than the paper to which Mrs Potter thought she was introducing me back in 1948. But it retains its freedom of spirit, its ability to laugh at itself as it laughs at others, and the clear conviction that the best story in the world ought to be written in a way that makes the words a pleasure to read as well as the facts exciting to learn. Those are the qualities that make *Guardian* articles worth reading a year after they are published. I have no doubt that I shall still be turning to this anthology with pleasure twenty years on.

# Once smitten, twice smote

It is now officially denied that the Prime Minister spat blood after the Falklands Service on Monday. In any case it had been assumed that Mr Denis Thatcher, if he used the phrase at all, was speaking figuratively. There are fairly strong episodes in the Bible, but no reference to blood spitting as a sign of rejoicing in victory. All the same, the church authorities did let pass a number of texts which would have been more appropriate to the occasion, for as the Book of Exodus says, 'The Lord is a man of war; thy right hand, O Lord, hath dashed in pieces the enemy.' And in the Book of Proverbs 'she hath cast down many wounded; yea, many strong men have been slain by her.' If the link with the State is to survive, the Prime Minister of the day is at least entitled to expect the Church of England to put on a performance to her liking.

For example, it is well known that Britain smote Argentina, and the Old Testament is full of references to enemies being smitten. Why, we ask with the Prime Minister, could not some of them have been used? 'And I contended with them, and cursed them, and smote certain of them, and plucked off their hair, and made them swear' (Nehemiah 13:25); or 'And he smote his enemies in the hinder parts: he put them to a perpetual reproach' (Ps. 78); or 'Hath he smitten him, as he smote those that smote him? Or is he slain according to the slaughter of them that were slain by him?' (Isaiah 27:7); or even 'And it came to pass that night that the angel of the Lord went out and smote in the camp of the Assyrians an hundred four-score and five thousand, and when they arose early in the morning behold, they were all dead corpses' (2 Kings 19:35). (In a more truly ecumenical service on the subject of war the passage could have been spoken by the Ayatollah Khomeini. The Assyrians, after all, were Iraqis.) 'I have wounded them that they were not able to rise: they are fallen under my feet. Thou hast given me the necks of mine enemies; that I might destroy them that hate me. They cried, but there was not to save them: even unto the Lord, but he answered them not. It is God that avengeth me, and subdueth the people under me. He delivereth me from mine enemies.' Surely Psalm 18 is more stirring stuff for such an occasion than Crimond?

Most of all, the occasion called for a special prayer, and its omission was inexcusable. O God, who hast smitten the Argy in the hinder parts and sent him packing to Comodoro Rivadavia, grant that the Falkland Islands shall have a closer constitutional link with the United Kingdom. Diversify the economy, O Lord, and lengthen the runway, that those things shall not again come to pass for which we await the results of Lord Franks's inquiry. Amen.

*28 July 1982*                                                          **Leader**


# The Divine Grace look

Reuben, fourteen-year-old son of the well-known London fashion designer, Marisa Martin, has left behind his 'almost punk' phase. Last night she helped him don frilly clothes and make-up to go to a pop concert. Next season she expects him to opt for a double-breasted suit, spats, and silver-headed cane—'the Brideshead look'. She herself plans to introduce silk and lace into her next collection of women's late day and evening wear. *Menswear Magazine* has just defined the look for High Street retailers.

'It's an indulgent, extravagant look – wider ties, cravats and bow ties. So opt for bold patterns for accessories – stripes, polka dots, Panama felt hats, braces and arm-bands for shirts.' *Harpers and Queens* has advised its readers to 'make a bid for decadence' by reverting to the more affluent styles of the twenties and thirties.

*Brideshead Revisited,* British television's *Gone with the Wind*, ended its fourteen-hour run on Tuesday night – leaving nine to ten million viewers with withdrawal symptoms and many marketing people with a surprised satisfaction that

Evelyn Waugh's study of 'the operation of Divine Grace' had started to ring the cash registers of the nostalgia industry.

Granada's serialisation never quite made the television top ten. But trade journals reported empty restaurants and theatres on Tuesday evenings. At the more fervent end of the market, an 'enormously successful' Brideshead exhibition at the National Theatre is repeatedly having to replace big photos of the two stars, Jeremy Irons and Anthony Andrews, stolen by teenage girls.

International sales have made it possible for British addicts to see the last two episodes again if they fly to Canada at once, and to watch the whole series again if they are in the United States from 18 January. The programme has been sold to Finland, Norway, Jordan, and Israel. Sales to Italy and other countries are being negotiated and Chinese television has asked to see a videotape.

An inaccurate newspaper report that Granada's publicity brochure was going on public sale brought the company thousands of letters and hundreds of cheques. The paperback of the novel has sold 2000,000 copies after heading the best-seller list for six weeks. The album of Geoffrey Burgon's stately music has sold 75,000 copies and is fiftieth in the hit parade. The single is sixty-fourth, and climbing.

'It is very surprising that music of this style and quality should sell so well,' said the publishers, Chrysalis Records, yesterday. 'We are more than pleased.'

The cassette industry is so impressed that it has called in Sir John Gielgud, who played Charles Ryder's father on television, to record an abridged version of the novel.

The paperback sales have raised hopes among publishers of a permanent surge in sales of Waugh's novels. The only precedent is the BBC serialisation of John Galsworthy's *Forsyte Saga* in the 1960s. That sold a million paperback copies of the novel and rescued Galsworthy from the risk of going out of print. Even now, the saga remains 'a good, steady seller in hardback', its publishers, Heinemann, said yesterday.

The Catholic Inquiry Office has noticed a 'good response' to its newspaper advertisements and church contact cards during the series. The Church is likely to mount a special re-cruitment campaign, linked with a repeat showing which Granada plans at a date yet to be decided.

'The trouble is that we didn't know in advance that it was going to be any good,' said the inquiry office.

'We have to be fairly sure in advance. If we had planned a campaign around the Borgias, for example, it would have been disastrous.'

Irony is seen in the success of a deeply Catholic story whose drama is based on 'pre-Vatican II' theology. A Catholic official said that if the heroine, Julia Mottram, had married the hero, divorced Charles Ryder, today, she would not necessarily have needed to fear mortal sin.

'There is more awareness of human problems today, more compassion and a more mature pastoral attitude,' the official said. 'Julia would not feel cast out. She would be told that the mercy of God can transcend Church law.'

One man has chosen to remain outside the stir over the series. He is Alistair Graham, aged seventy-seven, Evelyn Waugh's 'friend of my heart' at Oxford and the original of some features of the aristocrat, Sebastian, in *Brideshead*. Mr Graham, a distant relative of the Duke of Montrose, lives in a converted fisherman's cottage in the village of New Quay in Wales.

He has never spoken to biographers or literary historians about the friendship which led Waugh to destroy all his Ox-ford diaries. And – although he has had interviewers with cheques at his door and popular press cameras thrust in his face during the last ten weeks – he has maintained his courteous silence.

*24 December 1981*                                    **John Ezard**


## Boom

The world arms race has achieved a momentum unparal-lelled in peacetime. Military spending in 1981 reached at least \$550 billion a year, of which about one-fifth is being

spent on nuclear weapons. The five countries with acknow-
ledged nuclear arsenals have stockpiles equivalent to one
million Hiroshima-sized atomic bombs.

These figures have been compiled by a former head of the
economic division of the US Arms Control and Disarmament Agency, Dr Ruth Leger Sivard and published in Washington by sponsors who include the American Arms Control
Association and the British Council of Churches. In a fore-
word to the report, the former US ambassador to Moscow,
Mr George Kennan, comments that 'governments, obsessed
with military fears or ambitions, seem paralysed in the face of
this ominous state of affairs.'

Dr Sivard's information is drawn from such bodies as
NATO, the United Nations, the World Bank, OECD, and
the European Community. She notes that 'military budgets,
on close examination, prove to be frail foundations for the
assessment of military capability and even shakier for gauging
external threat.' The obsessive secrecy of the Soviet Union,
for example, has led the NATO powers to everestimate the
Russian threat and so 'to propel the budgetary competition
to new heights – with an increase of insecurity for both sides.'

In comparison of military and social priorities, the report
notes:

the world spends 2300 times more on military activities
than it does on peacekeeping;

rich countries give 4.5 per cent of national income to the
military and 0.3 per cent to overseas aid;

military forces now control governments in fifty-four
Third World countries.

'In the ultimate mockery of "defence", military power
turns inward to terrorise and destroy the people it is intended to defend. Of the fifty-four governments, forty-one
have records of violating the citizens' right to safety under
the law. The tools of trade for domestic control and aggression by military forces have been furnished in many cases by
the most highly developed and civilised countries of the
world. According to official US records on arms trade and
training the USSR sent these countries $32,000 million in
arms between 1961 and 1979, the US $27,000 million,

France and China $3000 million each, West Germany $2000 million, the UK, Italy and Czechoslovakia $1000 million each.'

Dr Sivard also questions the impact of military spending on the industrial countries. 'Among ten developed countries the slowest growth in investment and manufacture productivity has occurred in two countries – the United States and the United Kingdom – where military expenditures are the highest in relation to GNP. The best investment and productivity record is in Japan, where the military-to-GNP ratio has been very low and productivity has grown at an amazing 8 per cent a year.'

By contrast the productivity of nuclear weapons has soared. 'Since 1945 approximately 1300 nuclear tests have been conducted in the world. A principal objective is to improve the efficiency of the explosive, to pack it with more punch relative to weight. The progress made is remarkable. Between the bomb that levelled Hiroshima and the Poseidon warhead, the yield-to-weight ratio has increased 150-fold. A heavy bomber was necessary to carry the five-ton city-destroying bomb of 1945. Now one Poseidon submarine carries sixteen missiles, each with ten warheads, and each warhead with three times the explosive force of the Hiroshima bomb. That adds up to a larger explosive power than was used by all the munitions in the Second World War.'

Dr Sivard reports that the South Carolina plant producing plutonium and tritium for American warheads had 108 hazardous incidents in 1980, none of them made public. She also notes that the US missile attack warning system produced 147 false alerts in eighteen months, that the Pentagon has recorded thirty-two accidents involving nuclear weapons since 1950 (roughly one a year), and that thirty-nine airmen working at the Strategic Air Command headquarters in Nebraska had been arrested for drug offences.

(*World Military and Social Expenditures, 1981*. Available from WMSE publications c/o CAAT, 5 Caledonian Road, London N1 9DX.)
*7 December 1981*                                      **Harold Jackson**

15

# Carrington of the FO

Today is the 200th anniversary of the foundation of the Foreign Office and of the appointment by George III of Charles James Fox as the first Foreign Secretary. The present, and fifty-first, holder of the office of Her Majesty's Principal Secretary of State for Foreign Affairs is Lord Carrington, who counts his blessings and says he is doing exactly what he wants to do, and that, moreover, it is a job he always wanted.

Well, how long is always? Just how long had he wanted the job? When he was at Agriculture under Churchill, running the myxomatosis committee?

'The mixxy committee!' he exclaimed, delighted, as if at the mention of an old and dear friend. Now he could tell me a story about that one day.

But while he was consorting with rabbits the office of Principal Secretary of State for Foreign Affairs had been in his mind? 'Oh well, I didn't think I would get it. Make that clear. At the time I was doing mixxy I thought, and I still think, that I was exceedingly lucky to get *that* job. It was a rung up the ladder.'

But what had been the chances of his ever achieving that ambition? In 1959, when he was 40 and First Lord of the Admiralty, which was the first time he could really have thought of the job, the previous six foreign secretaries had all been commoners. And today, before himself, fourteen of the previous fifteen foreign secretaries had been in the Commons. So what were his chances?

'Negligible. Negligible. I mean, the first time it even became a possibility was when Alec (Home) became Foreign Secretary. If I remember rightly, the outrage (at that) was almost not containable.'

He was called Caligula's horse? 'That sort of stuff,' said Lord Carrington, and mused a bit, and then remarked, as if by the way, that he had possessed his ambition before he was a peer.

But since he had succeeded his father at the age of 18, this must have been while he was still at Eton, then? 'Oh yes, certainly. . . . I had a lot of people interested in politics around me at school. Believe it or not, I sat next to Julian Amery for four years or whatever it was. One talked a lot of politics.'

I remarked that he had now served under six Prime Ministers. This didn't seem to have struck him. 'Count it up,' he said. But there it is – Churchill, Eden, Macmillan, Home, Heath, Thatcher.

Had anyone else done this, served under six? 'Quintin? There must be some Labour ones.'

I didn't know there had been six Labour Prime Ministers. 'That,' he said, 'is part of the luck of the draw, isn't it? We got through Prime Ministers quite quickly a couple of times.'

How, I wondered, had he got started in politics? Alec Douglas-Home sat in the Commons for years before he succeeded his father, but Carrington had been unable to do that. So how? He said he had got elected to his county council, and done agricultural things. 'I have,' he murmured, 'some agricultural property.' And then, after the war, there had been many young peers in the Lords, and it was quite exciting, with a new Labour Government, but practically no Labour men in the Lords, and the Lords having to deal for the first time since 1911 with *political* things like town and country planning, and nationalisation. 'And it was fascinating to see how Bobbity Salisbury dealt with it. He was superb at it. The way he manoeuvred his way through the shoals of Conservative opinion. I then became a Whip, I think.'

How had he been offered his first real Government job, at the Ministry of Agriculture and Fisheries in 1951? By someone on behalf of Churchill, I supposed. 'By Churchill. I was out shooting (laughter), and somebody sort of bicycled up and said: "Mr Churchill wants you on the telephone." I said: "Don't be so ridiculous. Nonsense." But I went back and there he was on the telephone.'

He was appointed because of his farming interest? 'I doubt whether he knew who I was from Adam. I think he just got on the telephone, and said something nice, and banged it down. I was astonished.'

We went back 200 years. When Fox was first appointed, I said, he had Richard Brinsley Sheridan, author of *The School for Scandal*, as his second-in-command.

'And fourteen other people,' said Lord Carrington. 'Including a housekeeper.'

Well, as to Sheridan, Carrington had Douglas Hurd as a Minister of State, who has written novels. 'Yes I've got my Sheridan. A very good Sheridan incidentally. Very bright guy.'

Now Fox, I said, had his qualities: at fourteen he was gambling in Paris, encouraged by his father, at nineteen he met Voltaire, and he once lost £16,000 in a day on a horse. What could Lord Carrington offer to compare with all this? 'Absolutely nothing. A very conventional background.'

No wildness, I inquired hopefully, having it in mind that one of his recent ancestors, known as Champagne Charlie, drank with Edward VII. 'Well, you see, the wildness was slightly contained, because I was 20 when the war broke out. . . . And so, I mean, life got quite serious. I had a lot of fun of course. Apart from the bits when we were frightened or bored, there was an immense amount of fun. It wasn't quite the same kind of thing as Charles James Fox had, of course. After the war there was a lot of austerity; and you know, there were butterflies – you were a butterfly if you didn't work and people had to have their noses to the grindstone. We were really much worse off after the war than during the war. I don't think I was very wild.'

He thought the Second World War (in which, as it happens, he was a Guards officer and won an MC by taking a bridge in a tank) was not so terrible as the first, with those trenches. I said that evidently both Eden and Macmillan had been marked by that war; it was obvious when they talked. He said Harold Macmillan had sometimes talked to him about it, anecdotally, not about the horrors. But his own father, who died young, had been scarred by it.

Lord Carrington had earlier said the Foreign Office started with fourteen people. By 1914, just before the war, when

England was perhaps at the height of her power, the number was 176. What was it now?

He thought five thousand.

Yes. What did that show?

He replied that there were now 151 countries in the world, whereas sixty years ago there were only a handful of any significance. The Foreign Office was now concerned not so much with war and diplomacy as with commerce and the law of the sea. To those who said that Britain was no longer a militarily powerful nation, and asked therefore what all those people were needed for, he replied that you needed more people if you weren't powerful.

'I mean, if you could send a gunboat and settle the thing, it's quite easy. If you have to use diplomacy to do it, you need more.'

Had he ever regretted not being able to send a gunboat? 'But I mean there's no good being nostalgic. Gunboats very often settled things in Victorian days, and that was admirable, but as I said it's no good sort of swimming about in nostalgia. What you've got to do is deal with the things and the problems that you're faced with now. And, alas, gunboats won't do.'

I said nostalgia had been his word, not mine, and he laughed. 'I think that Palmerston probably had a more straightforward job as Foreign Secretary than I've got, because he had the military power. After all, we were the top of the lot in those days.' As it happens, we were that morning sending the last of the gunboats, a gunboat indeed about to be scrapped, to South Georgia. I didn't know until later, and I don't know whether Lord Carrington knew.

And now what we had was 130 international organisations? At this Lord Carrington turned his eyes to heaven.

Tedious? Too many? 'Of course. Of course it is. And some of them, it's difficult to see what some of them achieve. A lot of them are self-perpetuating.' But a lot, he said, were essential, and here he named the IMF and the World Bank. Then he continued, 'Even the least good of them . . .'

Such as the United Nations itself?

He gallantly defended the UN as essential. One didn't

applaud all it did, indeed one regretted a great deal it did, but one would rather it was there than not.

My mind running on papers and dispatch boxes, I mentioned that in the communications put before Lord Grey, Colonial Secretary about 1850, I'd seen his scribbled notes saying such things as 'Nonsense,' and 'Tell him no, quickly.' What did Lord Carrington scribble on papers?

'I think you'd find out there (gesturing beyond the doors of his office) on most bits of paper, either a tick or no comment; or a thing which says, "Speak." '

Like a schoolmaster's 'See Me'?

'I'd rather see the guy who wrote it and talk to him. Much easier, you know, seeing people – certainly for me – than the written word, because the written word is very, very – particularly here – very carefully drafted. These guys are all absolute wizards with the written word.'

I showed sympathy, at which Lord Carrington added, in what I think a memorably acid phrase, that his people could 'distil something rather ably on a piece of paper.'

Then we came to the Atlantic Alliance, of which Lord Carrington said that as long as he could remember people had been saying it was in crisis, that things were worse than they'd ever known, and that they doubted whether it could last till Christmas.

But one thing had struck him very much the other day, in the middle of a welter of talk about the Alliance falling to bits over Poland. There was a meeting of the NATO foreign ministers in Brussels. Now usually the communiqué took *hours* and *hours* and *hours*: he sometimes thought they took longer deciding what they had said than actually saying it. But at that meeting it was precisely the reverse. The meeting was over in two and a half hours, and the communiqué settled in 15 minutes. His conclusion was that when the chips were down there was a feeling, shared by them all, that the Alliance was the most important thing there was, and that went for America as well as Europe.

But things, I said, had come to the pass where a US Secretary of State, Alexander Haig, could call him a duplicitous bastard. I had thought he would pass this off lightly, with a well-chosen, though full and free, understatement. But he did not, at least at first.

He said, 'Well, I really . . .' and left me to reflect on the background to that piece of Haigspeak, which was that the Israelis, as usual, were in a terrible state, this time about America selling early-warning planes to the Saudis, and because Sadat had just been murdered.

The Israelis promptly turned round and bit Haig sharply on the calf, and Haig in turn was scared they would invade southern Lebanon or renege on the Sinai agreement. All very likely. Then Haig, feeling he had to do something to demonstrate brotherly love for Begin, turned round and bit Carrington, then president of the Council of EEC Ministers, whom the Israelis saw as running around the Arab countries promising that Europe would support a Palestinian state in Judea.

I returned to my question. Lord Carrington said 'You know, "duplicitous bastard" . . . I have said things in this room about people, which I should be less than happy to see reported in the newspapers (laughter), and I don't necessarily mean them quite as they sound. I don't think he did either.'

Hadn't Lord Carrington asked for the original of an *Evening Standard* cartoon that celebrated the occasion? 'Yes, and I got it. I mean, Al and I are perfectly good friends. Nobody believes that, but we are. We get on extremely well.'

Lord Carrington works, as every Foreign Secretary since 1868 has worked, in Gilbert Scott's magnificent Italianate pile in Whitehall. He has called it a mausoleum, though a splendid one. But apart from a few great rooms, the rest of it is in a state of unbelievable neglect, with barbaric bits tacked on here and there. I said that if I owned a listed building and treated it that badly, the GLC would properly do its best to see me in jail. Why was it such a mess?

It was going to be done up in three years' time, he said. His own room was mostly in its original state, with the original furniture.

Beautiful Queen Anne chairs, I said. 'Victorian walnut

copies,' he said. 'I think you'll find.' As of course they are, since there's a set of 20 or so.

'Good old Westminster sofa,' he said, patting it; and he was going to have a new carpet; and the curtains were falling to bits. 'We're getting it all done, but if you do too much of it you become like Judith Hart. Don't you remember her bathroom? She was Minister for Overseas Development, and she had a great suite made over there, with a bathroom and a changing room and one thing and another. Poor old lady never lived it down. Last thing I want to do is to be considered to have been extravagant. I think you've got to keep things up. After all, this is a room that represents Britain. I mean, people come in here.'

The pictures, he said, had changed. The portrait of George III over the mantelpiece had been taken down by George Brown. In its place there now hangs a picture of a Nepalese general, put up by David Owen. He himself had found a couple of Zoffanys in a waiting room, and they now hang on an end wall. But he thought people really wanted to see Palmerston.

By now I could see anxious private secretaries hanging round in the background, wanting to get at Lord Carrington. British passports, I said, used to carry an adjuration beginning, 'We, Ernest Bevin, request and require . . .' but now they didn't say anything about 'We, Baron Carrington . . .'

'Do you feel deprived?' he asked.

I did a bit, and should feel a great deal more deprived when the present passport was replaced by the proposed paperback thing.

'No you won't. You won't see any difference. It'll be exactly the same.'

I protested that at the moment the British passport was the only one that was a hardback. Lord Carrington asked if the new one wasn't too, and was told by an aide that it had to be flexible, to go through a machine, at which I said it would look like a limp Japanese or American passport, and Lord Carrington said the mock-up he'd seen wasn't too bad.

Ah.

Then he said, 'I'm rather sad about the whole thing. But the point is that it's machine readable.'

Was that essential? 'Well, it's going to help you going through passport controls here, there, and everywhere.'

But in Europe there were hardly any passport controls left, except in Switzerland. 'Well, all the experts assure me that it's going to help like mad, and if it doesn't help like mad, I'm damned if we're going to change our passport.'

The Minister for Overseas Development and a whole gang of people were now practically clawing at the door and howling to get in, but Lord Carrington was talking about the numenism of the room in which he was sitting. He could feel the spirit of Harold Macmillan there, though he had only been Secretary for six months or so, and the spirit of Alec Douglas-Home, and of Bevin.

Bevin? 'I see Bevin here very much, don't you? The sort of bulldoggy Bevin sitting round here, sort of going "Puff." (Here Lord Carrington blew out his cheeks and then exhaled.) You remember how he used to do that? I can see them all here, in their own way. Except the nonentities, whom I can't see at all.'

The incoming delegation had now established a bridgehead, but Lord Carrington was still standing urbanely in front of the great fireplace, to be photographed.

'Do you like Doris Day?' he asked.

What?

'Behind you.'

On a side table several colour photographs were displayed, one of a wholesome blonde.

Who was it?

'It's [much laughter] it's the president of Iceland. She was *charming*.'

What's her name? 'I don't know. What's the name of the president of Iceland?'

An aide told him. Vigdis Finbogadottir.

The Minister and attendant delegates swarmed in. This is a room to which people come. Those eager to be in on overseas development, Vigdis Finbogadottir, and no doubt good old Al Haig, next time he's passing through London,

England. The curtains may be falling to bits, but there's still a portrait of Queen Victoria at the foot of the grand staircase, and so, as to Mr Haig, 'an aspersion on his parts of speech,' as Richard Brinsley Sheridan said.

*27 March 1982*                    **Terry Coleman**

*Six days after this article appeared, Argentina invaded the Falklands. Three days after that, Lord Carrington, who had been so urbanely regretful that a Foreign Secretary could no longer send a gunboat, resigned.—Ed.*

# A bee erect proper

The fleet had sailed from Portsmouth, the course of Empire was in full flow, the mighty intellect of Al Haig was flying from Washington to No. 10 to succour our just cause, David Owen and Tony Benn were earnestly addressing the House in emergency debate, and William Whitelaw, in the Home Secretary's office at the Commons behind the Speaker's chair, was recalling the days when his grandfather was chairman of the LNER.

Once, when he was a boy, he said, and returning to school from Aberdeen, he booked a sleeper in the name of William Whitelaw and there at the station to meet him was the stationmaster, wearing a top hat, who was anything but pleased to see a fifteen-year-old boy arrive. And when the young Whitelaw got into the sleeper booked in that name, he found a large bottle of whisky.

His grandfather, whose name was also William Whitelaw, was severe. 'Never again will you ever, ever book yourself for anything in my name. You will have to use some other name – junior or something. And what is more, I do not wish you to mention to any of the family the question of the bottle of whisky.'

Mr Whitelaw's Tory antecedents are impeccable. The favourite name for Tory MPs to drop is Disraeli's, on any pretext, but Mr Whitelaw has a real connection, which is that his great uncle married Disraeli's niece, though as he says, they didn't have any children. William Whitelaw of the LNER was also briefly a Tory MP in the 1890s, but then devoted himself to the railway, and later warned the boy William off politics, saying it could lead only to disappointment.

Whitelaw Junior plainly took no notice, and politics has led him to be in succession Chief Whip, Secretary for Ireland, an unsuccessful opponent of Mrs Thatcher's for the leadership in 1975, and then Home Secretary at the time of the Brixton riots.

I asked first about Northern Ireland, which I supposed he must have thought, at the time, was the most difficult job he could ever be asked to do. 'Looking back on it now,' he said, 'one marvels at one's own temerity. Abolishing Stormont was a fantastic act . . . The whole of the Stormont civil service . . . well, as their whole government had been abolished, their loyalty to anybody coming in was by no means certain. Nor at that stage, I suppose, was the RUC's loyalty. And the dangers of a civil war were very great, and it looked indeed as if there was going to be one.'

As it happens, I remember interviewing Mr Whitelaw at that time, and this was very far from what he said then. This is not surprising. He is an instinctive politician, and, since men commonly admire in others the qualities they possess themselves, I think it worth quoting a little obituary tribute by him to Lord Blakenham, under whom he once served in 1962. It appeared in *The Times* last month, and said, 'He was masterly in dealing with people. Frequently I saw him persuade opponents not only to accept his point of view, but actually to go away believing that they had converted him to theirs.'

However, we came on from the fear of civil war in Ireland to riots in England. Last year must surely have been a bitter and difficult time for him as Home Secretary? 'Yes, I think that's right. Riots were very traumatic for this country, (but) I will always claim that we came out of the riots with the basic structure of our country unimpaired, and with the basic structure of the police also unimpaired.'

Had he feared these might not be unimpaired? 'On the second, yes. There was always the risk that once you had the police dealing with riots on the streets to that extent, you could end up with a much more military style police than we've always had, and I think that would have been a disaster.'

Coming back from Moss Side one night, hearing reports of other riots coming over the car radio, and then arriving back at the Home Office to find his own staff wondering whether there were riots in *their* streets, had he asked himself whether there would ever be an end to it?

While I was asking this question Mr Whitelaw was saying, Yes, yes, yes, and then he said, 'Oh yes, most certainly I did. That was, I think, the worst night. We got back to the Home Office and really the world seemed almost on the verge of collapse. But it wasn't. But it was a very nasty moment.'

That was the year the police first used CS gas, and the first time rioters threw petol bombs? 'Yes,' he said, 'All that.' But it was all in tiny areas. Railton Road in Brixton was all knocked sideways, but three-quarters of a mile away nothing had happened. But he hadn't seen anything like that devastation since Northern Ireland.

'And in a funny way,' he said, 'You simply have to learn to live till the next day, and you learn. Northern Ireland taught me the habit of living on till the next day . . . Living till the next day is an absolutely crucial factor in the life of any senior politician, a capacity for living to the next day and still being there the next day.'

I said that Lord Carrington had not, but Mr Whitelaw did not seem to hear. 'As long as you're there the next day. And the other thing is, you must never exhibit anything other, to the outside world, than calmness, and quiet determination. Nor to the people around you.'

Then what about the time two days after Brixton ('Yes'), when the police had made surprise raids ('Yes'), and he had been asked in Cabinet what good that had done?

Mr Whitelaw began to laugh heartily.

Hadn't he banged on the Cabinet table and said 'Nothingl nothing,' seven times?

More laughter. 'I'm not going to expose to you what I said, but I wasn't best pleased. At that moment I was obviously going to have to make a very tricky speech in the House of Commons . . . there comes a moment when you have to get the House of Commons somehow in one piece.'

I wanted to quote to Mr Whitelaw a couple of sayings of Darcus Howe, a Trinidadian whose self-given name this seems to be, and who is editor of *Race Today*. Mr Whitelaw nodded vigorously at the name.

After the Scarman report, which he dismissed as mere tinkering, Mr Howe wrote in *The Times* that within ten minutes of each incident beginning, a group of thirty young men appeared and began to organise a revolt; that scouts on roller skates brought information on 'enemy' positions; and that buildings were selected to be destroyed, and then destroyed. Such a body of men, wrote Mr Howe, existed in every black community in the country. He then forecast more and worse in the not too distant future.

'I think,' said Mr Whitelaw, 'that once riots start a whole lot of people jump on the bandwagon for a whole variety of reasons. Quite a lot of these reasons are purely criminal. They jump on the bandwagon for a jolly good bit of looting. It's as cynical and straightforward as that. . . . But I don't believe, and Lord Scarman didn't believe, that there was any deep-laid plan . . . I don't believe there was a great black insurrection, I really do not.'

And what of Mr Howe's reported remarks, made at the time of the Notting Hill carnival, that there had been a withdrawal of the black community's consent for the presence of police in their midst? 'Well, it's manifest rubbish. It's not true. Nor has it been seen to be true since.'

Did he ever get angry at such statements? 'Well, I think one's simply got to get used to them. You've got to get used to Ken Livingstone shouting his mouth off at every turn . . .'

But Mr Livingstone was not going to burn anything down. 'No, no. But he doesn't help, attacking the new Commissioner of the Metropolitan Police . . . So, I mean, one has got to get used to a lot of people.'

He wouldn't be in politics if he wasn't used to many

people, of whom his only great hope was that they would keep their mouths shut. 'But they don't, and there are an awful lot of them, and I'm not going to tell you who some of the others are, and I would be delighted to see their mouths shut, permanently shut, for a bit, just a little breathing space from their remarks, but there it is.'

Some of them must be in his own party? 'Well, yes . . .'

Look at the last Conservative conference at Blackpool, where he had been pretty well shouted down. 'No, I was never shouted down. You must be fair about that. No way was I shouted down.' He said that it was true that he had, for one thing, opposed the idea that people should not be selected as Conservative candidates unless they were pre- pared to support capital punishment. 'But if somebody doesn't take that argument on, then your party gets into a very bad state.'

But the trouble was, I said, that it was seen . . . 'It was seen by political commentators as if the Tory party, at a really right-wing conference, more right wing than in the past, had in some way worsted me. They certainly didn't like what I said. They were entitled not to like what I said. But there it is.'

But his own leader, Mrs Thatcher, had not supported him on that occasion? 'Well, this is always said. I know its's said. It's become a sort of myth. And I didn't feel it at the time.'

He had looked crestfallen enough. 'Well, I didn't look pleased. Why should I look pleased? Perhaps I have the trouble that I show too much on my face what I feel . . . But in any case it's written into mythology, and far be it from me to try and write out of mythology what's been written into mythology.'

We were coming up to the anniversary of last year's riots. If there were more, he had said that the police would go in hard: 'By which I mean, that I want to see the rioters nipped in the bud . . . I don't want to see the police standing behind shields with a great huge crowd gathering.' The police would go in and arrest the trouble-makers, and those arrested would be prosecuted.

I said there had been rumours that he was thinking of

leaving the Commons. 'That's not true.' He had never thought of not recontesting his constituency of Penrith? 'I obviously am at an age when I have to think of all these things, but I absolutely have no intention of retiring.'

So he would fight a redistributed Penrith? 'I would hope so.'

Mr Whitelaw is, as it were, a stable prop. *Burke's Landed Gentry* describes him as Whitelaw of Gartshore, Kirkintilloch, Dunbartonshire, and Ennim, Penrith. On the crest of his family arms is 'a bee erect proper.'

Was he disappointed at not having been offered the Foreign Office? (There had been more rumours that Lord Carrington would have preferred to see Whitelaw rather than Pym as his successor.) 'No, certainly not. No way at all. I've made it very clear to everybody that the one thing in the world I want to be is Home Secretary. I've all the trials and tribulations of being Home Secretary. I'm very fond of the job.'

With the Falkland Islands debate still continuing in the chamber nearby, and my mind running on the shouting matches that sometimes pass for debates these days, I asked Mr Whitelaw if the nature of people in politics had changed since he entered the Commons in 1955.

'Well,' he said, 'there's a much more professional line in politics. People are coming in much younger. People are coming in who don't have other jobs.'

In Mr Heath's government of 1970–4 was he perhaps the only man who could tell Heath he was wrong and get away with it? 'Well, I certainly did it. I suppose I got away with it. I'm still good friends with Ted Heath.'

He had not wanted that first election of 1974, when Mr Heath challenged the miners? 'No, I didn't, and Peter Carrington did, and it was the first and only time we ever fell out, in all those years together.'

Would it be true to say that in the present government only Lord Carrington (until last week), Mr Pym, and Mr Whitelaw, could tell Mrs Thatcher she was wrong? 'I think she has always been very generous in listening to my point of view. I'm not going to go further than that.'

He had never told her she was wrong? 'Oh yes.'

And she listened? 'Yes.'
And then she did what she wanted anyway? 'Yes.'
Prolonged Whitelaw laughter.

'And she's quite right. I mean, it's the job of a close colleague and friend to tell someone what you think, and if they then decide, if they're the leader, not to accept your advice, that's their affair. Lovely.'

*13 April 1982*                                           **Terry Coleman**


# The authentic accents of the MoD

Ian McDonald, the civil servant who quotes Hamlet, was asked yesterday whether we had meant to sink or merely cripple the cruiser *General Belgrano*, with its 1000 people on board. He said: 'My understanding is that, if a shot is fired, it is fired to sink.'

His answer carried the bluntness Mr McDonald has had to try to learn in his three weeks as the voice of the Ministry of Defence. When he first called journalists to daily noon briefings at the MoD building in Whitehall, he was much more elliptical.

He declared at the time: 'I may have nothing to say. But, like Mass, it will be said – whether there is anybody there to receive it or not.' He pronounced Mass 'marse' and called the flagship *Hermes* 'Hermays' like a classicist.

For well over a fortnight, he was an unnamed and off-screen ministry spokesman inclined to handle questions with a cryptic answer followed by a little giggle. Then he was catapulted to prominence by the urgency of presenting an internationally credible British version of the conflict over the week-end.

At peak viewing time for the past three days, the public has been given a rare glimpse of the forcefulness underlying the diffident patrician mannerisms found at senior levels of the civil service. Mr McDonald is a look-alike for Paul Eddington, the politician in *Yes, Minister*. But he is on the other side of the fence.

He is a career civil servant. His last job was as assistant secretary in charge of Division 14, the MoD's recruitment and pay section. In 1980 he was given a tour of duty as deputy chief of public relations, a job which normally inflicts no limelight.

He has found the period of the shooting war enough of an ordeal to make him take the unusual step – for a public relations officer – of forbidding his staff yesterday to give any

*'In the latest communiqué from Buenos Aires, the Chiefs of Staff claim that at St Mary's Hospital, Paddington, The Princess of Wales gave birth to a boy weighing 7 lbs 2 oz. In London, a Ministry of Defence spokesman said they had no knowledge of the incident.'*

*23rd June, 1982*

details of his educational or working background. His job has been to convince his listeners that, as he puts it, 'I will not say anything I do not believe to be true.'

As the weekend developed, his confidence grew until he felt able to disparage the reliability of his Argentine opposite number by quoting Shakespeare. He referred to the speech in Act Three where Hamlet asks his mother: 'Look here, upon this picture, and on this – The counterfeit presentment of two brothers.'

He used the reference to suggest that the Argentine was giving a grossly untrue picture of military events. He said it might be immodest for him to quote the next two lines, which say: 'See what a grace was seated on this brow; Hyperion's curls; the front of Jove himself.' Mr McDonald, who is a middle-aged bachelor, has the remains of what may once have been curly hair.

It was made clear yesterday that he has decided to behave a little more carefully in public. The stakes he is playing for were indicated by one reply earlier in his stint as spokesman.

Mr McDonald happened to say that, whatever might be happening in the Falklands, the MoD still regarded the Soviet Union as its greatest potential threat. 'The Soviet Union – not the Treasury?' asked one defence correspondent with mock incredulity.

Mr McDonald saw the joke. But, because of the microphones and cameras surrounding him, he had to deny to the world with a perfectly straight face that the MoD saw the Treasury as a greater threat than Russia.

*4 May 1982*                                                    **John Ezard**

*Does the lonely hearts column of* Nine to Five *magazine offer some hope of a peace initiative? : 'Latin-American Gentleman, 55, educated, tall, slim, elegant, silver hair – seeks English-speaking lady to enjoy nice restaurants, dancing, theatre, conversation, etc.' If only . . .*

*21 May 1982*                                          **Alan Rusbridger**


## Our boys

*Dear Mary*

If all this Argy-bargy over the Falkland Islands has done nothing else, it's acted on the males of this family like a sackful of Sanatogen Multivitamins with Added Cold Steel. Josh shed ten years the minute he heard they'd invaded and has frisked about ever since like a large pin-striped lamb, giving me loving little pats as if I were an Argentine Junta and personally responsible for the whole crisis. Ben, who has never noticed the faintest ripple of a current affair in the sixteen years of our acquaintance, is now au fait with every detail of the fiasco from the direction of the South Atlantic winds to the precise number of torpedoes on a Hunter-killer submarine (Tony Benn, please contact) and daily sings entire choruses of Rule Britannia in the loo. Tom rang up from Mousehole to remind us all that he was born in Comodoro Rivadavia, which irrelevant news was greeted by Josh and Ben with many congratulatory sounds, as if Tom had won something. What about CND, Tom? I said. Sea and what? he said.

Also, Mother rang up to give me her recipe for mock corned beef, since I wouldn't be buying the real thing any more. I never did, Mother, I said. You always told me how horrible it was, eating it in the war. That's as may be, she said, but we don't want those Argies thinking they're depriving us of anything, do we? They're a fascist dictatorship, Martha, you know. I know, Mother, I said. Only ten days ago, those would have been words of praise from my old Ma.

Only Jane and I remain consistent. Jane consistently calls everyone concerned, from M. Thatcher to the Falkland Island penguins, warmongering wankers and I consistently say, Oh dear, I hope nobody gets hurt. I did try to tell Josh what Lorna's hubby'd heard from a passing oil man, that their slogan was Keep the Falkland Islands Rhodesian, on account of the people being rather to the right of . . . but Josh cut me off with the sort of glare that said I was Lord Haw-Haw and ought to be shot at dawn. It is all very bewildering. My solution is to settle all the Falklanders on the good ship Canberra for a permanent round-the-world cruise but who listens to me?

Nor has there been any respite at Annie's Attic. Big Noreen's bloke, the born killer, was had up last week for bonking some man on the bonce with a bottle. It's not right, says Noreen. 'E thought the geezer was one of the Argies and e did is duty like a True Brit. Is pride overcome im, know what I mean? As for After-Shave Charlie, he's almost sobered up for the first time in a decade, solely in order to communicate to us a blow-by-blow account of exactly what he did to them cunning bleeders in the war. The last, the first, the Boer, *which* war, Charlie? I said. *The* war, acourse, he said. Tell you something, Missus. The sun has never set nor never risen nor never will without Our Boys is fighting some-one, somewhere in this world. Makes you proud, don't it? Charlie, I said, it certainly do. Does. The old boy would join up tomorrow if they'd have him and, I'll tell you, one blast of his methylated breath and Galtieri's goons would fall like ninepins, never to rise again.

The Attic closed for four days at Easter, just enough time for family hostilities to break out all over. Mother went to church on Sunday and returned blowing steam from all gussetts, a result of being forced to pray for peace by a vicar she threatens to denounce as Red under the dog-collar. She looked like a hot, cross bun and said poor baby seven times in a minute to the baby, who looked like a chocolate-coated Easter Egg.

Then Ms Irene Bossiboots turned up for a Resurrection Riesling accompanied by the roughest toughest hunk of knotted biceps I've ever seen. Tattered denim jacket, faded jeans, seven-league cowboy boots, leather strap round eighteen-inch neck, greasy bandanna round greasy head, a real bone-freezer. This is Ron, said Ms Boss, he's my hair-dresser and, my dear, what this man can do for my hair is *un*believable. She's right. Every time I see her hair, I don't believe it. Cheers, said Ron, downing the Riesling. Then he said did anyone here *begin* to understand why we were all supposed to go potty with rage because some itty-bitty island half across the globe had had its Union Jack taken off it? I could get all those islanders *and* their sheep into my salon and still have space for my Tint 'n Perm unit, he said. If he hadn't stepped on the baby at that juncture, raising the resulting Cain, I think Mother and Josh between them might have split every one of his ends.

Still, at least spring has sprung here, if only in patches. My friend Dorrie Carrie Bogvak writes from Boston that they've just had two feet of snow tipped over them and if she ever manages to tunnel out again she's going to emigrate with the twins to any old fascist dictatorship in any old banana republic that can guarantee her she'll never see another snowflake. She sounds very low, poor thing. She says time's running backwards in America, like a bad film, and she's hourly expecting to be put on trial in Salem and burned at the stake as a witch, due to campaigning for the Equal Rights Amendment and having a wart on her chest, which they'll think is a third nipple and proof of her witchery.

I wrote back and told her time wasn't exactly running forwards here and when it gets back to the Mayflower, she should nip on board and be reeled back to Southampton. I'd meet her on the quay in my wimple, shouting God Bless King James, and we could have a nice cup of tea before we went off to colonise the Falkland Islands.

Yours packing the hard tack,

*Martha*
**Jill Tweedie**

*14 April 1982*

*Sir,*
*Your Diary reports that Mr Tony Snow, a* Sun *and* News of the World *reporter, signed a Sidewinder missile on behalf of his readers with the words, 'Up yours, Galtieri.' This leaves me wondering what is written on the sides of Argentine missiles. Made in Britain?*

*Yours faithfully,*
*Gordon Falconer,*
*London SW4.*

*8 May 1982*


# Careless talk costs lives

There is something quixotic in this — for a post-imperial island nation, with an ailing economy to send out on three days' notice 26,000 men and a vast armada to the opposite end of the oceans in defence of a few hundreds of its own nationals threatened by an invading tyranny.

It is in defiance of all calculations of interest. There is no realism about it. And it is this which has caught, for a moment, the heart of half the nation. Those who suppose the British to be a nation of shopkeepers are riding for a fall.

They can also be a nation of romantics. They like to argue their politics, not in terms of interests, but in terms of oughts. This is true of the British Labour movement also. Inside every shop steward there is a Don Quixote struggling to get out.

The British are also a rather old seafaring nation, the island anchorage of the greatest naval imperialism ever known to the world. For 500 years the ships have set out, from the Thames and Medway, from Plymouth, Portsmouth, the Clyde, to quarter the globe and to accumulate that extraordinary empire by acts of aggression a great deal less decorous and less bloodless than the invasion with which the Falklands War commenced. It is odd that we should be so moralistic today about other nations' faults. We expect them to grow up instantly to our own senescent sanctity without passing through our own adolescent sins.

The whole British people had a part in this naval empire. It was not just a preserve of the ruling class. They were the common people who built and manned the ships and whose families awaited their return. Naval victories were a staple of popular ballad and broadsheet. Drake and Nelson were genuine national heroes, not invented from above.

There is a long resonance in this, and an old resource for Tory Populism. Naval officers have been the most competent cadre of the British ruling class – as seamen, navigators, administrators. Some even, through shared hardships and loyalties, became democrats or Friends of the People.

And there is another ancient resonance, which one can sense to be vibrating now. The English nation came of age with the defeat of the Armada. The naval battles which first secured our empire were mainly with Hispanic peoples. Our privateers scoured the oceans, robbing the King of Spain of his treasure and singeing his beard.

The European maritime nations exported their rivalries and fought them out before astonished native audiences at the furthest ends of the earth. 'We did maik them such a breakfast as I do verielie think was neyther in the way of curttesy or unkindnesses well accepted.' So wrote Captain Thomas Best in a despatch of 1612 recounting the Battle of

Swally Hole – one of those sharp engagements in which the English gained dominance over the Portuguese in the contest for ports in India.

'The Dragon, being ahead, steered from one to another, and gave them such banges as maid ther verie sides crack; for we neyther of us never shott butt were so neere we could nott misse.' The fight took place 'in the sight of all the army of the Muslim Governor who stood so thick upon the hills beholdinge of us that they covered the ground.'

Manners have changed today. We do not have to wait for Captain Best's despatch to come to us by sail around the Cape. We are told about it all – or we are told as much as some official thinks it proper that we should know – the next day by Mr Ian McDonald. There has been some loss in the vigour of the language, as well as in veracity. But that is a small price to pay for progress.

And progress has made other gains. This is an electronic war, a war of top technicians. Our men-of-war no longer steer between the enemy and crack their sides. Torpedoes and missiles are launched at twenty or more miles. All that opponents may ever see of each other is a radar blip.

And there is no astonished army of the Muslim Governor now viewing the Battle of Falklands Sound. The audience, thick on the hills, are not only the sheep – or such of the sheep as have not already been changed, by the opposing forces, into mutton. It is also that of the arms traders and war gamesmen – the 'experts' of the whole world.

These are rapt in attention. Shares are rising and falling. Sea Harriers are up but aluminium frigates are down. Since the *Sheffield* was sunk the makers of the Exocet have already received new orders for sixteen hundred (or was it sixteen thousand?) missiles. Full order books for that. And 'lessons' are being learned. United States naval strategy is already undergoing major review. Too late for us, of course. Progress is going on, and we are the price.

We can see, more clearly than we could two weeks ago, the features of World War III. It is not only that the Falklands War is being fought with nuclear-age technologies in which only the nuclear-tipped warheads are missing. It is also that the consequences of the militarisation of the entire globe have become transparent.

This is not just a matter of the export of sophisticated weaponry from the advanced to the Third World: sales to Argentina of the Exocet, of Skyhawks, of Sea Wolf and Sea Dart, Type 42 destroyers (sister ships to the *Sheffield*) and the rest. No doubt our forces in the Falklands are already reflecting upon that, and in due course the British public may give it a thought also.

It is also that, with the weapons, the advanced world is exporting – directly or indirectly – military juntas. Look where you will, the pressure is that way: Chile, Guatemala, El Salvador, Argentina, Poland, Afghanistan. If we want to crusade against fascist juntas, we need only scan the list of our own best customers for arms. Our loyal NATO ally, Turkey, is a junta of that kind, with above 30,000 political prisoners in its jails and with the executive Committee of the Turkish Peace Association at this moment on trial. This year the United States has increased its hand-outs to the Turkish junta of military aid.

The peace movement has been warning of this process for years, but our government took notice only when a junta blew up in its own face. It is not as if our governments (Labour or Conservative) were given no warning. In 1978, to his credit, President Carter cut off military sales to the Argentine on the issue of human rights. France, Britain, Israel and Germany eagerly stepped in to take up the slack. If (which God forbid!) one of our nuclear submarines should be sunk, causing a major reactor disaster in the South Atlantic, it would perhaps have been located by a Lynx helicopter (Westland Aircraft Ltd) equipped with Ferranti Seaspray radar and Decca electronic supports.

Helicopters in the Argentine have had other uses. It is said that some of the thousands of 'Disappeared Ones' – oppositionists seized by the junta's security arm – were simply dumped from the bellies of helicopters into the South Atlantic. An American businessman recently overheard Argentine officers jesting about 'the flying nuns' – two French disappeared nuns who were dealt with in that way. It is a convenient and clean means of disposal.

It is an odious regime. Yet there is something a little odious also about the hypocrisy of politicians. We are now, very suddenly, in a war to the death with a fascist regime. Yet our government has no interest in liberating the Argentine people, or in strengthening the democratic opposition to General Galtieri. On the contrary, by taking recourse to military measures, instead of diplomatic and economic sanctions, it has strengthened the junta and given it a surge of populist nationalist support.

To be honest, I do not think that Mrs Thatcher – and still less President Reagan – want to see the fall of the Argentine junta. They would like to humiliate it, to be sure, and to see it reshuffled into more accommodating forms. But they do not wish to threaten juntadom, whether there or in Chile. For if the junta fell under pressure from its own people, something far 'worse' – an Argentine Allende or Castro might come to power.

If the West had wished to destabilise the junta it had the means to hand. The Argentine is one of the most indebted nations in the world. And why? Because Western banks have loaned to Argentina the wherewithal to buy expensive Western weapons-systems. If Western banks had been willing to pull the plug and default the junta, in a few month's time unrest might have overturned the military rulers.

But this would have been a desperate remedy with an uncertain outcome. It would have caused pain in the ledgers of the Western banking system. It was better to settle the matter in traditional ways, by the loss of blood rather than the risk of money. It was better to send out a task-force.

And do we realise – does *anyone* yet realise – what we – or our betters on the front benches of all the major parties – have done? In that quixotic moment of injured national pride and historical reminiscence, we have sent 26,000 men 8000 miles away, without adequate air cover, to confront some of the most advanced weaponry yet devised.

The politicians squint at us complacently from the screens,

39

one eye on the cameras, the other on the opinion polls. They are confident that they – or at least those poor bastards out there in the South Atlantic – will pull it off. Yet romanticism married to that kind of calculation of political advantage is a poor guide to reality.

Careless talk costs lives. It is costing lives now. Talk of paramountcy, sovereignty, flags, unconditional surrender; careless talk on the Jimmy Young Show and at the Scottish Tory Party conference; the careless roar of the House of Commons at feeding-time. Now they have got their meat.

It is impossible to write a line on the impending outcome of the Falklands War without hazard. To write is like rolling marbles on the deck of a ship in a storm. I write this now on Friday. What will we learn when this appears on Monday? Will Port Stanley have fallen to British marines? Will one of our capital ships have been sunk? Will a cease-fire have been enforced by world opinion?

I wish only to say this: we have done a dreadful and unthinking thing. We have allowed a desperate gamble to take place with human life, in preference to a longer course of diplomatic and economic attrition. The gamble may pay off (and greatly to Mrs Thatcher's political advantage), owing to the immense resources, experience and skill of the British forces.

But it is not inevitable that it will, and it is necessary that someone should incur the odium of saying so. Our task-force is now at risk. Its air defences, always inadequate, depend upon two carriers. If the *Hermes*, instead of the *Atlantic Conveyor*, had been sunk, then the terms of battle would have tilted dangerously against us.

And what would happen then? Will 500 years of imperial naval history end in a tragic encounter in Falkland Sound? And how will the land forces be rescued and brought back? How, across those 8000 miles, can we mount another Dunkirk?

Our politicians and much of our popular media have been guilty of appalling levity. The sinking of the *Belgrano* and the *Sheffield* ought to have enforced a change of tone, an interval of reflection. I would have been opposed to the sending of the task-force even if I had known that it would bring a quick, and almost bloodless, victory. Our proper course was always pursuance of the full terms of UN Resolution 502, in *all* its parts, and with the endorsement of world opinion. Our resort to force has already endangered the peace of the world by weakening the authority of the United Nations, which, ineffectual as it is – and as we have made it – is yet the only institution which points forward to an international rule of law.

But we are now, as I write, brought to a desperate situation. A major British defeat could have appalling consequences within our culture: it could turn us into something much like a junta ourselves. Already the authoritarians of every hue are having their festival. After the careless talk ends, the really ugly talk begins.

That is why the peace movement must now go out into those storms outside and rescue what is sane and pacific in our culture. It may also have to rescue our fleet. If the first thoughts of all of us are with our brave lads in the South Atlantic – as it is obligatory for every political speech to commence these days – then our second thoughts ought to be how to get them out of that cold and hostile place.

I can see no way in which CND's demonstration in Hyde Park on 6 June can fail to be also a demonstration to halt the Falklands War and to pass it back into the hands of United Nations negotiations. I know that there are some notable critics of our resort to force in the Falklands who are not nuclear disarmers; and I know that there are some nuclear disarmers who think that the Falklands War is not a proper issue to concern CND. But I think that we must all, calmly and in good order and in the greatest possible numbers, go to the Park together. This is a crisis of historic dimensions, a crisis in our culture and our polity, and an ideological confrontation which we refuse at our peril. And, even more than that, it is our urgent duty both to our kin and also to their Argentinian fellow-sufferers in the South Atlantic.

We never know anything of the truth of wars until a few years have passed. It will all trickle out later – the crises of supplies, the official lies, the troops sickening in the ships, the equipment bogged down on the islands. We may also learn of episodes of skill and courage which we can celebrate with a whole heart – above all the extraordinary rescue operations (on both sides) of the hundreds who have already been tipped into those seas.

But now this is a war which must be stopped. Even if – as with the Peruvian or the Secretary-General's formulae there is a little loss of Mrs Thatcher's face. That is in the true interests of all parties, including the Falkland Islanders.

It is also in the interests of a threatened world. The peace movement did not deserve this tragic diversion. It has been in recent months, steadily expanding, both in numbers and in geographic extent. New publics are entering the international campaign. Last week some 70,000 marched through Vienna; half a million have marched in Tokyo; on Saturday Dublin will see a major demonstration; in two weeks the United Nations Special Session on Disarmament will be signalled by a demonstration on a quite new scale by the American peace movement in New York.

It is more necessary than ever, at this very difficult moment, that the British peace movement should resume its presence in the nation's life. 6 June may be the most important event we shall ever hold. Militarisation is now global and the defences against militarist passions must be global also. There can be no gaps in that line.

Speakers and contingents are attending in Hyde Park from around the world: from the United States, from Iceland, from Japan. I have heard it said that the British peace movement is finished, knocked sideways by the Falklands war. It was a fair-weather movement only – a peace movement which fainted at the sight of a real war. I ask you to walk out quietly and without provocation into that opposition, and to answer it with your numbers.

*31 May 1982*                                        **E. P. Thompson**

# If I'm paranoiac, so is half Europe

*Dear Mary*

My back is still aching but wasn't that a great party? About half-way through the day, I felt exactly as if I, personally, had thrown it. Martha, At Home, 24 October, Hyde Park or Thereabouts, 11 to 6 p.m., Banners Will Be Worn. I kept spotting people I hadn't seen for yonks. At Charing Cross, those three lovely Danish women who were at Manchester one year. In Trafalgar Square, Hans-Helmut hanging from a lamp-post, that nice German punk I got stranded with in a train strike. Along Piccadilly, Marie, Lorna's French au pair, and then all those women from Birmingham where we stayed on that Women's Conference and, guess who, Miss Mc-Donald, our old maths teacher, wheeled down from Edinburgh and still going strong at eighty, and the two Liverpudlians who gave us a hitch that time in Brighton and Jenny Cartwright up from Derby and Mrs Next-Door, still laughing herself silly, and Ron from the hairdressers and about thirty people from our street and, oh, about a hundred others. I'm hoarse from catching up with the news, shouting across streets, bellowing over tankards. Marie's had a baby, Kirstie's got married, Manuella from Rome has moved to Paris, Jenny's divorced, it just went on and on.

Going for a sausage roll, I bumped into my own ex-spouse, too. All the way up from Mousehole with a girl called Olly, aged about five and dressed like a Red Indian. I gave her a big hug. Well, she'll need it, being with Tom. I'm only here for the beer, said Tom, and I believe it. He was more or less legless already and we were only on the Embankment. Look, I said, you come round and see your children before you scuttle back to Cornwall or *else*. I don't know if he got the message . . . we were parted just then by some street theatre – but, judging by her expression, Olly did. She probably didn't know about her new man's past. I'm the only person Tom is tight-lipped about.

And then, best of all, meeting you! There I was, slogging past the Haymarket behind these two huge papier mâché figures, Thatcher and Reagan groping each other in the most disgusting way, when out from under them for a breath of fresh air pop you and Mo! We must have held up the hordes for at least six minutes, jumping around. That bloke you were with, the one with the green hair and the gasmask, he was a dish. We met up later, you know. Jammed against the journalists' barricade under the speakers' platform and, from what little he said, he really fancies you. Then he took his

*'In this week's improvisation class I want you to imagine that the Russians have invaded Europe and President Reagan has dropped the Neutron bomb. Now : – Paul and Cynthia, you'll be people, John, Fiona and Julie will pretend to be buildings . . .'*

*11th August, 1981*

gasmask off and, Mary, if you don't fancy him right back, pass him on. What eyes!

He nearly started the only fight of the day though. There were these two journalists in front of us and one said, 'Here comes the King,' and the other said 'You mean, the Prince of Darkness', and we looked up and saw they meant T. Benn. Well, before you could say CND, your bloke was tightening up their ties for nooses. I see why journalists have special barricades – it's to keep them safe from the public.

But it was a downer, coming home. The baby, on my back the whole day without uttering a squeak – obviously he only ever needed a quarter of a million other people around to

44

keep him entertained – took one look at home sweet home and began his first bit of serious protest. Josh, who hadn't come on account of he thought Irene might be up in a helicopter and finger him for a fellow-traveller, was sitting there grumbling about how Thatcher was caving in by rescuing·the BBC World Service.

What's the point, he complained, financing a lot of frogs, or worse, Englishmen *pretending* to be Frogs? Joke, he said, hastily, seeing my face, but I know enough about that man to know his elaborate jokes merely conceal elaborate truths.

It's like that woman said from the CND platform, Mary. The world is run by old men. Old Reagan, Old Brezhnev and behind them, shuffling the papers, my very own Old Josh. Each one sunk in a fantasy of being Gary Cooper in *High Noon* when what they actually are is Count Dracula back from a good night's necking to keep his cheeks rosy. Josh says I'm paranoiac about Cruise etcetera but I say if I'm paranoiac, Josh, so is half Europe and how are you going to find a bin big enough to take us all?

Next day, mother phoned and said had I seen all those Communists in London and wasn't it sad, my aunt phoned and said had I seen all those Lunatics in London and wasn't it amusing, and Tom appeared accompanied by Olly. Poor man. I think he's actually afraid of his own children – he looks at them as if they were fireworks gone off at the wrong time. No wonder. Daughter Jane doesn't look too much older than girlfriend Olly, which must be a trifle unsettling for them all. No good, really, using Grecian 2000 and sucking in your beer belly when Jane's around to blow the gaff.

I wish there was a gardening programme that advised you about husbands instead of plants. Dear Percy Thrower, My husbands aren't doing too well. One is curling up at the edges and losing its leaves and the other has blight. What should I do? And dear Percy Thrower could tell me to spray them with derris and all would be well.

Yours, preparing to dig them both over,

*Martha*
**Jill Tweedie**

*28 October 1981*

# Exigencies of the service

Gregory Dixon, just eighteen, was pedalling home on his bike at eleven o'clock in the evening. He had taken his girl friend on a date, seen her on to a bus home, and was cycling back to college, where he was studying for A levels. His front and rear lights were in good working order as he rode down the Woodstock Road in Oxford.

In a transit van near the city centre, PC John Wood and two other policemen were parked, waiting for something to happen. A call came through asking for assistance at a Trust House Forte hotel car park. Some youths had been spotted breaking the windows of cars – there was no suggestion of violence or danger. PC Wood set out to the scene of the crime, blue light flashing, but sounding no siren and travelling, some witnesses said later, at 60 miles an hour. He claimed he was driving at 50, in a 30 mph zone.

He crossed over two red traffic lights, thundered down the Woodstock Road, reached a bollard in the middle of the road, and swerved round the wrong side of it on to the right-hand side of the road. There he crashed head on with Gregory Dixon on his bike. The young man was killed instantly.

When the case came up in court the jury found PC Wood guilty of reckless driving. To the surprise and shock of Gregory Dixon's family, Judge Mynett, passing sentence, gave PC Wood a £100 fine. He did not take away his driving licence, or recommend that he should stop driving for the police.

It is now a year after the accident. Gregory Dixon's parents are outraged by the sentence, and are campaigning to have tougher restrictions enforced on the emergency services. PC Wood is still in the Thames Valley police force. Is he still driving? We don't know, since the only response to that question was a stone wall. According to the Acting Deputy Chief Constable 'This is an internal discipline matter and as a matter of policy, we do not discuss it.'

Mr and Mrs Dixon, Gregory's parents, feel they are entitled to a better answer. 'The judge said PC Wood had suffered enough. What has he suffered compared to us?' Gregory's father said, choking back tears. 'If it had been any other driver, apart from a policeman, he'd have had his licence taken away for a long time, and he'd have got a heftier fine. He might even have gone to gaol.'

The Dixons have been sending out letters to friends, relations and well-wishers, asking them to lobby their MPs, write to Ministers and demand a change in the laws that condone reckless driving on the part of the emergency services. Ray Whitney, MP for Wycombe, has written to the Lord Chancellor, outlining the facts of the case and expressing the great concern of the Dixons and the general public in this matter.

No one, it seems, has done any proper research, weighing up the benefits against the dangers of the emergency services' constant breaking of the Highway Code. No one has tried to estimate the number of lives saved by fire, police and ambulance services arriving at the scene a few minutes sooner than they would have done if they had kept to the speed limits. There are plenty of people who gratefully acknowledge that they owe their lives to the bravery and skill of these services, but how many 'emergency' calls are real emergencies? At least the fire and ambulance service break the speed limit with the intention of saving lives. But the police, more often than not, are out to apprehend criminals. There are no figures for the number of deaths and injuries to the public caused by vehicles being chased by the police. It is the job of police to catch criminals, but at what risk to the general public?

Figures are hard to come by, or to make sensible use of when you can get them. The Ministry of Transport reports that on average there is an accident every 50,000 car miles. This is, they say, a great underestimate, since many accidents are not reported. Compare that to the police statistics. In 1980 Metropolitan Police cars recorded a rate of one accident every 10,856 miles driven – three times higher than the average for all cars. According to the Chief Inspector of Constabulary's report for 1980, 737 police officers nation-wide were convicted of traffic offences (321 of which took place off duty), fifty-seven were disqualified from driving.

The Metropolitan Police has 2054 cars, and in 1980 was involved in 3889 accidents. Those figures on their own are only an indicator, and they don't tell the whole story – since they include minor bumps and scrapes. But an accident rate three, or possibly more, times higher than the average needs some explaining. How many of the accidents took place during emergency calls? How many members of the public were injured? The Metropolitan Police couldn't answer that. But then they are the ones making the accident reports and collecting the statistics in the first place.

The London Ambulance Service has 1020 vehicles on the road. In 1981 they had 1426 accidents. 120 patients were injured while being conveyed by ambulance. They have no estimate of the mileage per accident rate of the service. In Oxford, however, they had seventy-two vehicles on the road last year and only twenty-four accidents, which suggests that there are considerable regional variations.

The London Fire Brigade's most recent figures are for 1979. They had 610 vehicles on the road, and 721 accidents. (A third of these happen in the station yard, they say.) Two members of the public were killed in traffic accidents involving fire engines. Forty members of the public and twenty-eight members of the fire brigade were injured in traffic accidents involving fire engines. In all, the fire brigade rescued 684 people that year. But included in those rescues are children with their heads stuck in railings, and people stuck in their cars. How many of those serious accidents happened when fire engines were going to a fire involving real danger to human life?

The 1979 Road Traffic Act specifically exempts the emergency services from observance of speed limits and traffic lights. 'No stated speed limits apply to drivers of vehicles being used for fire, police or ambulance purposes if the observance of those regulations would hinder the execution of those duties,' says the law. So long as they don't have accidents, that gives the emergency services freedom to drive as fast as they like, since it does not specify the circumstances that would justify breaking the speed limit. Speed limits 'hinder' all kinds of people in a hurry.

Life in the inner cities these days is often tense. I live on the edge of Brixton. The incessant screech and yowl of emergency sirens, and the flashing of lights, police cars screaming round corners and hustling down the wrong side of the road does much to upset the calm in Lambeth streets. People freeze, stop talking, stare after the vehicles, wonder what's going on. Is it death and disaster? Is it near? Is it a riot?

Having driven in police cars on a number of occasions I've taught myself to be cynical about those sirens. A couple of months ago I was in a South London police car, where the driver had no siren or lights, and was not supposed to use the car as an emergency vehicle. He heard on the radio that some other police cars were chasing a suspected burglar's car in a district only vaguely described.

There was no particular emergency about the call. Drivers were asked to keep their eyes open for the suspect's car. But this driver, bored and not over-anxious to return to more routine work at the station, accelerated off to the approximate area, and combed the streets at top speed. We met several other police cars doing the same thing, dashing up and down watching for a brown Cortina.

A message came through later. We were all in the wrong area, the brown Cortina had long departed before the call went out, and the suspect hadn't done anything. He was merely acting suspiciously. But a jolly good chase was had by all. None of the police I saw wore seat belts either. The policeman I was with shouted and yelled at the public outside, cursed and bellowed, treated them with utter contempt. Who was he protecting against whom? How many lives was he risking?

Of course, if a mad axe-man was hacking down the door, every second would count, and in some calls it isn't clear whether there is an emergency or not. But Chief Constables seem to turn a blind eye to the fact that the police use almost any pretext for driving like madmen. After all, if they are seen needlessly crossing red lights, and breaking speed limits, who is to catch and arrest them? *Quis custodiet ipsos custodes?*

Russell and Valerie Dixon want some answers to these questions. They intend to pursue the matter through the civil courts, not because they want the compensation money – they intend to give it to Stoke Mandeville – but because they want more publicity for the case. They want Judge Mynett reprimanded for the sentence he handed out. They want facts and figures on emergency service driving. They want firm restrictions placed on emergency services in the way they drive, and the occasions on which they are allowed to break the Highway Code. Russell Dixon says: 'I calculated that if PC Wood had kept within the speed limit, he would have reached the scene of the crime at the hotel car park only two minutes later. My son was killed to save those two minutes. And PC Wood was only going to a bunch of kids breaking into cars. That's what my son died for.'

*21 January 1982*                                    **Polly Toynbee**


# The approaches of strangers

At the height of the recent furore about rape and rape sentencing, I met a man who told me he was very worried by the implications of tougher legislation. As my brow darkened he said, hastily, yes, yes, he *knew* that rape was often not a sexual act but GBH (Grievous Bodily Harm) and he *knew* male attitudes to rape were frequently abysmal and he knew it was all unforgivable in every way.

But, but, he said. He, for example, worked with adolescent boys and youths and he also knew how often what might seem rape to an outsider was actually what he called 'a mess, a great sad mess.' The boy thinks the girl thinks the boy thinks the girl thinks. He starts, she stops, he pauses, she smiles, he starts again, she lets him, she squeals, he pauses, she giggles, he doesn't understand, she doesn't understand, disaster looms. Both have their wires inextricably crossed, both are unsure what is expected of them, both are intent on acting out what they see as their masculine or feminine roles. And we must all admit, if we are honest, that such wire-crossing, such deplorable ineptitude, does happen – and it is not confined to the young. If we could film one such encounter in slow motion and add a dose of ESP, we might well discern a hundred tiny hesitations, a hundred moments of total confusion, in which emotions war with attitudes and attitudes conflict with temperament and neither party can guess what on earth the other wants. Like puppets on a string, the couple play out society's stereotypes and then must take the consequences as individuals if things go badly wrong.

And one of the reasons that things can go badly wrong is that rape is only the extreme end of an otherwise entirely acceptable spectrum of male behaviour.

A man feels masculinity demands that he be the initiator of sex, a woman feels femininity depends on her show of resistance. This is society's expectation of male and female behaviour and, obediently, this is how we do behave, even in the marital bed. He makes the pass, she evades it. He woos, she is wooed, he must reveal his intentions, she must conceal hers, he must insist, she must resist. Anger at the imposition of such roles is never far from the surface, an anger that divides the sexes. He is, after all, only doing what he thinks he must and so is she. The result, as the man said, is too often a great sad mess.

There is no rape in the animal world because animals are neither capable of, nor equipped for, ambiguity. They do not act, they react. The female sends out clear sexual signals and presents herself for sex, the male avails himself of her offer. The sexual waters are not muddied by pretence, by any impulsion to live up to an image or by other, more devious, aims camouflaged by the sexual act. Human beings, on the other hand, are infinitely more complex and more pretentious creatures who cherish ideas of ourselves far above and beyond our physical gender. We do not define ourselves by who does what to whom but by a towering edifice of images and symbols and learned behaviour, so that men measure masculinity by anything from their jobs to their drinking

51

habits and women their femininity by anything from frilly blouses to being unable to repair a fuse.

But because we have little genetically programmed sexual behaviour, because being human means being adaptable, we could – without too much effort – turn all our present standards on their heads and define ourselves anew, tomorrow, if we so chose. At present, for instance, being a 'macho' man means, among other things, taking pride in sexual aggression. Yet it does not overly stretch the imagination to envisage quite another norm in which a macho man is one too proud to make any sexual moves at all towards a woman unless she makes her desire for him crystal clear, in word and deed.

Indeed, even by existing standards, doesn't that make more sense? What kind of a male creep is it, for goodness sake, who is so repulsive to the opposite sex that he must force himself on a woman? What kind of pathetic twit has so little confidence in his own powers of attraction that he must constantly be pushing for sexual favours? Given the power of social conditioning, wouldn't it be easy enough to make laughing-stocks of men who are sexually aggressive, even in talk, so that boys grew up with the absolute conviction that even to coax a woman for a kiss was – to the extent he had to coax – obvious proof of his undesirability? No doubt we should then create a percentage of men who were impotent *unless* a woman urged them on, which would be a lot less extraordinary (and much safer) than some men today who claim openly inviting women makes them impotent. What, when you think about it, could be a more ludicrous complaint than that? And yet some of us offer them sympathy and castigate the women.

Recently, a man put a lonely hearts ad in a magazine and wrote of his reactions when he received letters from women in response. He said he found himself 'enjoying an entirely novel experience . . . I was receiving the approaches of strangers.' He went on to say that, for women, this is not only a familiar situation but one they learn to be wary of. Yet for a man to talk to and meet women who have already stated their interest, however tentatively and conditionally, is unique. She is stripped, he says, of the weapons with which she has been armed from childhood. She must come as a man.

'She can't be falsely modest – she's given herself a good write-up in advance. She can't be coy – who asked her to write in the first place? The logic of the situation demands that she make it clear either that she is attracted or that she isn't. If she is, and he isn't, she has the pain of knowing that she made it clear and was rejected. Men are faced with these problems all the time. Women have one set of social pitfalls to contend with and men have another and through their maturing years they each have to develop their particular strategies for dealing with them. It needs a special kind of courage to throw off that conditioning and have a stab at the other role.'

Quite so. And at the heart of these 'particular strategies' lie the roots of the anger between the sexes and many of the misunderstandings – her anger that she is forbidden to show her interest straightforwardly, his anger that he must. Each blames the other. Each signals clumsily to the other because she must seem to be reluctant, even when she is eager, and he must seem to be eager, even when he is reluctant. In a logical world, truly interested in safeguarding women and in making as sure as possible that we choose the fathers of our children, it would be the other way round and rape would only, ever, be a twinkle in a *woman's* eye – she couldn't do much about it if she tried. Because of our present illogic, rape is seen as women's shame when it is men's, in the most basic sense, evidence of their utter rejection, their real emasculation.

The way things are, harsh sentences for rape are necessary and long overdue but they change nothing. Indeed, they divide the sexes even more, making men resentful of women and women afraid of men. What we ought to do is to stop playing roles, resist the backlash by those who claim permissive sex has gone too far and acknowledge that it hasn't gone half far enough. The more absolutely honest and open we can all become about our real sexual feelings, men *and* women, the more we will learn to trust each other and, paradoxically, the less we will be harassed if we say 'no.'

The rapist, then, will be seen by this properly permissive society for what he actually is – a violent, crippled, deviant wreck of a male – and not at all (as too many of us still see him) a man who has merely gone too far along a normal masculine path.

*15 February 1982*                                    **Jill Tweedie**


# Anglo-Argentine schooldays

The Malvinas Islands are Argentine. I have known that since I was six and General Juan Peron, sometime dictator of Argentina by popular acclamation, ordered that it should be taught in all schools. I admit to being rattled somewhat by last week's military confirmation of the assertion I had learned as a child. After all, I did not need convincing.

Anglo-Argentines, that grey component of British nationality that constitutes a community in Argentina, have never doubted that the Malvinas belong to Argentina. But there was also always a certain inward comfort in the knowledge that the British way of life – or the colonial version of it – had not been withdrawn completely from the continent and endured at a smidgen over 300 miles off the coast of Patagonia.

There was a time when Scots residents in Argentina, fortune seekers who had made their farming empires with masochistic pleasure in taming inhospitable land, visited the islands regularly from their own farms in Patagonia. Many had small coasters and trading stores on the mainland, friends and relatives on the islands. The Welsh in northern Patagonia traded with the native Indians and settlers on the mainland and with the native Scots on the islands.

That was in my father's day, in the Thirties, when he had started farming in Patagonia – in the days when Britain still controlled Argentina's economy and when Britons still talked about the 'Battle of the Falklands', in its earliest edition during the First World War, as if it had taken place the week be-

54

fore. It was the closest the war had come to them. The Second World War changed customs, the private coastal trade declined, and the visits to the Falklands did too.

After the war there was the *SS Darwin* which ran between Montevideo and Port Stanley. It must have been a new ship at one time but that was a part of its past that the *Darwin* kept well hidden. It was also strange that it was named after the naturalist – a little offensive really as he had called Patagonia one of the most barren places on earth. That association was not made however and the *Darwin*, a very ordinary tramp owned by the Falkland Islands Company, remained all its steaming life Port Stanley's only way of catching up with a world that had raced away out of reach.

The *Darwin* took Gilbey's gin and newspapers and Cadbury's chocolates to the kelpers and brought to Montevideo some of their wool clip for transhipment. Much of the wool was shipped direct to British ports by freighters that called every three months.

The *Darwin* also meant school holidays, their beginning and end – a novelty for those of us who lived in Buenos Aires. For islanders going to Britain it was the compulsory first stage of the approximation to Nirvana which for the British colonial was the slow boat 'home'.

The *Darwin* must have called at other places at some time, but in my memory of those days there seemed to be no others than Montevideo and Stanley. It was a strange and fascinating voyage. Argentina's South Atlantic coast was never far, a bewildering view of endless beaches and rock cliffs off which sand curls twirled, blown by the endless Patagonian wind. But the coast might not have existed, for it was politically not there to the *Darwin* and the Falkland Islands Company.

The *Darwin* did not call at any Argentine port, so 'Anglos' from Argentina took the nightboat from Buenos Aires to Montevideo and there boarded the *Darwin*.

Apart from the *Darwin* there was *HMS Protector* twice a year. It was a converted Second World War minesweeper with a helicopter deck and we called it a destroyer. It carried dozens of sailors who on arrival in Montevideo would spoil all the fun for us because they wooed – though they never had quite enough time to win – all our girlfriends at the British School. The sailors got very drunk at the Montevideo Cricket Club and the petty officers got too sunburned to complete the two-day cricket tests against the community sportsmen or the top form of the British School.

The sailors had the advantage of uniforms which attracted the girls. But we won in the end, not just when the *Protector* sailed away. The British community may have been true Brits but that did not mean that mothers trusted fellow Brits in naval uniform. So we had to chaperone the girls to tours and teas on *HMS Protector*. I liked it better than the *Endurance*, which always has seemed like a floating wool shed.

After *HMS Protector* had sailed, the girls – and sometimes their brothers – occasionally received postcards of the jetty at Port Stanley. In Montevideo the cards were stolen in the post office. In Buenos Aires the stamps bearing the silhouette of the monarch's head were damaged, which distressed stamp collectors at school.

I went to school in Buenos Aires and Montevideo, that is why the memories of the two cities mix.

At Saint Albans College, in the Buenos Aires southern suburb of Lomas de Zamora, and at St George's College in another suburb that owed its life to the British railways in Argentina, there were boys who were boarders. They were from the Falklands. Their parents, perhaps not wealthy enough to post them to a school at 'home', settled for the British community's imitation of a public school in Argentina.

The custom of sending boys to school in Buenos Aires, where the British had built the best of these establishments in South America, remained from before the Second World War. But after the war there was Peron, who imposed the school rule that 'the Malvinas are Argentine by right of inheritance from Spain and they were usurped by Britain in 1833.' God, were we sick of that line.

The boys from the Falklands, though British subjects, had to recite that with the rest of us at ceremonies to mark the 'Day of the Islas Malvinas'. Whenever that was I have forgotten because there is a 'day' for almost everything in

Argentina and some days take in a couple of 'days' because otherwise the year is not long enough.

And on the 'day of the Islas Malvinas' school inspectors would descend on all English-speaking schools to hear the little Brits and Anglos recite that line. Then they would ask the Falkland boys to repeat it several times and mimic them and mock their funny English accents when they spoke Spanish. The boys went to bed exhausted and in tears.

The islands grew as a political curiosity. Buenos Aires bookshops became populated with a growing variety of treatises – brief as well as bulky – giving the grounds for Argentina's claim. With the accumulation of such texts, schoolboy memories of cricket matches and of an island community which sought to be preserved in a colonial past, became papered with political pontificating. The books were all boring, terribly boring, which the islanders – all beautiful people – and those strange islands really did not deserve.

I forget how many books of such repetitive contents I have read, each of them recalling that the British ship *Endeavour* removed all British colonists from the islands in May 1774 under pressure from Spain. Argentina considers that was an acknowledgement of Spanish authority, which reverted to Buenos Aires after independence in 1816. The argument began in January 1833 when Britain objected to the Argentine claim. Britain's seizure came on the heels of a dispute between the United States and Buenos Aires because the Falklands governor – a delegate named by Buenos Aires – had captured three North American sealing ships for not paying him a tax on their catch.

In a way it is a relief that this boring story is about to come to an end. It is a pity that life beyond politics must be consigned to nostalgia. I always knew that the islands were Argentine – I learned at school that they were on the continental shelf off the mainland and I learnt when Argentina, then known as the United Provinces of the River Plate, became independent of Spain. But it was comforting to know the British were still close. I just regret it had to end this way. I never thought it would end in tears.

However, I am assured that the dispute goes on at another

level. Somewhere in Buenos Aires province, on a ranch owned by a Briton, two large Amazonian parrots, taught by their owner, start each day with the same exchange:

'Keep the Falklands British,' says one.

'Rubbish,' the other replies.

*10 April 1982*                                          **Andrew Graham-Yooll**


## Language barrier

The trouble with this sort of thing is that you can so easily sound like Professor Colin McCabe. But it is interesting, is it not, to observe the kind of language being used – no names, no pack drill, but mainly in the *Sun* – to chronicle the unhappy goings on in the South Atlantic.

Nothing terribly new about this. Paul Fussell, in his book *The Great War and Modern Memory*, drew up his own list of poetic and euphemistic language used in that conflict. A few examples: A horse was a *steed* or *charger*; to conquer was to *vanquish*; the front was the *field*; warfare was *strife*; to die was to *perish*; the army was the *legion*; the dead were the *fallen*. And so on. 'This system of "high diction",' commented Fussell, 'was not the least of the ultimate casualties of the war.'

He was being premature. The last few days have turned up a list just as impressive as Fussell's Great War catalogue, and the shooting has only just started. A few examples: The Union Jack is *The Flag of Freedom*; the South Atlantic is *the cruel waters*; British soldiers are *our brave boys*; British commandos are *our tough guys*.

The language is unashamedly discriminatory. British casualties tend to be the *price of victory*, which doesn't seem to be true of Argentine casualties. Sea Harriers tend to be *lost* or *shot down*; while Mirages and Sea Hawks are, as a general rule, *blown out of the sky*. Argentine gun boats, by the same formula, are *blasted to smithereens* while British ships are generally *sunk*.

Britain's 'brave planes' carry out bombing raids or strafe

enemy ships; Argentine pilots, by contrast, embark on *desperate suicide missions* or carry out *merciless air onslaughts*. And talking of 'brave planes,' you may have noticed that *HMS Antelope* (alias *HMS Valour*) was a *brave little frigate*, not so much blasted to smithereens as *stricken*.

*You will remember me introducing you to the Professor of Accounting at Belfast University, Professor Perks, earlier this week. Allow me to do the same today for the Professor of Accounting at Birmingham University: Professor Trevor Gambling.*

*27 May 1982*                                    **Alan Rusbridger**


# 'You can't get away from the guns'

When the Americans brought the word 'combat' into the Anglo-Saxon military vocabulary, replacing the more neutral 'action', they reinforced the persistent tendency to romanticise and misrepresent which has always accompanied the business of war. It is a tendency which has been far from absent in the Falklands conflict, to the point where an Exocet attack on a British ship is treated, obliquely, as if it were somehow 'unfair', or the beginnings of an atrocity tale are made out of a pile of napalm bombs at Goose Green.

In truth, something like 'combat' occasionally, and sometimes critically, occurs in modern battle, usually when small numbers of infantry meet in an unexpected or surprise encounter. But most soldiers, most of the time, are not 'fighting' in the sense of trading fire with identifiable, visible enemies. What they are doing, instead, is either delivering or receiving high explosives, in all the many varieties that military technology has devised.

That is the way war works, and it is no discredit to the British assault troops and their superior skills at both fighting and moving to say that what they have done is only a preliminary – an essential one – to a slaughter of the Argentinian troops around Stanley by an intense shelling and

59

bombing, against which they have few, and dwindling, defences, and no effective protection.

Most of the young men pictured on Argentinian television poking their sub-machine guns out of foxholes will never see a British infantryman between their sights. They will have been killed, or wounded, or forced into retreat, most of them, long before that moment arrives.

To be subject to accurate and sustained artillery fire is one of the nastiest experiences in war. There is no recourse in action, for the guns are much too far away, and there is no respite, no way to control, or to respond to, or to diminish the enemy's rain of fire. John Masters, describing a Chindit 'block' under Japanese fire during the Second World War, wrote of 'forty-five helpless casualties in the dressing station, all space full, and more coming. Minutes later two direct shell hits solved some of these problems with murderous thoroughness.' Or of the slow-motion dreadfulness as his inadequately protected unit was smashed to pieces: 'The shells fell slowly and burst with long, slow detonations, and the men collapsed slowly to the ground, blood flowing in gentle gouts into the mud.'

A shell from one of the British 105 mm howitzers is capable, as it bursts and spews its metal fragments, of killing or badly wounding an entire squad of 14 men. The naval shells which British warships can deliver in such quantities – although probably only at night, to avoid Argentinian air attack – can be just as lethal, even though not principally designed for killing people. To the shells have to be added the cluster bombs of the Harriers. A cluster bomb breaks up into a number of individual bomblets which, exploding simultaneously, fill an area half the size of a football field with lethal shards. Against this assault by metal, which has already begun and which will now intensify, the Argentinians have only the most inadequate defences. They have their own guns, of course, and they will attempt counter-battery fire. They have anti-aircraft weapons, and the mainland air force is still capable of intervention against British ships, planes, or troops. But their guns will be progressively taken out by British fire before they can register the changing positions of the British tubes; their AA will be similarly ploughed up; and their mainland aircraft have so little time to operate over the Falklands before returning home that their effectiveness against land targets will be minimal.

Worse, for the troops on the bleak grassland around Stanley, there is no adequate protection. It is possible to protect troops against shellfire by putting them under concrete, which the Argentinians have had no time to pour. A good second best is a stout combination of timber, sandbags, and earth, in which, for instance, many troops, of both sides, sat out bombardments in Vietnam in relative safety. Command post bunkers of that ilk would often have overhead cover four foot thick. But timber is virtually unobtainable in the Falklands, and the water table is so high that trenches cannot even be dug deeper to compensate for the lack of overhead protection.

The boys pegged out in holes in the peat around Stanley are going to take a terrible punishment, and, if they retreat to avoid it, the increasingly compacted main garrison will take worse punishment in turn – unless they surrender. That is what, stripped of euphemism, we are now saying to the Argentinians. We are not saying: surrender, or we will engage you in infantry combat – although we will do that, ultimately, or before then, if easy opportunities occur. We are saying: surrender, or we will gradually and painfully blow your infantry to pieces, without you being able to exact any kind of serious price from us.

That threat is in keeping with the tradition of nineteenth-century British war-making to which, in so many curious ways, the Falklands conflict is a return. Kipling put into the mouth of his master gunner these lines, chilling in their jovial brutality.

*For you all love the screw guns – the screw guns they all love you.*
*So when we call around with a few guns, O' course you will know what to do – hoo! hoo!*
*Just send in your Chief and surrender – it's worse if you fights or you runs :*

*You may hide in the caves, they'll be only your graves,*
   *but you can't get away from the guns.*

The American military historian S.L.A. Marshal, writing of troops under shellfire, said: 'No one has ever managed to diagnose the emotions of fish in a barrel.' That is what the Argentinian garrison is well on the way to becoming – fish in a barrel.

It would be ludicrous to suggest, of course that the British commanders should thrust their men into the attack just so the Argentinians can have the satisfaction of a 'fair fight', or so they can be brought to defeat with an infantry casualty list three or four times as long as the one we will, thanks to the guns, otherwise face. But the price of minimising our casualties is to maximise theirs; and in venting our indignation at Argentinian stupidity, or intransigence – or napalm – we should surely bear in mind how inevitably brutal our own plans for victory are.

*4 June 1982*                                **Martin Woollacott**


# A country diary: Kent

Two swans trod tentatively across the ice. One hundred yards behind them was open water with a mass of gulls, tufted duck, mallard and Canada geese. Yet the swans persisted in their isolated track, webbed feet pointing slightly inwards, heads down. Then the cob sat down. Fell down, I thought at first, but the action had an air of deliberation. The pen caught up with its mate and the cob stood up again. There was a pool of water on top of the ice where the bird had rested, thawed by the warmth of its body. The two carried on determinedly. There were creaking noises, the groaning of ice about to break, then the cob sat down again and there was even more water about when it stood up. The pen, following a parallel course, repeated the action.

The process began to look like deliberate action rather than random exploration on thin ice. The two of them sat down hard together. The ice creaked, the surface broke, and the swans moved their broad breasts rhythmically from side to side, freeing more of the ice, then they dipped their heads deep into the icy water, probing the unseen depths. Using their bodies as ice-breakers they continued their procession until they reached another stretch of open water near a small waterfall which had kept the water moving enough to prevent a complete freeze-up. I wondered why the two birds should make such efforts to break new ground, or rather new ice, when open water was already available. Was a new feeding area of such importance? The function of the webbed feet and the long powerful neck is familiar, but now the broad front of the birds showed a function I had not really noticed before. The sheer weight of the swans, at forty lbs one of the heaviest of flying birds, gives them the role of ice-breaker which no other bird can match. The birds royal completed their pioneering progress and fed contentedly.

*22 January 1982*                                           **John T. White**


# Winning is only half the battle

There is never a day now for clear thought. Either Argentine jets are high-technology coffins cartwheeling in profusion from the skies: the days when victory seems easy. Or our frigates and destroyers and supply ships are blazing hulks: the days when it is weakness to talk of any thing but hardened resolve and ultimate triumph.

Yesterday was one of the bleak days. The *Coventry*, exposed on picket duty, was at the bottom of Falkland Sound. The *Atlantic Conveyor*, mistaken perhaps for *Hermes* on Argentine radar screens, was an Exocet-battered wreck. Ministers and MPs gathered again in mutual grief, consoled themselves that the loss of life might have been worse and, with barely a questioning voice, decided to push onwards.

No one in these islands is free from either the grief or the impulse – under wounding attack – to strike on. But there must, somehow, also be a time for clear thought. Military thought, first of all. Our troops are established around Port San Carlos. Our flag flies once more over the Falklands. There can be no serious doubt that, in time, we can repossess the islands. It may take longer than the proclaimers of instant victory thought. There is a shipful of stores beneath the South Atlantic now. The Argentine air force, with suicidal courage, comes and comes again, taking an almost scientifically calculable toll of Britain's naval protective cover. But, in the end, their resources will expire before ours. Their garrison cannot be resupplied. They will lose.

It may be swifter and easier than that. Perhaps the Argentine army – the shivering eighteen-year-olds, of whom we hear so much – are less stalwart than the Skyhawk and Mirage pilots. Perhaps they will crumble fast as the paratroopers push beyond the bridgehead. But perhaps not. The jet pilots tumbling from the sky betoken the dogged, unthinking heroism of war, and of a cause – Argentine patriotism, the Malvinas – which the British have tragically underestimated. Six weeks ago our television was full of 'dagoes' fleeing at the first sight of 'cold steel'. They are ill-coordinated and poorly led. But they are brave, on their record, and trapped out with the sophisticated weaponry of Western export drives. And we may have to blow many hundreds of them to bits around Port Stanley – clinically bombarding from vulnerable ships offshore – until the white flag flutters. There is carnage now. There is more carnage to come. And it is necessary, alas, to set such bloodshed present and bloodshed future against the stated aims not merely of this Government but of all those, across the parties of Parliament, who see no break in conflict.

Britain's stated aims have changed in the seven days since the Cabinet finally sanctioned re-invasion. Mr Francis Pym, last Thursday, after that decision had been taken, was still explicitly anxious to find a peaceful solution. The UN Secretary-General could continue to draw on the 'constructive support' of Great Britain. Over the weekend that changed. Downing Street foresaw no outcome but 'complete Argentine surrender'. Mrs Thatcher and Mr Nott talked afresh about paramountcy for the islanders. Mr Nott said sovereignty could 'never' be given up. That would be 'absurd'. Mrs Thatcher who, a week earlier, had intervened to chide him for saying 'never', this time gave only reinforcement. Mr Pym, before an American audience, talked of six or twelve-month cooling off periods. His Prime Minister, scornful of such tap dances, put only British administration and paramountcy and complete island vetoes on the table. She believes in the 'status quo ante'; she believes that the Falklanders must then choose, declaring that they cannot conceivably choose Argentina; and then she talks of her belief in negotiation. But she does not say what there will be left to negotiate about.

It is, of course, hard to concentrate on differing ministerial pronouncements when men are dying and ships are sinking. The business can seem carping and unreal, dwarfed by the reality of war. But our brave and phlegmatic task force was sent into action over just such carefully drafted formulas; and when the shooting stops, those formulas will be of paramount concern again. The present concern is that nobody can tell what they will be or how, emotionally, this will match the blazing action on Falkland Sound.

Yet it is vital to consider them now, since not only will they end the fighting but determine, at the close, what the fighting was about: why, in short, so many died. And here the void of thought or purpose grows distressing. Mr Pym says the future after re-possession is 'uncertain'. There will be 'consultation with many nations' about 'some pattern of defence'. Could he be more specific? 'I cannot be.' Mr Nott, too, floats ideas of security guarantees from regional powers. Including Argentina? Not including Argentina. He seeks a 'sensible and wise and peaceful accommodation with the countries of South America'. Including Argentina? He tells the Falklanders, by radio, that 'they might like to think in terms of independence, secured by some international agreement . . . a very small nation on its own, of course dependent on the goodwill of its neighbours.' The goodwill of Argentina, or are there other neighbours we have not heard about?

Those Falkland Islanders who are refugees in Britain are

already being led to believe – indeed told directly – that the status quo ante, the right to remain exactly as they were, with a £10 million new runway, a strong British garrison and unlimited trade subsidy across eight thousand miles of ocean, is theirs for the asking. Meanwhile the Falklanders on the islands are being told of a different prospect: 'very small' independence with 'goodwill' – in return for what? – from Buenos Aires. How can we be specific, say the Cabinet, until we have consulted the islanders in freedom? Maybe. But the questions that will be put to the islanders in freedom, the options that Britain can present to them at that moment, are at the heart of the reason for continuing conflict: and it is an abdication of political responsibility not to rehearse them clearly. What could be more pointless or cruel than to seem to hold out the status quo ante at this moment whilst knowing, in sotto voce calculation, that it can never be restored?

This is not malevolence on the politicians' part: it is simple, fatal muddle. It calls into being international arrangements which do not exist (and cannot be presently discussed) which pretend that Argentina, imbued with the bizarre passion for the Malvinas, spilling blood copiously for it, can somehow magically be transformed from rabid wolf to toy poodle at the snap of Mrs Thatcher's fingers.

That is self-delusion. The more Argentines we kill along the road to Port Stanley – and the more of our troops who give their lives – then the less possible becomes the aim of the entire task force expedition (a lasting peace) and the more inconceivable any 'fruit' of victory except the one we have striven for twenty years not to win: that is heavily armed, immensely costly possession in perpetuity of distant islands we do not want and shall have no practical use for.

Our allies – meanwhile – look on in apprehension and perplexity. They berate the Argentine aggressor. They understand the inevitable motors of military action. They revile the chaotic imbecility of the junta. But they know, too, that all our woolly phrases about 'international guarantees' and 'regional protection' is so much mindless buck-passing (to them, and they do not want it) unless there is something at the end to negotiate about, some compromise for peace that takes the Falklands off the agenda for ever; and they cannot see what no ceasefire, UN vetoes, total victory at whatever cost, leaves as a basis for any arrangement or any 'goodwill.'

We are, in short, ruling out a negotiated settlement – indeed any outcome other than patchy, sporadic exchanges between mainland and island garrisons – if we leave nothing for the Argentines to negotiate about. We quote again – because it is the voice of an ally beyond the hot-house of British opinion – from the Washington Post: 'Does the Thatcher Government expect to retain the support it now enjoys for war aims it has yet to define? Does it believe there is any ultimate way to ensure the future of the islands without consulting the Argentines directly? It was, after all, inattention to the Argentine interest and the Argentine passion in the first place that got Mrs Thatcher into the situation she is now attempting to redeem by arms. She has right and reason to oppose Argentine aggression but, now that she is fighting, she cannot ignore the central political reality; there is really only one other nation with which Britain must work out the fate of the islands – Argentina. The sooner that process can resume, the fewer men will die.

Talk of a ceasefire, then, is not the puling of voices afraid to fight or queasy at the seepage of blood. A ceasefire with our troops firmly on the island, the flag planted, the supply ships pouring in, is not the ceasefire of weeks ago; a tossing stand-off on the ocean. It is a pause before inevitable but costly Argentinian defeat. It gives the chance of withdrawal that the generals, in the face of desperate losses, have been preparing their public for. It allows Mr Perez de Cuellar (and perhaps 'magnanimous' Mr Haig) their chance to return. It permits a settlement. Yet day after day now, in tones that make political retreat increasingly difficult, we are led to believe that the possibility of ceasefire is damp cowardice. Better the certainty of complete military conquest and the 'uncertainty' of future diplomacy.

That is not a tenable or logical belief. It dismays the peace-makers. It promises only everlasting misery for the tiny community of Falklanders – especially the old and infirm trapped in Port Stanley. Our troops, with fortitude, are enduring and

67

succeeding. But they know – and Admiral Woodward has said – that only the politicians can make peace. It is not strength in a politician, amidst the clamour from the back-benches, to shun that obligation, to hold that only pounding bombardment and shattered limbs can bring conclusion. It is weakness; weakness of perception and of imagination. The diplomats now offer the hard road: the road of hard reality, hard truths, hard speeches, hard thought yesterday, as for a few seconds in the House, Mr Nott appeared to shuffle in that direction: and the UN is stirring. There must be a moment soon, perhaps in the shock of loss, perhaps on a tide of optimism, when our politicians abandon the blankness of the days since re-invasion and begin to lead again.

*27 May 1982*                                                    **Leader**


# Living like a camouflaged frog

To be ill-equipped both against the killing cold of the Antarctic nights and the enemy bombs was an unexpected challenge. Believing that four days aboard a heavily laden ammunition ship under daily attack was extending one's luck to an unreasonable degree, I escaped ashore by helicopter at San Carlos, and after fifty-one days at sea, savoured for the first time the smell of grass, the sight of children at play, and sheepdogs. There was almost a deafening quiet on land after so long living in the constant noise and motion of a warship.

But it seemed that even the dogs were a menace, for they were infected with a liver fluke which lived in the waters of local streams. I only found this out when a Special Boat Squadron man saw me patting one. He was an officer I had known from the days on Invincible, and he was horrified to hear that the reporters who came down to the Falklands attached to the Navy had not been able to benefit from the full military kitting-out that had been given to other correspondents who sailed down with paratroops and marines. 'You'll never survive dressed like that,' he said. I was wearing jeans, a waterproof jacket and my shoes were completely masked in mud. My civilian canvas hold-all was falling to pieces from the continual soakings.

My friend from the Green Death – affectionate service slang for the elite unit who wore jungle-camouflaged fatigues – took me back to his unit base, a privilege I would have relished in other circumstances. There, in a deserted white-washed cottage, the special forces had made a little home from home. As we approached the house, the delicious smell of roast goose came floating through the air, just like the Bisto Kid advertisement, and I realised that I hadn't eaten properly for some days.

I spent that night sandwiched for survival between the sleeping bags of the SAS and SBS who talked, long into the darkness, about the philosophy of war and its poetry, and the latest books. One commando was an expert on George Bernard Shaw, and quoted him at length. The Green Death, who specialise in covert activities, then devised a plan by which they would each go out and 'prof' (i.e. acquire) some clothing for me.

These were no masked assassins blasting their way through the windows of the Iranian Embassy but gentle – to me at least – and thinking people. My experience with them was just one facet of the friendliness shared by men in the midst of war. In three months, I never heard a cross word spoken, but many a helpful and humorous one.

In the early hours I began to shake with cold, for the peat stove which had cooked the goose had finally burnt low. Gingerly picking my way across the sleeping bodies arranged across the living-room floor – for it is not a good idea suddenly to waken a member of the Green Death who no doubt could bite the head off a flying bat – I walked into their radio room established in the back kitchen among pots and pans. I was just in time to hear the SBS radio operator intercepting an Argentinian message which said that the enemy had fixed our position in their night sights and were about to start an artillery bombardment centred on our cottage.

The sleeping Marines were given a gentle shake. But their reaction to the threat was simply to start brewing a massive grenade-container full of tea. Then they all went back to sleep again. 'Sleep, you know,' said a Scottish sergeant-philosopher, 'is one of God's greatest gifts, and you must accept it whenever you can.'

In one of my many personal escapades to try to cadge clothing, one night I crossed San Carlos bay three times in a Gemini rubber dinghy which skimmed the surface of the waves, sometimes narrowly missing the blacked out shapes of other ships in the anchorage, and literally taking off into the air as we hit the wakes of other invisible vessels which were dashing around in the night.

I was looking for a place called Blue Beach Two where the SAS had reported seeing a mountain of kit. We finally found the jetty and a voice said from out of the darkness: 'Password?' I replied, rather feebly: 'I'm very sorry, I don't know what the password is tonight. No-one has told me.' I heard the sentry cock his sub-machine gun and froze on the ladder up to the jetty. 'Well, who are you?' he asked. I told him.

'Oh, the *Manchester Guardian*. My Dad reads that. Well, look, the password tonight is Open House. I say Open and you say House – no the other way around. And then I say "Advance friend and be recognised. Okay?"' I thanked him, and we proceeded with the dialogue as directed.

But there was no kit available on Blue Beach Two so I crossed the water again.

I went back to sea and this time my new ship was an empty Royal Fleet Auxiliary which immediately sailed from San Carlos out towards the two carriers in the Total Exclusion Zone.

We all wondered why we had been given such a strange order. But then it became clear. For five days, the Sir Geraint acted as an Exocet foil, for after the sinking of the Atlantic Conveyor when she attracted a missile away from the Invincible, it had become very clear that the best way of protecting our vulnerable carriers against Exocet was to place 'sacrificial' ships all around them. But we survived another three Exocet attacks that week.

The overwhelming mood among the British servicemen was one of comradeship, but tension and sheer fatigue took their toll as the weeks turned into months at war. On the Invincible, during one missile attack, I found myself at action stations with a group of sailors in what was effectively a sealed compartment. We were, anyway, living most of the time prepared for attack, but somehow the jarring klaxon of action stations always jangled a man's nerves.

We were sitting on the deck, many feet below the water-line, believing that at any moment our compartment could be either flooded or blasted by an explosion. One young sailor next to me had in his cupped hand a photograph of a young woman with a baby in her arms, and he was crying. When I later included this in a report, one of the officers vetting my copy said: 'I find this extremely difficult to believe.' It was the only time in the whole experience that I had heard anyone accused of lying. But despite the obvious trauma of the Navy, as a traditionally 'silent service', at having a number of their natural enemies, the press, living with them, correspondents were treated with great courtesy and friendliness.

The attitude of a very few officers to their men was, however, surprising, and when the deeply unpopular decision was taken not to grant the usual additional pay in the form of LOA – Local Overseas Allowance – one commander said to me: 'They are pretty lucky to be here in regular employment, and not on the dole queue at home.' By contrast, the relationship between officers and men in the land forces was markedly more relaxed. Everyone dug his own slit trench and the biggest crime was to try to impose on the privacy of the muddy holes in which the owner crouched on a stone above the surface of the water, like a camouflaged frog.

Air raid warnings on shore were signalled by a blast on a whistle and the shouted words 'Air raid warning Red.' Within seconds everyone had taken cover and there would be a complete silence as people strained their ears for the sound of an approaching jet engine. After a time of inaction a head would pop up out of the ground and ask 'Is it Yellow yet?' The Yellow state was the all-clear but the question was too often misheard and shouts of Yellow would be mistakenly passed from trench to trench. Then as people started to emerge from their holes, almost inevitably someone would shout 'It's still bloody Red!', and the whole demented panto-mime would start again.

Life aboard ship was far more formal and disciplined. The day would start four hours before dawn broke, with a prayer from the padre over the Tannoy. I remember well the day after *Sheffield*, when 'anxiety', as the Navy nicely terms fear, was very high. After a word from the captain about the prospects of 'a very interesting day lying ahead which will challenge us all' the padre came on and began a special prayer 'for those of us who today may die.' Up until that moment the sailors around me at action stations had been forcedly cheerful. But their morale sank as suddenly as any ship we were to see. The padre never used that prayer again.

The presentation of the Falklands war has been carefully sanitised. Pictures and descriptions of casualties have been discreet, and I believe rightly, for the sake of relatives. Even now to attempt to describe some of the more horrific sights and sounds of a war would be unkind.

But the ballooned faces of badly burned men whose clothes had been welded on to their bodies by the searing flash of an explosion; the screams in the night from the dormitories on the ships acting as refuges for the survivors: these can never be erased from the memories of those who saw and heard them – nor should they, for this was so often the price of victory in a bloody campaign. 'Warmongers and people who delight in death and destruction are not welcome in this department,' said a notice taped to the door of a com-partment on one of the ships. In the Task Force, if not in the saloon bars of England, there was little taste for glory achieved at such a cost. Even seasoned officers said they never wanted to return to Goose Green, the insignificant hamlet where 300 men died in a few hours. The scene after the battle was ghastly. There were rows upon rows of corpses badly charred by the phosphorus of artillery shells. In several places there were rifles stuck in the mud with helmets on them, marking where men died. Days later, Argentine prisoners went round the trenches of their fallen comrades, yanking out bodies by the legs and throwing them in a pile on a tractor trailer. There were bits of human remains almost everywhere, and there were pigs rooting around the battle-field. I saw one pig lazily scratching himself on the side of an unexploded 1000-lb bomb.

Scraps of paper being blown about with the wind turned out to be good luck cards drawn by Argentine school-children. They were very similar to the drawings that British children sent us: the kind of simple drawings you would see on the wall of any primary school.

A mass grave on a hill overlooking Darwin, only two miles from Goose Green, where the bodies were taken for a brief service conducted jointly by an English and an Argentine padre, was itself a continuing horror. As the days went by and the water began to rise from the clay, the bodies wrapped up in drab green ponchos would start to float. Only the sight of two black boots sticking out of the battle shrouds gave any real clue that these pathetic bundles were once human.

At the airstrip in Goose Green there were tons of canisters of the most feared weapon of modern war: napalm. Britain had agreed never to use it but it seems that the Argentine intention had been different. Some senior officers were horrified by the number of napalm canisters and said that their use against our troops could have altered the whole course of the campaign.

Even without napalm, flash-burns were the most horrific-ally common wound, especially among Navy personnel. You could always tell burned people from a distance, for they moved about often shaking their hands in their efforts to cool the burning skin. Some people with burns were given plastic bags to wear on their hands. The bags were filled with a bleach-like powder which eased the pain to some little extent, prevented infection, and promoted healing. But for the men who were literally skinned by the explosions there was only the fitful escape of morphine-induced sleep.

Although one of the hospital ships was staffed by psychiatrists who were there to cope with the stresses of war on the minds of men, many survivors who were ostensibly bright and cheerful during their waking hours, would suddenly scream and shout in their sleep. One night I spent in a dormitory for wounded men. One of them abruptly howled in his sleep, setting off a bedlam chain reaction from the others, who awoke in panic.

The people who coped best with the horrors of war, it seemed, were the Falklanders. More often than not they went about their daily lives as if the troops swarming around them did not exist. In Port San Carlos a hostel used by the sheep-shearers had been converted into a casualty clearing station and the scrubbed pine kitchen table was an operating bench, lines with surgical instruments, saline drips and huge wedges of field dressings. Almost inevitably the living room next door had a picture of the Queen and Prince Phillip, and in an adjoining room a family of Falklanders were enjoying yet another meal of lamb chops.

The islanders never seemed particularly glad to see us, although that could be put down to their natural reserve and shyness with strangers. One man told me that they wouldn't know the full cost of the war for as long as seven months, when the sheep were gathered for shearing. This was said in Goose Green.

My enduring impression of the British at war is one of incredible courage and professionalism throughout all the serving men. As one sailor told me: 'We have enjoyed years of peace and sailing to glamorous parts of the world to show the flag. But now we are doing what we were paid to do all along. Although we have been trained to fight, there was never any way in which we could have been prepared for some of the terrible things we've seen.'

I have brought back with me from the Falklands one small poignant, tangible reminder of the human loss of the grief which follows a war. At Goose Green I was given a spare pair of combat trousers, from a pile of Argentine clothes which had been left in a house. In one of the pockets I found a plain silver wedding ring inscribed in Spanish 'To My

Darling'. I am sending the ring back to a padre in Buenos Aires whose address I have been given. Whether its owner will return, I will probably never know.

*3 July 1982*                                    **Gareth Parry**


# Ends, and an oddity

Some statistical odds and ends of war have been quietly tidied up this week amid the joyous homecomings and the Inquiry debatings. Casualties, for example, can now be properly assessed: 1032 (255 dead, 777 wounded on the British side); 1798 dead, wounded or missing among the Argentinians – a figure which may yet err evasively on the side of understatement. In total the Falklands claimed at least 2,830 dead and wounded.

One end, however, has actually grown rather odder through the last seven days. It will not, one guesses, be much inquired into. It is a small patch of cloud in a blue sky of heroism and achievement. Nonetheless, the oddness of the conflicting evidence should not go entirely unremarked.

On May 2 – before a single life had been lost, before the *Sheffield* and the rest – HMS *Conqueror*, a British hunter-killer submarine, torpedoed and sank the vintage Argentinian cruiser, the *General Belgrano*. At first it was feared that as many as a thousand seamen had died. In the end the figure was set at 368, the biggest toll in a single incident throughout the campaign. There followed, predictably, many political and diplomatic waves. No episode did more to create Latin American and UN problems for Britain.

Much agonised questioning within Britain and inside the House of Commons ensued. And General Galtieri, for what it is worth (which may not be a great deal) later blamed the 'outrage' of the *Belgrano* for the failure of Mr Alexander Haig's peace shuttling.

What was said at the time? On 4 May, announcing matters to the House, Mr John Nott described the *Belgrano* and its two accompanying destroyers as 'a heavily armed attack group close to the total exclusion zone and closing on elements of our task force, which were only hours away.' The escorting destroyers, he believed, 'were equipped with Exocet anti-ship missiles.' The threat, he said, 'was such that the task force commander could ignore it only at his peril.' Only the *Belgrano* was attacked, 'so that the escorting destroyers should have been able to go to the assistance of the damaged cruiser.'

Mr Denis Healey, active in the cause of accuracy, understood that the action took place thirty-six miles outside the exclusion zone we had publicly set, and asked how far away the task force actually was. Mr Nott said thirty-five miles, and then thirty, but declined – for security reasons – to reveal how far distant the fleet had been. 'Only hours,' he repeated. Mr Healey would know 'that communications are not necessarily received instantly by a submarine. It sometimes takes time for communications to be made for reasons that have to do with the natural concealment of the submarine. . . .' Pressed again, he reiterated that 'delay in communications.' Pressed once more, the following day, he said: 'The actual decision to launch a torpedo was clearly one taken by the submarine commander, but that decision was taken within very clear rules of engagement which had been settled in London and discussed by the Government.' The message was clear enough to all in Parliament who heard him. The commander of the Conqueror had taken his own steps within existing guidelines. He had blown up the *Belgrano* because he considered it a threat.

A week later Mr Nott was back, late at night in Westminster, to amplify his answers to the dogged (and jeered) Mr Healey. The distance between *Belgrano* and the task force was now known: 200 nautical miles or 'five or six hours,' assuming they had been mutually converging at speed. The total exclusion zone, however, was 'not relevant in this case.' We had apparently told the Argentinians ten days before that any vessel which posed 'what amounted to a threat to interfere' would encounter 'the appropriate response.' 'Under certain rules of engagement already agreed,' the submarine thus attacked the cruiser. The task force in general was 'at all times under political control.' Mrs Thatcher was having regular, 'almost daily,' meetings with everyone concerned. The House took a second message that the *Belgrano* was actually rather a long way distant, but that if Rear Admiral Woodward thought it a threat – zone or no zone – then that would be supported. In any event, the *Sheffield* had by then gone down and the *Belgrano* had faded here as an issue.

This week Commander Christopher Wreford-Brown and the *Conqueror* returned to Britain. He had, he said, been tracking the *Belgrano* for hours. Communications, though, do not appear to have been a problem. 'I was under direct orders from Fleet Headquarters and they were confirmed to me directly before the attack.' It was not his decision, nor Admiral Woodward's; he had asked Sir John Fieldhouse, Fleet Commander-in-Chief at Northwood, and been told to sink the *Belgrano*. Northwood chimes in to point out that, after the encounter, the Argentinian ships were pinned apprehensively in their home ports. A success. Commander Wreford-Brown says the *Belgrano*, too, had Exocets. Rear Admiral Woodward says the people he blames for the large loss of life were 'the escorts, who ran away, which is not the sort of behaviour I would expect from anybody.'

There are discrepancies here of a curious kind. Mr Nott begins by referring to the exclusion zone and ends by claiming it wasn't relevant. The looming threat of a task force clash, after ten days, pondering, turn out to have unloomed across 200 miles. Exocets suddenly sprout on the *Belgrano* (assuming a public significance that, before the *Sheffield*, they didn't have). And 'communications difficulties', repeatedly cited, still enabled the *Conqueror* to chat directly to Northwood, quite bypassing the task force commander on whom Mr Nott had earlier been anxious to lay a second tier of responsibility. Communications, indeed, are the oddest link in this chain of contradiction and inconsistency. Either they were very bad: in which case everything Mr Nott said to the House can be explained. Or they were very good, as Commander Wreford-Brown's account would have us believe: in which case Mr Nott was tap dancing. There is

77

nothing wrong intrinsically with the two versions of events –
one a lonely captain beneath mountainous seas using his own
best judgment, the other a fearsome central lesson designed
to send the Argentinian fleet scuttling home – but the two
versions simply don't fit together; just as Sandy Woodward's
notion that the Argies were too thick to see that we'd be too
gentlemanly to attack the escort rescuers doesn't fit with Sir
John Fieldhouse's notion that of course we were free to
interpret our 200-mile zone in any ungentlemanly way we
pleased.

In victory, of course, hair shirts are not worn; nor is
querulous introspection encouraged. Nasty things do happen
in war: this nasty thing happened. We shall forget it: and be
pained, perhaps, to discover at some later date that the
Argentinians – or at least 368 Argentinian families – may not
be so keen on forgetfulness. Fortunes of war, no doubt:
exigencies of the service. But it is necessary, nonetheless, to
register amid so many deeds of untrammelled heroism that
the old *Belgrano* lies fathoms deep in a rather greyer and
uneasier grave.

*10 July 1982*                                             **Leader**


## An acre of sadness

When people are in love, it seems, they write much nonsense.
When they grow out of love they do much the same, but
backwards. Like, as it were, Hebrew.

That is straining the metaphor until it creaks, but you
know what I mean.

It took the Israelis two thousand years to achieve their
homeland; it took them another generation to make it
flourish and bloom, and greatly did the Western world
applaud and respect their tenacity and courage and purpose.

It took them just two months to bring that respect and
admiration to dust, to change the image of the gallant victim
and survivor to that of the braggart and bully. It required a
man of the dedicated charmless insensitivity of a Menachem

Begin to lose for Israel, simultaneously, immense resources of international goodwill and domestic unity. Neither will now be easy to restore.

As a goy outsider I was personally a part of that birth-of-a-nation process from 1948, and even before, so paradoxically did I become involved first in the small accomplishments and then the bigger ones. I recognised the sentimentality, but I was hardly alone in that.

I now suddenly remember that in fact long ago I was formally and officially given a notional acre of a hundred trees of Israeli woodland somewhere or other in Galilee; I never learned exactly where nor did it ever occur to me to find out, if it in fact exists at all other than on the piece of paper they gave me thirteen years ago.

Now, however, it strongly occurs to me that I should return to claim my gift-right, and declare in my little acre a kind of UDI in protest at the outrages in Lebanon.

Is this apostasy? If so, I share it with countless Jews and even Israelis now made aghast at the obsessions of Beginismus.

Begin of the Irgun resistance in the 1940s was one thing: Begin as the embittered mini-fuehrer of the 1980s is another. That one can even use the words would have shocked and horrified David Ben Gurion, the first Premier, and indeed his successors, and it now shocks me. The words are not even mine; I lift them from an Israeli paper. The Israeli press is censored but not supine. It is the most intelligent press in the Middle East. I am glad I do not have to work for it.

It is clear that whatever happens to Lebanon now Beirut can no longer be worth looking at or trying to save, and that can be of no advantage to anyone. Thus goes the only large city of any urban civility in the Middle East, since you could hardly so describe the hideosities of Damascus, Baghdad, or Tel-Aviv.

It is immensely significant to see how the British press has almost gone into reverse over the last month. Correspondents who over the years have been understanding and even sympathetic to the Israeli situation are now impelled, albeit reluctantly, to reflect the regret and bitterness at the brutalisation inflicted on the one Middle East state that never formally took up arms against Israel, that retreated into neutrality even to the point of national humiliation and that is now crushed perhaps forever between the upper and the nether millstones.

The initially proclaimed Israeli plan was to clear a forty-kilometre cordon sanitaire in the Lebanon north of Galilee. They achieved that perhaps too easily; the chance of eliminating the PLO became too tempting, and Israel fell into its own trap.

It is being said today that the forty-kilometre 'cordon' was a stratagem anyway, that the blitzkreig was intended from the start. If so it was a negation of Israel's pretensions of 'solely defensive' wars – which previous conflicts had indeed been – and Israel cannot again claim to be a beleagured enclave of democracy in a hostile Arab world. That will be a pity especially for the like of us, who created exactly that image so long ago, in another world.

Do we ask too much of those we once admired? Why should there be anything special about the Israelis because they are the Chosen People?

Only the other day in the *Guardian* the Chief Rabbi Jakobovits told Terry Coleman: yes. 'It is part of the liturgical vocabulary, and we thank God daily for being chosen.'

Is 'liturgical vocabulary' a sanction for blowing up Beirut? It is hard to believe that the mountebank Yasser Arafat could so readily have created for himself the role of martyr. It has always been the tenable Israeli case that the PLO have been indifferent to causing civilian casualties and casual about their own. To the PLO Arabs have been as expendable as Jews. Now they have manoeuvred the Israels into slaughtering Lebanese just because Lebanon was used by the PLO as a sanctuary, and while that may make a sort of military sense it makes for disastrous public relations. The wounded babies in the photos now are Arab; that never happened until Beirut.

Israel may win the immediate battle – she always does – but she has lost something else, and if Israel does not regret it, her friends most bitterly do. Long years ago William Ewer wrote: 'How odd of God – to choose the Jews.'

God did not choose the Jews. The Jews chose God, because they invented him.

Does anyone want my Galilean acre and my hundred trees?

*10 August 1982*                                  **James Cameron**


# A fight for life

It's not all beer and Hush Puppies being a TV cameraman, I can tell you. One minute it's, 'We're off to cover a heart transplant at Harefield. You're assistant cameraman, Paul. In case Pat and Tony keel over. Time and a half lads, cocoa money and all the nurses you can eat.' The next it's, 'Did you know you're B positive? Have you had any of these diseases? Lie down here.'

Paul Cave's face as he realised that he was the only one in the TV team with B positive blood reminded one strongly of the great archetypal blood donor Tony Hancock. ('A joke's a joke but I'm not walking round with an empty arm for anybody.')

Pat or Tony – there is very little camaraderie among cameramen – recorded the eloquent play of expression on a face which, despite the brave moustache, was quite young. 'I don't like blood,' he said touchingly. 'Don't look then,' said the nurse.

Cave was one of thirty-five people who gave blood when Vaju Manek began to haemorrhage badly in *A Fight For Life*, the second in the *Heart Transplant* series (BBC-2). Fresh blood with the clotting factor intact was needed and it was most moving to see how people came in the middle of the night from their beats, from their beds, from the BBC, to help this stranger. A man from the nearby RAF station, a uniformed policewoman, the daughter of a former transplant patient and her friend. This one had an Irish accent. That one was black. Hauled out of one bed and told to lie down on another, half dazed, nearly dreaming. 'At least that's worth being woken up for,' said the RAF man when he was told why the blood was needed.

Vaju's wife Pushpa, and his daughter, Neeta, had been the first to give their blood. Neeta, a doctor, must have guessed what this desperate thirst for blood, five times the usual amount needed for a transplant, indicated.

It was a bloody operation but far too engrossing to be distressing. Personally, I would have liked to have seen precisely what the surgeons were doing rather than guess it, by implication. Startling humdrum comments like 'put your finger on this one', which would make you uneasy if uttered by plumbers, made you long to jostle for a better view.

A heart transplant is high-class plumbing and the sound of it was wet and splashy or like those sucking noises you hear in a dentist's chair. Blood flowed, nearly flew, down tubes. There were literally bags of blood. A surgeon's mask was smeared with it. I thought at first that the lamp over the table was splattered with it until I realised it was a mirror, reflecting Manek's open chest.

When they opened the chest the team discovered that his heart was stuck to his breast bone. His aorta punctured, blood welled out of him and his circulation was stopped to find the damage and prepare it. This was when Uxbridge was shaken awake with desperate requests for B positive blood. The operation took twice the normal time, eight and half hours.

Bruce Anderson, the heart patient who had been passed over, in favour of Vaju Manek, woke and told the nurse he had been disturbed all night by the sound of the plumbing. A coincidence that made me jump. Pushpa and Neeta turned their strained faces to the surgeon, Mr Yacoub, who said Vaju was all right but it was early days yet. 'We are behind you. Thank you very much, sir. Oh God,' said Neeta kissing her mother. And, quite suddenly, you could not see.

Vaju Manek died the next day. At Harefield a group of women were talking about Pushpa: 'She was so upset I just didn't know what to say to her. I cuddled her a bit but what

can you say? There are no words.' Sitting at the next table,
waiting for the next heart, Bruce Anderson said nothing.

*2 April 1982*                          **Nancy Banks-Smith**


# Cut to the bone

My international fame as an economist is not great but I shall
never learn unless I try. My household economy might seem
odd, but it is no dafter than that of the nation.

I spend £25,000 a year on smoked salmon and I have a
£10,000 burglar-alarm to protect my ten-bobs'-worth of
knick-knacks, but I cannot afford to buy bread and butter.
I have replaced the tiles on my roof with steel armour at a
cost of about £13,000, but my drains have not worked for
years. I earn in money about 28 per cent of what I spend; I
grow progressively poorer in real terms and I go on bragging
about what I pay my bodyguards. I go about, as I have
always done, as a national exemplar of my native glory. I am
a Ditcher who calls himself a Thatcher. I wish it were a new
joke, but alas there are no new jokes now.

It must have been rather blush-making last week for Sir
Geoffrey Howe to find himself announcing a planned rise of
£5000 million for next year's planned public expenditure on
the very day that the Westminster Hospital revealed that it
had had to let ninety-seven children die waiting for bone
marrow transplants that the hospital could not afford, because they cost about £7000 each.

Professor John Hobbs, who is in charge of the Westminster transplant programme on a budget of £180,000 a
year, of which £46,000 comes from charity, asked for another £114,000. Not a chance, said the Treasury; we have
got to feed another £480 million into, you know, Defence.
But, plead the hospitals, this *is* defence; it saves children's
lives. With £480 million we could save them all. Killing
comes dearer, says Defence, exiting Right.

Enter, to a muted fanfare, the Fairy Godfather. He is Mr
John James, described as a millionaire philanthropist. With-

83

out wasting time (babies are waiting) he reaches for his chequebook and makes out £100,000 for the Westminster's transplant programme. Professor Hobbs says: 'It means we shall no longer have to make heart-breaking decisions about which children should live or die.'

Sir Geoffrey Howe says nothing. Why should he? He has saved perhaps the cost of one-and-a-half minutes of his Defence budget. And that by an act of private charity.

I do not know whether it is possible to shame Sir Geoffrey Howe, or indeed any Chancellor, but this irony should surely help a bit. I do not know whether Sir Geoffrey has even sent a thank-you note to Mr James; I should suspect not. It would be an embarrassing exercise.

'Dear Mr James: Many thanks for your welcome little handout to the Westminster and the Royal Free. I hope it didn't put you out, not that I suppose a hundred grand makes much of a hole in your piggy-bank, ha ha. I have to think carefully about these little sums now; it costs almost as much these days to run a hospital as to maintain a missile-silo, and much as I dote on the suffering kids one must keep one's priorities right. . . .'

It sounds more and more like a 'Dear Bill' letter in *Private Eye*.

I have been for years a regular customer of the Westminster and an intermittent one of the Royal Free. The first is dowdy and old and the second is grand and new, and they have both done much to keep me operational, and were my surname what my first is I would gladly kick in the occasional £100,000 to them rather than to Sir Geoffrey Howe, who cannot be trusted to spend it wisely, as is now clear, even if it were not before.

Would it not even now be possible to persuade Professor Hobbs to give the Chancellor a bone marrow transplant? It might provide him with what he clearly lacks: a spine.

*8 December 1981*                                    **James Cameron**

# Life's negative

Most of the time, the world is properly coloured in. Grass and trees are green, buses and roses are red, people in their clothes in their rooms are an interesting jumble of blues, yellows, pinks, mauves. Thus it is and then, suddenly, isn't. One day, while the back is turned, some vast vacuum sucks all the colours into itself. Grass, trees, buses, sky, people, streets, all are drained of pigment and left an insubstantial grey, their outlines drizzly, drawn with a wavering pencil. The black magic of depression has struck and everything that, yesterday, was positive is negative. Everything.

Like pain, the depredations of depression are impossible to recall, once gone. I have been on nodding terms with the fell disease for stretches of my life and still, when a friend is depressed and I am not, the fascism of things going right easily rears its head, a kind of bullying jollity. Come now, what's wrong? Think of those with *real* problems: famine, poverty, war. Count your blessings, stiffen your lip. Look at the beauty of Nature and lift up your heart. Get *on* with it. All very worthy and well-meant advice, except when the stifling blanket descends on me and I recognise anew the sad sound of whistling in the dark. In depression the essence of life has been withdrawn, the spring has broken, facts and words become meaningless, the everyday bustle signifies nothing.

One of the most frightening aspects even of momentary depression is the impression of reality it reveals, as if contentment or happiness were merely a veil now blown away, mirages in a desert conjured up by thirst-crazed travellers to keep them going. Nature's confidence trick. You need water? We'll pretend an oasis. It's not there, of course, but it may get you over a bad patch. If you can be made to believe that the barren sands around you, through which you could not make your way if you saw them too clearly, are actually blooming, verdant with palms and springs, the hope thus provided may spin out your efforts, keep you intent enough on survival never to ask the question that has no answer: what for?

In my youth, I dived into depression without restraint. Almost, I embraced it. The tidal wave washed over me, washed everything away and left me stranded on a strange beach. But in youth everything, even depression, has its compensations. Within the most stygian gloom there lies a black pearl of drama. Look what is happening to me, *can* this be happening to me? Alone in your bed, in your bedsit, a part of you may watch the other parts with some interest and no edifice around you is threatened. Later, encumbered with home and children, bills and work, the downward spiral of depression has dire effects. If you put up your arms and go under, so may they all along with you, tumbling pell-mell into the charybdis you create, toys, shoes, dishes, nursery flotsam left on the surface like traces of a sunk ship.

It was only when I decided to kill myself that depression finally lost its power over me. I determined on an altruistic suicide – my existence was a burden to everyone, I would be doing the world a favour in despatching my lumpen flesh but I did not wish to distress anyone who knew me by allowing them to find me in a mess they could never forget. So I would have to go to an hotel, to be found by strangers and tidied up before being put on display. But what hotel? And how? Did hotels admit young women without luggage, for an unconvincing night? Would I have enough change for the gas, would there be gas? If I took pills, would they work before the chambermaid broke in? I couldn't jump from the window, not with my height-sickness and I couldn't cut my wrists, not given my faintness at the sight of blood. After a day spent wrestling with such details, I saw that I was not willing to kill myself and so there was nothing to do but live and nowhere to go but up. Or uppish.

Depression never hit me full force again. When it hovered, I treated it politely but as a transient. I had lost my faith in its absoluteness, I knew it for as much or as little a fraud as happiness and it knew I knew. Now, it makes its entry like a bad actor, blustering and mugging, hamming it up, fluffing its lines, gesturing grandiloquently, rolling its eyeballs and displaying, too carefully, its once heart-stopping profile. True, even a bad actor can have convincing moments, carrying the audience along in his very desperation; but the illusion, once shattered, cannot easily overwhelm.

Now, when I glimpse depression shuffling in the wings, waiting to come on, I have tricks up my sleeve to forestall it. I think, for instance, of optical illusions. That box, drawn on paper, that seems to project its closed end towards you but, at a shifting of the mind's gears, becomes suddenly open, hollow, so that you can look inside. Those pencilled lines of identical length, one with arrows at its ends pointing outwards, the other with arrows pointing inwards, the first seeming half as long again as its apparently shrunken twin. Marks on paper that serve as reminders of some possibility of control over reality, if only in the mind's eye.

I have other remedies, too. I no longer allow the blanket to fall without a struggle – instead, I force myself to track that fall to its source. The mind veers away, reluctant to reveal the awesome pettiness, the huge egoism that often sparks mild depression, the bloated baby that screams in all of us and blackens our horizons with its bawling for attention. Once the baby is discovered, though, the blackness lifts. Also, I attend to my body, something I once thought far too undramatic and suburban a thing to do. My soul in upheaval and you talk of a tonic or Vitamin C? Cold showers? Walks round the block? Would anyone have dared suggest such cures to Byron? Still, the links between body and mind are indissoluable and the banal fact is that forcing oxygen through the lungs does, sometimes, set the mood afloat again. Other people have their own methods of rupturing the dark circle. One woman goes away, anywhere, if only for a day. Another, reasoning that while she feels like death she might as well do the deathiest chores, does so and recovers. Yet another, drained of all energy, reads *Moby Dick* for the umpteenth time and forgets herself in Ahab's chase.

Useful devices all and enough to push most of us onto an even keel. Nevertheless, ex-depressive as I am, with only the occasional lapse, I cannot dismiss the idea that the vision of life seen in depression has the truth in it, the bare-boned skeletal truth, and an intrinsic part of depression is knowing this and being told it is not so. Reality, however terrible, is bearable if others allow its reality. When they refuse you that, when they skip around you pretending you've got it wrong, that's rock-bottom time.

*12 April 1982*                                    **Jill Tweedie**

## A gale of gloom, but few ripples

A curious mid-summer amorality seems to have descended on the country. People are bored by unemployment, the politicians say. People just do not care any more. Everyone knew that unemployment was going to go on rising. A cool 3.19 million? The worst total since official records began? More than a million out of work for more than a year? Could be worse, they say: 'Only' a rise of 129,000 in a month, and most of them school leavers who will be mopped up by youth opportunity schemes by Christmas. In all the catalogue of certainties which are being torn up by the roots in early eighties Britain, one of the most surprising – indeed, alarming – is that unemployment on such a scale has ceased to stir our national conscience. Juxtapose the calamity of the dole queues with the success of the Prime Minister and her Government in the opinion polls: Gallup in the *Daily Telegraph* on 15 July showed a further rise in the Conservative Party's support to 46.5 per cent, quite enough to send the remnants of the Opposition into electoral orbit for another five years.

'Unemployment is a very serious problem,' explained Mr Cecil Parkinson, the Conservative Party chairman, to *Newsweek*, 'but recent election results have shown it needn't be the over-riding consideration. Don't forget, nine out of ten people in the country are still working. The public realises that the cause of unemployment goes back years and that no political party is entirely blameless.' How convenient this new electoral geography must seem for Mrs Thatcher and her ministers. The Prime Minister always believed, and was once even tactless enough to say, that unemployment was a 'problem,' but inflation was an 'evil.' Inflation hits everyone, including the 86.6 per cent of the working population who are still lucky enough in Mrs Thatcher's Britain to have jobs. Unemployment hits relatively few. For the one million who are the long-term unemployed, it is a personal catastrophe. For the 342,000 who have each month joined the register since April, or the 315,000 who have left it, it is a passing problem, a few months of anxiety and straitened

'*Apparently when you've finished the Youth Opportunities Scheme, you then go on to a Government Retraining Centre and from there into early retirement*'.

*21st October, 1981*

circumstances. As long as they do not riot, it seems that the unemployed can be kept out of sight and electoral mind.

But it is also true that the Government has successfully fostered the myth that unemployment is somehow a necessary phase; the pay-off for the bad old ways of its predecessors; no fault of its own. Others, once associated with rodomontade defences of the Government's prescription, now seem less sure. Mr Samuel Brittan, the commentator of the *Financial Times*, is at last calling for a budgetary stimulus to the economy, and is being berated for his pains by those of his erstwhile co-religionists who still cling to the original faith. It is hard, in truth, not to pin the blame for the largest part of the increase in unemployment since 1979 on Government policy. On the latest standardised OECD figures – rather than the farrago of national incompatibilities which the Department of Employment likes to publicise – Britain had the highest unemployment rate of any of the developed economies, after many years of suffering no more than an undistinguished average. If the cause of unemployment is so deep-seated why did our jobless so suddenly rise in 1980 and 1981? Why did Britain, enjoying self-sufficiency during the oil crisis, see national output fall while output elsewhere only rose more slowly? Why has our unemployment risen so much more than unemployment abroad?

Mrs Thatcher and her team have squandered North Sea oil on the support of ever-lengthening dole queues. They have laid waste the economy with an efficiency unparalleled since the thirties, and they have fewer alibis for their foolishness than any inter-war government, since they were copiously warned by the mainstream of the British economics profession that their cures would prove worse than the disease. Yet they are, where it counts, getting off scot free. They may have transgressed the ten commandments, but they have kept the eleventh which says 'Thou shalt not be caught'. While the voters refuse to look beyond the Falklands bunting to the shabby and debilitated economy which is Mrs Thatcher's true memorial, the Cabinet 'wets' will continue to creep out of Downing Street like small boys after a salutary wigging. Reflation? An alternative? Politicians are jacks of all trades, but masters of sailing with the prevailing winds. And the winds, at present, are still blowing Mrs Thatcher home to port.

*19 July 1982* **Leader**


## Lost in the Twilight Hotel

'The only way out is when you're blanked,' says Andy. 'Things just get worse and worse.' Being young and homeless in central London used to be a staging post, maybe, to housing and a job of sorts. But the streets are dead ends these days. For a growing number of young people, homelessness is becoming a way of life. And they are finding out younger what that means.

How do you live if you're Andy, now twenty, who left local authority care in London with the promise of a place to live and no education at all in how to handle it, who after a spell in the army and a chance of employment blown, has now been around the streets for a year or more? Or if you're Garry, who first left home in Liverpool at fifteen and now, give or take the army and the ups and downs, reckons to have ten years of street-wisdom behind him?

Official responses sound like a vicious game. There is no social security without an address to deliver it to and no possibility of an address without an income. It can take two days or more to get seen and there's abuse when you are. If you are Andy, there are days when you just can't take the hassle any more and opt to sleep out.

When the £7.60 the hassle produces for establishing an address can buy you, maybe, bed and breakfast which amounts to a dirty bed in a room shared with three others, a bit of bread left outside the door and the chance of catching nits, sleeping out begins to sound like not such a bad alternative. When Centrepoint tell you that its night shelter must take new and very young arrivals to the West End, and that you are too old or too long on the scene; when you're barred from the Department of Health's own casual ward, or refuse to accept its regimentations; when you're young and like to keep yourself clean and wouldn't sink to a bed in a dosshouse. there doesn't sound to be an alternative at all.

So if you're Andy, or Garry, or another of the regulars that cluster by day in the New Horizon Centre in Covent Garden, you end up in Leicester Square when the pubs close and the cinemas finish, and you wait for the night to start.

You can tell the people who have a place to go from those who don't by the way they move. Not much point in hurrying, after all, if tonight's choice is between Cardboard City down at Charing Cross Station and the Twilight Hotel of St

James's Park. Not much point, that is, until the police vans start their routine sweeps through the square. You scatter then. Who needs yet another CRO, that walkie-talkied computer read out to see if you're wanted this time?

Midnight: Start with another cup of tea, laced strong with sugar against the hours ahead, at one of the all-night cafes. By now, Cardboard City is in the building, boxes dragged into service from the shops' throw-outs, black plastic sacks emptied for blankets, to stake a claim to the nooks of the subway, the places under the railway arches. If I were not here, Andy and Garry could be staking their own claims; the locks and patrols in the Embankment Gardens mean one option fewer. But their London is what they're showing me this night. So we keep walking, marking the boundaries of their patch from the Embankment up through Soho and down again. South of the river belongs to older men, the ones who still carry the stereotype of the homeless. You go there in winter, maybe, because they have fires. But you only go when there are plenty of you, and not with a visitor.

2 a.m.: The lights are out in the Twilight Hotel of St James's Park, and you tread softly as you skirt the bandstand, because it's been taken over by the drinkers and their tempers are uncertain; these days you wouldn't go there to sleep on your own. But this is a large hotel, and away from the crowd you can build shelter with deck-chairs and find peace on a summer night. Garry is persuaded as we sit on a bench by the lake to recite a poem that has just come into his head – a gentle hymn to the stars and a girl he wishes he was with. But the peace doesn't last.

They are alert to the police cars almost before they appear across the lake, these two. They see the torches almost before they flicker on the water. Five cars. That's trouble, maybe someone in the water. People do die in the night. Garry once found a man in a public lavatory with a syringe stuck in each eye. You get used to it. You'd be sorry if you knew them, but you can't afford to care.

The all-night cafe between the park and Charing Cross draws its regulars from both and neither – a motley of older men, of skins, of young men working the gay clubs. Friends pass in the street. One young Scot is on the run from his girl friend. She clapped him about the head with a saucepan when she heard he'd spent the Giro, £45-worth, on drink.

You buy what escape you can when you can from this life; otherwise, tomorrow might seem too like today. Another young man is on the run, too. But this time, it's from the police. He's been picked up four times in the last twenty-four hours and he doesn't want to make that five. There's research to show how this life and offending go together. Who's surprised?

They get younger all the time, says Garry. He wonders if anyone cares that kids are selling themselves for the prospect of a bed for the night, or less. A beautiful youth in the cafe works around Piccadilly. Down from Liverpool, just seventeen, his dark eyes, glazed with tonight's mixture of drugs, his hands shaking round the cigarette. They get younger all the time.

And no less desperate. In among the cardboard boxes in the Charing Cross subway, in among the scattering of young couples, not far from Scottish Dave, scrounging a cigarette through a haze of cider, in among the many more older men, is the young girl we last saw in Leicester Square. She's sixteen, says Garry, goes with men for £1 or less. He's given her 50p himself to try to dissuade her. But she's crazy. She should be in hospital, like quite a few others he knows.

Up at Mortimer Street, the north end of the territory, the cardboard houses make the queue for the casual work that might just be on offer when the Job Centre opens, and likely won't. That's not what Garry, qualified chef, is after. But how do you find a real job when someone has stolen your knives and your whites, when you've only got the clothes you stand up in to impress the interviewers with, when the Job Centre just doesn't want to know when you haven't got an address to apply from?

4.30 a.m.: The light is up. In St James's Park, the birds have shaken their feathers and the bandstand has emptied before the police start their morning clear-out. In the Charing Cross subway, they are stirring to beat the hoses which can soak you if you're not quick enough – though this morning seems to bring a dispensation from that, at least.

The night's bravado seeps away. It is very cold. The cafes are shut. There's breakfast at the Hare Krishna temple, but they want you to pray for it. The early workers have somewhere to go; that just underlines our aimlessness.

6.30 a.m.: Only now do we find a cafe open for breakfast. It's months since Garry and Andy had a cooked one; most usually, breakfast comes from the rolls and milk cartons stacked against cafe walls. But the anticipation of the day's coming hassles with social security, of working out where you sleep the next night, blunts the enjoyment. Garry is exhausted. He has a bad stomach ulcer. Two nights ago, he collapsed and friends took him to hospital, but he wouldn't stay, he hates the places. There's research to show that living rough over a period damages your health. Who's surprised?

7.30 a.m.: The day centre doesn't open until nine. Normally, this early morning would have been hours longer. Where do you go? The lavatories are already full of people getting what sleep they can; Andy has to pretend he's police to get in to one at all.

At least at the New Horizons day centre there will be the chance of a shower, a shave, and sleep undisturbed. But the place closes at 5 p.m. The St Martin's youth club closes at 11 p.m. That, says Garry, is when the loneliness really sets in. But who wants to know? They've got their cars, their families, their little house. Oh, yes, they've got a house.

*11 August 1982*                                          **Ann Shearer**


## Dreams come true

Keith Hearne's dream machine – which he hinted might be possible in a *Guardian* Futures article last year – has become a reality. It means that for thousands of people the nightmare might soon be over. Ultimately, dreamers may be able to control their fantasies.

94

The machine is based on a tiny sensor, clipped onto the nose to measure inhaled and exhaled air. It is connected in turn to an alarm. When you dream your breathing rate rises. When you have a nightmare it rises even more. The device is adjusted to trigger the alarm at nightmare-breathing level. The result: when the horrors begin, the alarm goes off and you wake up.

The nightmare interruptor will go on sale early next year for £99. If all goes well, this device will be followed in the summer by a more sophisticated version, at about £150, which converts ordinary dreams into lucid dreams, in which you know you are dreaming, can control your actions, and remember what happened. This time, since the object is to stay asleep, the alarm is replaced by four tiny impulses, generated by a battery, delivered through a wristband, and triggered when the sensor realises you are dreaming.

'The subject is told that each of the four impulses corresponds to a word: This . . . Is . . . A . . . Dream. You might be walking down the road in your dream, the impulses hit your wrist, you do a double take (because it is an incongruity), you look at your wrist, you don't see any wires, and it clicks that this is the cue, and you are lucid. Once you realise you are dreaming you are in a fantastic world, and one man had three lucid dreams in one night. They usually only last for two or three minutes, but they can last for half an hour.'

However, there are problems to be ironed out before Britain becomes a nation of beautiful dreamers. Mr Karl Weiss, managing director of Incam, the firm which holds the rights to the machine, said yesterday that while they could guarantee the nightmare interruptor, the dream machine does not work for some people. For others the strongest shock is only sufficient to trigger lucidity, yet some find it extremely unpleasant. There is also the problem of potential customers who might be reluctant to go to bed wired by the nose to a battery.

*27 January 1982*                                    **Andrew Veitch**

# 7000 loiter in the Palace shrubbery

About 7000 people visited the Queen yesterday, but not in her bedroom, and not without invitations. None of us was wearing the sort of clothes you use for shinning up drainpipes, except perhaps before a May Ball, or at Blandings Castle.

The first post-Fagan garden party was held in the forty acres of lawn and flower bed, menaced by thunderstorms, but never actually deluged. If there are really sensors buried behind the delphiniums they must have been deafened, as guests went exploring to prove their theories about the Intruder's route.

Gentlemen ushers moved in at sensitive points, but the freedom given to garden party guests was pretty thoroughgoing. You could stroll directly beneath the private apartments (no signs of burglary to be seen), or plunge into the wilderness which fringes the main lawn to examine the gardeners' leaf pile.

Security was discreet, but would have been more so if our hostess had been the mother of numerous marriageable daughters. Few garden parties can ever have had so many single, well-built male guests, who were outnumbered only by the vicars.

There was so many of these we might easily have been in Heaven. Indeed the party was a sort of heaven for us eavesdroppers. A Golden Treasury of remarks about the Intruder could have been compiled, including my own favourite: 'But what on earth will other countries think?'

Queen Mother hats and heady perfumes were everywhere, but the democratic nature of the party, the first of this season, showed the difficulties which now face security. One guest from Sudbury turned up in an old van with a notice saying: 'For sale, £300' beside his royal car park sticker.

Determined efforts were made by the grubby fourth estate to extract a security angle from the slightly-dazed guests who had been hooked from the crowd by Court aides to chat with the Queen.

'Did you compliment her on her coolness in a tight situation?' was the usual question. It was inevitably deflected by replies like, 'Oh no, but she was very interested in my work for the Soroptimists.'

Famous faces were to be seen among the uniforms, top hats and patrols from the 15th Finchley Scouts who had been drafted in – future Fagans please note – to give the police and

'*But didn't Mrs Thatcher say in her letter that the garrison of forty-two marines stationed in The Queen's bedroom would be sufficient to deter any invader . . . ?*'

*13th July, 1982*

soldiers a hand. Mrs Thatcher was there with a clutch of Cabinet ministers who get invited to all three parties every year, and less eminent, if more exciting political stars.

'Look,' said the man behind me in the queue, 'There's that Tory MP who was involved in all the scandal.' A group of us turned up our eavesdropping devices to full volume for the denouement. 'Oh, yes,' giggled the man's companion, 'He must think this is a tea dance.'

*15 July 1982*                    **Martin Wainwright**

# Across the river and into the trees

Last year Victor Zorza, for long this newspaper's resident Kremlinologist, decided to go to live in a remote Indian village. Instead of analysing the global intentions of the Soviet Union, he is going to write a weekly column in the *Guardian* about rural life in the Himalayas, beginning on Monday.

Such a switch in a successful career sounds like the action of a romantic character in a Joseph Conrad novel but Zorza, a man dedicated to the pursuit of reason, rejects any romantic notions and claims his decision was soundly based on the evidence his eventful life had brought him.

'Thirty years ago, just after the Second World War, I wanted to fathom the mystery of the Kremlin's actions.' Zora told me in New York shortly before he left for India. 'Our ignorance was dangerous, and I tried to collect and pass on what knowledge I could. Now I feel the same away about our ignorance of the Third World.

'I don't think we can solve the problem for them. That's something they'll have to do themselves. We may be able to help, in comparatively small but crucial ways. But if we are to do so, we must understand the problem first, and not just intellectually – we must become emotionally involved with the way the other three-quarters of the world's population live.

'I want to live in one such poor Indian village and convey what I find to western readers. What might help is the human story of the joys and sorrows, the progress and the setbacks, the triumphs and the defeats of a villager's life as noted by alien eyes and ears through a whole year's cycle and the four seasons.'

It is easier to follow how Zorza came originally to Kremlin-ology than how he has now reached India. He was born in Poland fifty-six years ago – in the eastern part now absorbed by the Soviet Union – where an understanding of Russian actions is part of every child's education.

He was only fourteen when the Nazi invasion wiped out

his family. As a young Jew trying to avoid a similar fate in a concentration camp, he found safety in Siberia of all places. Then he was befriended by the Soviet writer Ilya Ehrenburg, who helped him to reach the exiled Polish Air Force in Britain.

Zorza dreamed of becoming another Joseph Conrad and writing great novels in his newly adopted language, and in the meantime he worked as a translator for the BBC and then began to write analytical articles about Stalin's Cold War plans that brought him to the attention of the late A. P. Wadsworth, then editor of the *Manchester Guardian*.

Several times his predictions – such as the Sino-Soviet split, the fall of Khrushchev, and the Soviet invasion of Czechoslovakia – were proved right when the CIA and other Western intelligence services were wrong.

He moved from London to Washington (where his weekly column appeared in the *Washington Post* and was required reading in the White House and the State Department – not to mention the CIA). Neighbours on NW 44th Street in Washington grew used to seeing famous political faces get out of limousines and go into the Zorza rented residence for a consultation or a brisk walk through the nearby woods. No party-goer or Georgetown swinger, Zorza had to be sought out at home among his bulging files.

Kremlinology and his family were his life – and then disaster struck as it had in his boyhood. His twenty-four-year-old daughter, Jane, developed an incurable cancer. Zorza and his wife, Rosemary, returned to London to be with her. She died in a hospice, one of the new hospitals devoted to the terminally ill, and her parents were so impressed by the help Jane had received that they wrote a book about her final months, *A Way to Die*, in the hope it would help other cancer victims. They also raised money for hospices on both sides of the Atlantic.

Up to then Zorza had been a relentless achiever, a work-aholic dedicated to striving after greater and greater success. His daughter's death checked and changed him. He had once taken Jane on a trip to the Third World and the poverty in India had made a profound impression on her. She had asked him to write about it one day instead of Kremlinology. At the time it had seemed impossible to him, but now this conversation kept coming back to him. He was asked to resume his Kremlinology column, but instead he immersed himself in reading about the Third World.

Then disaster struck again – he had to have a heart bypass operation. He made a quick recovery, but the operation hadn't been as successful as hoped. His doctors told him he might have only a few years to live.

'As soon as I heard this,' Zorza told me, 'my mind was made up. If I only had a short time left, I wanted to do something really worthwhile with it.' He booked a flight to India and packed his bags.

If the new column describing the dramas of this village life has the same success as his Kremlinology (which was syndicated in twenty-five countries), then Zorza will consider his time in the Third World well spent. He is aware of the difficulties in trying to stimulate more understanding in a largely uncaring world. Preaching can't do it, but reporting can – and Zorza is setting out with the urgency of a reporter who feels there is no time to lose.

*20 February 1982* **W. J. Weatherby**


# Village voice: the drummer's tale

The old village drummer rushed into the temple square, his face bleeding. His two sons and their wife followed. I joined the small crowd which began to gather round them. A rich farmer had driven them from their field and proclaimed it his own.

'He can't do that to you,' I said.

'You try and stop him, then,' the villagers challenged me.

The small field, confiscated from an absentee landlord, had been given to the drummer half a dozen years ago by a government determined to emancipate the poor. The family worked hard to clear the rocky, barren slope of stones. They levelled the ground, terraced it, and built a wall to keep wild animals and straying cattle away. But after their first good harvest three years ago, a rich farmer accused them of appropriating his land.

The drummer promptly produced the government land deed, but the farmer tore it up, abusing him roundly. 'The government can't touch me,' he shouted. He said that he had bought the field from the absentee owner. No government had a right to give it to the drummer. Yet he made no immediate move to evict him.

The drummer was the first villager with whom I struck up a friendship, probably because he had more time to talk to me. While the others were in the fields, he had to stay in the village square to beat the drum for the temple services, five or six times a day, and to act as the village barber. He was one of the poorest men in the village, and one of the happiest – always smiling, singing, joking and asking questions about the strange world I came from. What was it, I once asked him, that kept him so cheerful?

At first, he recalled, he had owned nothing. Even the drums belonged to the village. Then he got the land. The village bought a wife for his two sons – polyandry is a time-honoured custom here – and now he had a growing family. With their new field, they no longer had to rely entirely on the charity of the village for their food. 'Wouldn't you be happy?' he asked.

But soon I noticed that his family were spending more time in their field, and less on the open windy platform by the temple which the village had given them for a dwelling. Someone still had to be there most of the time to beat the drums for the temple services. But when a villager wanted a shave, or a village elder needed a messenger, the drummer was often in his field. 'You're a landowner now,' the villagers teased him. 'Barbering is beneath you.'

It was all quite good-natured at first. At harvest time the drummer still went from house to house to collect his gifts of grain. A villager could still have his shave, though sometimes he had to wait two weeks instead of the usual one. The payment was one roti – a pancake made of coarse grain – for shaving one week's growth, and two rotis for two weeks', so the drummer was no worse off.

Gradually the mood changed. The drummer wasn't always so sunny. At harvest time some families sent him away empty-handed. 'Don't you grow your own grain now?' they asked. After a shave, a villager would tell him to collect his payment later. Yet, when he tried again, he would be told to return some other time.

But the old drummer was still the friend of the village. His platform in the temple square, the only home with no walls to keep out friendly or idle neighbours, is a natural gathering place. The villagers linger round the platforms to exchange gossip, to argue, to flirt. After dark the drummer sometimes beats his drum, his son blows the horn, and a line of dancers winds sinuously round the square, singing. A crackling fire-brand, held high to light the square, gives off a pleasing, pine-like smell.

The routine of village life obscures the tensions. They need his drumming to wake them at half past four every morning so that they can get to the fields at first light. And they need it to sound curfew at ten every night. Reveille also wakes the village gods; while curfew warns that anyone venturing abroad risks an encounter with evil spirits – who take over while the gods sleep. The village wouldn't want to lose its drummer, even if he has his own land now.

The drummer and his sons saw little of the rich farmer after their initial confrontation. He lives in another village. He was biding his time until they had done all they could to improve the land. The blow fell one morning at planting time, after they had toiled for weeks to prepare the soil for the new crop. At daybreak they found that the farmer's men had planted the field with rice by moonlight, braving the evil spirits. The drummer pleaded, shouted, cursed, then attacked with bare fists. The farmer shook him off, and his men beat the drummer until they drew blood.

In the village square the drummer wiped the blood off his face and appealed to the crowd for help. None was forthcoming. The villagers were glad he had been put in his place.

'But you haven't lost your land,' I told him. 'All you have to do is to take the case to court.' He couldn't afford a three-day trip to town, he explained patiently. There would be the cost of searching the records, copying the documents, bribing the clerks. Even if he won, the farmer would appeal, the case drag on, the costs mount.

With his land gone, the age-old relationship between the drummer and the village was restored. The villagers won't let him starve. They do their duty by him, as long as he does his. Of course, he will again be utterly dependent on them for his living, but that is as it should be. That's why the gods ordained that there should be a drummer caste, and that its members should own no land.

*1 March 1982*                                          **Victor Zorza**


## Village voice: a mark of distinction

At first I used to sneak out of the village before dawn, under cover of darkness, but always with a sense of being watched. Already there were people about.

The drummer had sounded the reveille, and everyone was hurrying to the edge of the village to answer the call of nature. But they didn't all make it to the fields and I often stepped into a mess on the path. The village elders would not let me build a privy. 'We've never had one here,' they said. When I persisted, a friendly Brahmin took me quietly aside.

If I used a hole in the ground, Joshi explained, the contents would pollute the soil and cause illness. But, I protested, it was far more unhealthy to leave the stuff lying all over the village. It was this, I said, heatedly, that spread disease.

That was a mistake. Joshi didn't like being lectured. The village council had carefully considered my request, he said coldly, and most of the elders were against it. Theirs was a more natural way. The sun burnt excrement to dust, which the rain then washed down the hill. But a hole in the ground would be a trap, he said, because only a thin layer of earth covered the solid rock.

If the majority were opposed to my request, I reasoned, there must be some who were in favour. Would they help me, to talk the council round? Who were they, I asked Joshi. 'Me,' he answered with a sly smile, and walked away.

Joshi, one of the richest men in the village, is always up to his ears in schemes to increase his family's wealth and prestige. Middle-aged, with sharp, hawk-like features, he had gone out of his way to be friendly. But I kept my distance because the Harijans had warned me that he was a ruthless exploiter.

When it became known a few years ago that government doctors would be allocated to some villages, he built two rooms on to this hut to accommodate a clinic. But first, of course, he made sure that the rent would repay building costs within a couple of years. After that it would simply swell his income. The doctor, trained only in native medicine, took one look at the village and fled. He came back occasionally mainly to sign the government register. Joshi went on collecting his rent.

Perhaps he might also be able to turn my need to his advantage. In the meantime, I had to overcome my reluctance to relieve myself in public. I sought privacy further away from the village, but was always nervous of being observed.

I was climbing a little higher every day, finding round every bend a view so beautiful that I almost forgot the pressing need that drove me on. In the end nothing would satisfy me but to reach the peak, a 40-minute climb from the village. Sometimes I raced the sun, due to rise at any moment over the furthest range, to watch it strike the snowy summits. I would arrive breathless, drunk with the pure morning air, exhilarated with the scenery, alone at last. The changing panorama as I slowly turned a full circle, the feeling of ease as I finally squatted down, brought on a state of complete wellbeing.

It became a daily routine. But the local food could play havoc with my morning schedule. Sometimes I had to run to the edge of the village during the day, unreasonably irritated by the curious looks I imagined were following me.

I still needed that privy. Perhaps the Harijans, untouchables, who were also represented on the village council, would help me. I had more friends among them than among the Brahmins, who always looked uneasy when they saw me fraternising with the 'lower class'. But the poorest villagers proved also to be the most conservative.

I told them that nearly half the Indian children who died under the age of five were killed by diseases spread by poor hygiene. That was another mistake. They didn't believe me. Then Joshi approached me again. If I agreed to build my privy on his property, he would persuade the other elders to give their consent. Was there a catch? But he wanted no money, just the prestige. I had once stayed in a village in South India where the richest man had built a shiny toilet and kept it unused, as immaculate as a temple. It was a mark of distinction.

I told Joshi I would build on his land, provided the village agreed to send two men to the city to be trained in the art of privy-building. A Unicef official I know has promised to make the necessary arrangements. When I depart, I hope to leave behind me not only a new structure in Joshi's field, but also the desire to use it, and craftsmen who could satisfy a new demand. Some hope.

*19 April 1982*                                    **Victor Zorza**

# On the track of the maharajahs

*Dear Richard*

That evening you – as a very old, envious and railway-fancying friend – heard that I was off for a long weekend in India to tour the old Maharajahs' palaces in the old Maharajahs' luxury train, you punched me on the knee and said: 'It sounds like *Brideshead* on wheels.'

Well, it was and it wasn't. I must apologise for failing to bring back the £20 worth of snapshots of clean loo seats which you earnestly authorised me to commission so that you could talk your wife into doing the trip when it becomes an official package holiday. And you may like to know why a chain pipe-smoking holy man in the far Aravalli hills of Rajasthan is now struggling to pump butane into a non-rechargeable lighter bought at my Essex corner shop.

How pleasingly you winced at the invitation. Come with us on the Palace-on-Wheels, it said – the trial run of a train taking tourists for a week around six of the great palace cities of the north-west Indian state of Rajasthan, including Bikaner, Jodhpur, Jaipur, Udaipur and Agra, where the Taj Mahal is.

It was 'to consist exclusively of saloons built for the former Maharajahs and Viceroys', resotred to their former opulence and hauled by a vintage-class steam engine. Each 'brass and ornate' coach would have its own lounge, dining room and bedrooms. In the communal part of the train, there would be a dining car, an observation-cum-lounge car, a post office with its own postmark and even with a professionally staffed children's play room. And this usually abstemious land would provide 'miniature spirit bottles in refrigerators kept in each saloon.'

Not until we reached Delhi, briefed to expect English summer weather, did the gods begin to get their talons into the dream. As we walked down the gangway, we felt a forest-fire heat coming from the direction of the 747 engines. We stepped hastily away, into worse heat. It wasn't the engines at all. It was the sun; an unseasonable and, for our whole stay, unremitting 95°F, in a buffeting aroma of incense, curry, bodies and drains. One's instinct was to get straight back on the plane. Instead, we went to a hotel where there were more servants soliciting work than Lady Marchmain ever employed. In the bedside drawer, in place of the Gideon Bible, was the *Bhagavadgita*. 'One cannot separate in theory what is not separable in life,' it says.

Safely re-installed in air conditioning, the tour operators were avid about the prospects for Palace-on-Wheels holidays, although they disliked the Railways Board's slogan. One said – not unprophetically – 'I do not like the word wheels. It reminds the customer of vibrations.' The British operator talked of marketing it as 'The Maharajah Experience'. The French, determined to work in an echo of the *1001 Nights*, opted for 'Seven Nights with the Maharajahs'.

Heads full of marketing dreams and possibilities, we drove to Sarai Rohilla station, Delhi, behind five new tractors which farmers were driving 150 miles back to their villages to save on rail freight charges. Most of the villagers had come with them by bike. They all blew horns in celebration as the procession headed into the night.

The train was on platform 1. While its plaque said 'Palace on Wheels', it was from the outside a worryingly blank train, white with heavily curtained mosquito mesh windows. Still, we said, didn't the English palaces of *Brideshead* period screen themselves from the populace behind high park walls, trees and gates? In such cases, we reassured ourselves, the real opulence is always inside.

We climbed inside our coach, into at first glimpse all the opulence of an ex-colonial temperance hotel in Bognor Regis. The uniform Burma teak panelling was drab under the faint lights. The furniture appeared modern, with floral, Marks and Spencer-style antimacassars. The ceiling was undecorated, unlike the Maharajah's ceilings we had just seen in Delhi's engrossing railway museum. The dresser contained no china. The fridge offered six small bottles of Coke and bitter lemon. The wall plaque said, 'This coach belonged to the erstwhile Bihamer State Railway.' Not a word about Maharajahs.

We belted down the platform, checking all seventeen coaches. It was the same story. Two plaques mentioned links with Maharajahs. The rest spoke of occupancy by railway managers, senior railways officers and Agents-General. Almost every senior functionary in India seemed to have used the coaches, except Maharajahs.

There was one small dining car, little bigger than a British Rail buffet, with a bar holding a single empty, dusty wine bottle. There was an observation car so tiny that we calculated that if all the passengers decided to use it simultaneously, it would have made the Black Hole of Calcutta look like the Albert Hall.

Worst of all, for the tour operators, there was no interconnection between carriages. So – we asked – how do tourists get to dine, drink and observe? When the train stops at a station, explained an official. How often did the train stop at a station? 'Only when you get off.'

The British operator looked at his watch and put his head in his hands. 'I've got a disaster here,' he said, 'I've got a brochure done showing rubies and diamonds. I've got two directors flying out first class and it's too late to stop them.' The Frenchman said more generously: 'It is big. It is even huge. But it is not rich. How can I advertise Seven Nights With the Agents-General?'

It was not a particularly restful night. Our coach suspension was designed in 1898; Indian Railways are not all continuous welded rail. Those of awake at rosy-fingered dawn peered through the mesh and saw farmwrokers defecating in the fields before beginning the day in a landscape which looked much as the English countryside might have looked if the great drought of 1976 had lasted almost unbroken till now.

Our loo *was* spotlessly clean. The four of us had two attendants to keep it so. It also vented undisguisedly on to the track through a cavity nearly a foot wide. Around 7 a.m., I found it necessary to pull the chain. Simultaneously, a cheer went up from outside. I went to the window and found we had stopped at Agra Fort station, where every railway worker for miles had marshalled to greet the great white hopes of Indian tourism. I suppose I had provided some slight proof that the palace train was inhabited and stirring.

Many handshakes later we left, garlanded with marigolds and roses, to wash away the blear in day-rooms at the Agra Sheraton before starting our sightseeing. You may think it kinder to draw a veil over the next three days. Not so. They were delightful days. Partly it was that we acclimatised (on the second day we asked proudly for the air-conditioning to be turned down), lost our Western irritability and weariness of mind. But mostly it was because we attuned to the places as well as the palaces.

We walked round the intact Xanadu which Akbar, the greatest Mogul invader of India, erected as his capital at Fatehpur-Sikri, near Agra, then abandoned for another capital fifteen years later. You could get Castle Howard, Blenheim and St Paul's inside its walls and still leave space for half the City of London. Shelley forgot about Rajasthan in that poem we both read at school. There the works of Ozymandias, king of kings, hardly decay.

We rode elephants painted with flowers up a small mountain to the Amber Fort, near Jaipur, a castle arrayed by a 12th-century dynasty of Rajputs, the indigenous warrior caste of Rajasthan, along eight miles of battlements. It proved undefendable. And we saw the Taj Mahal, the only wonder of the world built as a memorial of human love.

As a lawyer, you will find that the Taj seals an instant contract with the human eye. It will float off, as easily as an English thistlehead in September, if you stop looking at it. So you need to set aside lots of time.

We grew fond of our train. It proved a more comfortable way of covering the 200-mile palace city itinerary than car or ordinary railway couchettes. The causes of its shortcomings seeped slowly and obliquely from board staff. The Palace on Wheels is a top level project. The idea came only this year to the board chairman, Mr Mohinder Gujral, in the kind of vision by which legend says the Taj design was vouchsafed to Shah Jehan.

Mrs Gandhi – no less – enthused but made two conditions. It must be spotlessly clean (as your commissioned photographs will show it was when they reach me through the bureaucracy at around the time of the next Mogul invasion). It must also be a perfect reconstruction of the original lifestyle.

Hardly had the 5000 staff of the Ajmer loco workshop begun finding and restoring the coaches when a new directive burst on them. Their superiors – noticing that the international railway executives conference was opening in Delhi in October – decided to hold the trial run then. In two months' time, less than it takes to negotiate the installation of a screw on BR's Advanced Passenger Train.

If one bears this in mind, our train was remarkable. Ajmer found, marshalled, and made trackworthy twelve coaches once used by Maharajahs. The problem was that Maharajahs changed their coaches as often as their Rolls; the coaches passed down over the years through Agents-General to track inspectors, undergoing progressively inferior redecoration and repainting each time. What Ajmer could not hope to do in two months was to trace and reproduce the original architecture. Their compromise was the serried Burma teak we found at Delhi station. Between Delhi and Jaipur, they sneaked on a steam loco, the Desert Queen, a Y-gauge engine built in 1960.

They gave us a firework display, which would have scandalised the British Home Office, on our last night in Jaipur. Men held the setpiece frame, brushing the sparks unregardingly from their shirts and hair. They badly wanted the train package to work. So did the tour operators by the time we returned to Delhi. After thirty-six hours of talks with Indians, they came out with a package to recommend to head office. It included fully restored coaches, fewer early morning starts, camouflaged loo vents and a foray by camel to a desert palace, costing around £750 for nine days inclusive of the flight. It's likely to start next winter, possibly with an optional second week on a beach or game reserve. Watch our travel pages for final details.

'It's far too early to be showing this to the press,' complained an operator. Yes. But we'd had a privileged, exceptional, warts-and-all glimpse of a holiday in the making. Now, if you're going to save up the money and spend 12 hours flying out there, you'll try to avoid flying back after nine days. You'll need to unwind after the train.

Two of us looked briefly at one possible unwinding place, the 800-square-kilometre Sariska game reserve near the palace town of Alwar, four hours' drive from Delhi. Overtaking innumerable bicycles and passing innumerable wheatfields, we saw only two tractors. The good soil was being worked by men, women and particularly children, pulling oxen or hand ploughs in the worst of the sun. I belatedly saw the point of that tooting little procession of tractors out of Delhi three days earlier. That morning's *Times of India* ran an investigative story about a dispute between 'rich' and 'poor' farmers over routeing a new road: poor farmers were defined as those supporting a family of six on half an acre; rich farmers as those having six acres.

Sariska is one of only eight Indian habitats where a tiger

can survive. It has been left to grow for 22 years, with little arable farming or other human use. That makes it an aching contrast with what else we saw of Rajasthan. It teems with deciduous trees, brush and grass. In Lutyens' Delhi, they water the grass three times a week in winter to keep it alive. At Sariska, they don't have to. 'Much of India used to be like this before overpopulation,' said the reserve field director, Jai Singh. The chief editor of the *Hindustan Times*, Kushwant Singh, is said to remember his father shooting tigers fifty years ago on the now baked, deforested land where Delhi Airport stands.

By a trackside clearing under a gorge, we found Sariska's strangest inhabitant, its holy man. He is an ex-factory owner, with large, very astute brown eyes. He has lived there for ten years under a vow of silence; but his sign language is precise. He says the tigers come down with padlocked teeth and share his fire during deep winter ('when the temperature sometimes falls to *one degree of frost*').

Of spiritual matters, we said nothing; we found ourselves bonded in the freemasonry of pipe smoking. We swapped tobacco. His, made from leaves rolled on molasses, was superb. He said that he would show me how he could smoke my tobacco in his pipe without coughing as I do. He inhaled seraphically. We waited. His eyes became preoccupied. His cheek twitched, his lungs went into rictus and he let out the gut-wrenching roar common to heavy pipe-smokers of all creeds. Matter so often triumphs over mind in affairs of nicotine.

He gave me one of his eight clay pipes. I gave him one of my two briars. He showed eager interest in my throwaway lighter. I warned him that it was non-refillable: but his acolytes seemed to think they could find something that would do the trick in Alwar. Having later seen the shops of Alwar, I doubt it, Richard, though one must never underestimate the resources of a holy man – Yours,

*28 November 1981*                                    **John (Ezard)**

# Village voice: ritual revisited

The buffalo festival, now the happiest day of the year, used to be the bloodiest, and there are those who would like to bring back this centuries-old ritual. The nervous glances which greeted the group of strangers approaching the village temple gave just a hint of trouble.

The festival usually draws people from many neighbouring communities, but these visitors were different. They came from a hostile village which, enraged by the abandonment of the buffalo sacrifice, had instigated in previous years a boycott of the celebration.

Originally, the senior priest would first make obeisance to the buffalo. Then, with a sharp blow, he would send it galloping out of the temple, the crowd in hot pursuit. The frantic beast, beset by a mob wielding sticks, stones and knives, usually made for the fields as it struggled to evade the blows. The chase ended only when one tormentor brought the buffalo down, generally by breaking its leg. The head was carried solemnly back to the temple, once again an object of worship.

In the early seventies a government social worker came from town to persuade the villagers that hacking a buffalo to death was cruel. There was a law against cruelty to animals. The high-caste Brahmins retorted that the new ritual he proposed would cause the angry gods to punish the people with cholera and other plagues. The visitor was chased out of the village.

But he kept coming back. First he won over the low-caste Harijans. The sacrifice, he explained, was designed to unleash their primitive instincts, to brutalise them. They were venting on the buffalo the suppressed fury they harboured against their oppressors.

Then he persuaded the Brahmins to accept that they would continue to receive the traditional offerings of rice and oil from the surrounding villages, even without the sacrifice. The headman alone remained obdurate.

The headman in the village has always been a member of

the same family, even though the once-hereditary office is now elective. The Brahmins vote for him because the high castes stick together, and the Harijans because they are intimidated. He lives on the other side of the hill, in the richest of several communities which make up his constituency.

The social worker was on yet another visit to the village when the senior priest became seriously ill. He rushed the Brahmin to town for an operation and was credited with saving his life. At the next festival the buffalo was spared. But the headman goaded his own community and several others into boycotting the new celebration. He fomented quarrels and instigated fights.

Half a dozen years later, the rift between the villages still seemed unbridgeable. I was at the festival when the headman's men arrived unexpectedly in the square.

The singing and dancing became ragged and died out in confusion. Then something strange happened. The drummer resumed his insistent beat, as if to challenge the intruders. First one, then another of the visitors tapped his foot in time. A young man took a step forward, as if to dance and smiled. One or two faces in the watchful crowd smiled back. Hesitantly the newcomers edged ahead until, encouraged by cheers, they had danced their way into the middle of the square.

At the festival the drummer, the village's humblest servant, was always the central figure – treated with respect and offered the choicest morsels. The Harijans could for once eat their fill. The five half-starved children of Kedu the cripple stuffed themselves with pancakes. Dinu the debt-slave, gloriously drunk, appointed himself master of ceremonies, and even the most exalted of the villagers obeyed him in good humour. It was Dinu who pushed back the crowd to clear the space for the sacrifice – a coconut to be halved by one stroke of the ceremonial sword.

Laughter mingled with drunken shouts as teams from each village danced in the competition which has now replaced the buffalo chase. The arrival of the previously hostile villagers remained unexplained until some time after the festival.

The merry-making continued late into the night. A fierce-looking youth complained drunkenly that without the buffalo chase he had no chance to show his mettle.

A teenage girl detached herself from the group of women. 'A buffalo is a human being, too,' she shouted at him, 'it suffers like we do.' She intoned a song and the other women took it up: 'I give you milk, I give you dung, but still you kill me. Please don't. . . .'

That day the village was not the sad place I sometimes felt it was. Progress had been real – for the buffalo at any rate.

*29 March 1982*                                         **Victor Zorza**


## Oh, Calcutta!

For the third consecutive time a Test match in India has forlornly petered out into a tame, sad draw. Yesterday at Calcutta, in the fourth of the six-Test series against England, India scored 170 for three wickets, having been asked to score 306 to win the match. Gavaskar, their skilfully resolute, Job-like little captain, batted all day for 83 runs.

Well, not all day actually, and there was the tragic rub, for on this final day an earlier start than usual was made and, as ill luck would have it, Calcutta's regular morning smog lingered longer than usual. The first seventy minutes of the day were lost and the match was ruined. Gavaskar thereafter had no realistic reason to chase runs, and once he and Srikkanth had batted out the remaining fifty minutes to lunch there was not really a possibility that England would take all India's wickets.

Immediately after the interval Srikkanth was very well held by Botham at mid-on off Emburey and English hopes were raised briefly. Then Vengsarkar stayed with his captain to put on sixty in just over an hour and a half. The fact that the slim, elegant No. 3 batsman was dismissed by Fletcher, the England captain, who has only one other Test wicket in his long career – though Bill Lawry, no less, at Brisbane twelve years ago – gives you some idea of how England had just about given up the ghost by then.

Even the immediate duck by Viswanath scarcely caused an eyelid to be raised in expectation. There has been a lot too much expectation in this series that has been well and truly doused as soon as one has fallen for it.

For what it is worth, and that's very little in retrospect, Emburey bowled well and menacingly while the game was 'on' in the morning, Gavaskar was a model of patient rectitude all through, Patil looked more ridiculously jittery than ever as he played out time with his captain and might well have been caught three times.

Gooch, for the last trick, had the huge and honest crowd in fits as he borrowed a pair of spectacles and mimed an over by the studious Doshi, left arm round, moving a fielder a fraction before every ball, asking twice for the ball to be changed. As usual, Jacques Tati would have approved, and some might remember it as the highspot of a sadly dreary day.

Then the evening mists rolled up from the river to be met by the exhaust fumes, and once again the dark blanket wrapped itself over the city. The series was, one suspected, dying on its feet.

Smog stopped play. I daresay it used to at Lord's in the days of London's old peasoupers, before the Clean Air Act. Every morning and evening, especially in the exhaust fumes of the rush hour, the smog here has been almost unbearable. I know it is the least of Calcutta's problems, but, for the record, all of us have been sick or nauseous if we've ventured out in it.

It cannot have helped Boycott's sickness at all, though he ventured out yesterday to watch the last rites performed. He, Botham and Willis (the last two with their wives) will miss the trip for the three-day match to Jamshedpur which starts tomorrow and have a short holiday on the beaches near Madras. It should help decoke their lungs.

When the umpires came off after just one ball, the sun was just breaking through the dully echoing, milk-white mists. Fletcher and the England team pointed to the shadows on the turf, and though the Indian batsmen and the umpires were off at a rate of knots, the England captain, plus Emburey, Gooch, Gatting and Lever, remained on the pitch in some playful sort of sit-down strike. After ten minutes they moped in. They were off for a further hour, and so, in a way, the four previous days had been meaningless.

England had batted on at the start the day before, but in truth it was much worse yesterday. It was an eerie feeling sitting above this vast cockpit – another 85,000, and some said it was an all-time record Test attendance. Not a slow handclap was heard. A patient throng was marooned in a ghostly silence. Our favourite landmarks had vanished. They were somewhere out there.

There can be no other place that remotely resembles Calcutta. Certainly there is no cricket ground like Eden Gardens. It is an absolute tragedy – though, in one major way, ironic justice, I suppose – that one of Calcutta's great jamboree weeks of its year, so longingly looked forward to and triumphantly organised, should be blighted by one of the many blights that the city is heir to.

World health authorities say the smog and pollution levels here are seven times higher than should be acceptable. It has been quite a week. But we will not be sorry to leave our sore throats behind.

As I write, the crowds are departing the stadium, disappointed but still raising a smile. And as the evening rush hour starts, the sun is being obliterated again. Exhaust is never exhausted. But expectation is.

*7 January 1982*                                    **Frank Keating**


# Who's for Solidarity, and why

During most of the past year – quite apart from the machinations of the Soviet Union – we have been playing our own propaganda game with Poland, booting that battered football of a country up and down an increasingly muddied field between two goal posts: the Western Left and Right. We play the game in all seriousness – there is little else we can do in the way of more constructive activity but draw lessons from Poland to strengthen our Left *v.* Right fixtures At Home. So far, it seems the Right have scored.

Three things account for this. Poland is Soviet-dominated; therefore any Polish struggle for autonomy presents itself as a struggle against the Soviet Union and against the Soviet system. Secondly, the Poles are, on the whole, a religious people. These two ingredients fuel the Right and leave the Left defensive, a position made the weaker by a random geography. What happens in the USSR's backyard happens in our frontyard (Czechoslovakia, Hungary, Romania, Poland) whereas events in America's backyard (El Salvador, Nicaragua, Argentina, Chile) are even more distant from us and so can be safely ignored. The Left may mourn these far greater horrors but they pose no more than a moral threat.

As for the religious aspect of the Polish struggle, that has been co-opted as of right by the Right, who count God as an automatic ally, dismiss as aberrations such anomalies as Italian or French Catholics who are also Communists and refuse to contemplate the very idea of Catholic Socialist Poles or Solidarity members who are also atheists.

The third ingredient is the nature of the Western media, run – on the whole – for profit, skilled in reporting East–West confrontations and unmotivated in conveying the subtleties of a particular event as seen through the eyes of the partici-pators rather than providing a grindstone for those with their axes at the ready.

The Left, more aware of these subtleties, is caught be-tween the devil of Soviet totalitarianism and the deep blue sea of an America intent on using Poland for its own hawkish ends. No wonder, before the London march for Solidarity, the Left was confused. When the Right is out in full strength to support a cause, the Left is bound to fall back perplexed, scratching its forehead and wondering just how many of its enemies' animosities can match its own.

How many bishops cancel out how many trades union leaders? How many nuclear hawks clear the streets of nuclear doves? Should a Bernard Levin presence mean a

Paul Foot absence? What does Shirley Williams represent in the SDP, never mind marching for Solidarity? If Margaret Thatcher supports Solidarity, does Solidarity know? If President Reagan approves, can the holocaust be far behind? If the Pope stands for Poland, does Poland stand for the Pope? Or, as a fighter for working people everywhere, should one put all petty sectarian issues aside and do what the Polish workers clearly request – support their demands? Surely one thing remains certain at the core of all politics: the right of a nation to determine its own fate?

Unfortunately, to add mud to muddied waters, the demands of Solidarity have been presented to us, in the West, under one umbrella word. Freedom. Which, interpreted, means 'What we have.' But the generally unpublicised fact is that what Solidarity stands for is a Socialist freedom and that in a more radical and far-reaching form than Mrs Thatcher or Mr Reagan could imagine in their most frightful nightmares or even Mr Foot easily contemplate in his most utopian dreams.

If Western trades unions are the (just) acceptable form of Socialism here, then Solidarity in Poland is a face not to be tolerated for a moment by the Right, here, should it dare to raise itself in their domain.

We can all accept that Solidarity began as a fight to form trade unions. That alone, in a country where workers' interests were held to be identical to the ruling party's interests, was a revolutionary demand though not without its tiny parallels in our own party politics. Solidarity's demands exposed – not Communism – but what should much more accurately be called Sovietism: Soviet rigidity, Soviet sham, Soviet failure. Just as, one could add, El Salvador exposes America's democratic sham, were the same people interested.

But that once understood, the Right drew huge conclusions. All the gallant Poles want, they said, is free trade unions. Pushed, some added 'and the right to strike' – a right none are too keen on in their own countries, a right they often attempt to curtail. Fair enough. Given the vote, such curtailments can be fought. Silence, however, reigns when it comes to publicising Solidarity's accompanying aims, beside which the aims of our own Ken Livingstones and Peter Tatchells pale to a watery blue.

Solidarity has 'views' on what should happen in all firms as well as in municipal and district councils. It maintains that leaders at all levels should be elected and should be responsible to its electorate. It wants councils in every organisation to recruit directors by open competition and selection. It asks for the indexing of wages, all wages, to inflation. It requires the abolition of privileges for Party members (in the West read company cars, interest-free loans, all executive perks).

It requests that all public officials gradually become subject to social control. It stands for real Press freedom. And it demands for its workers the right to the same pensions and family subsidies as the police and the army (high student grants, subsidised housing, private schooling, home help, moving costs, transport costs, early retirement – the list is long). Cry your eyes out, Tony Benn.

The Soviet Union is shocked by such demands. And its natural bedfellows in the shock unit are Margaret Thatcher, President Reagan and almost every other establishment figure in the West, were the same demands to be levelled at them. Beside Solidarity, our own unions noiselessly gnash their gums and disturb no-one. The Pope himself would be forced (if logic prevailed) to advise the Poles against such earthly revolution as he did the Latin Americans, who live under far more dreadful conditions.

Yet these realities continue to be ignored by the West so that we may point, with false naivety, to our carefully constructed image of the brave Polish worker who wants only to get out from under the Russian boot with the help of a nuclear missile or ten from his friends. How still and small the voices of those who support Solidarity in its real aims, in spite of the Russians and in spite of the West, too. How even stiller and smaller, the voices of those who would implement Solidarity's aims here, in Britain, for the British.

*4 January 1982*                                    **Jill Tweedie**

# Poland from the back of the queue

A solitary armed guard lazily inspects every new arrival. Yet you hardly notice him, for there, shimmering in the distance, the airport balconies are full of frantically waving strangers, of noisy, cheering silhouettes. As you step off the plane, you feel like a Beatle arriving at Shea Stadium.

The spell is shattered by the airport bus which takes an unusually long time to arrive at the bottom of the steps. Perhaps the armed guard wasn't joking when he said that it had run out of petrol. Then your first Polish queue winds in several directions at once around the arrival hall and your first Polish argument develops. A priest had tried to push to the front muttering something about a mass. After an hour news reaches those of us at the back that the Passport Controller isn't even in his booth, that he went off some time ago for an unspecified break. Welcome, indeed, to Poland.

Several hours later I finally break through the airport's outer cordon – of tugging hands and insidious voices whispering 'Change money?' in your ear, of anxious relatives inspecting your face, of shifty-eyed taxi-drivers offering you bad deals – and I board the articulated bus for Warsaw. It soon fills up with chattering soldiers and an over-laden party of Poles back from holiday in Bulgaria. Almost immediately someone on the other side of the aisle notices my luggage labels and begins a conversation.

He had come to the airport in search of some elusive spares for his Polish Fiat. I tell him that it isn't that hard to get most spares in England but no, I didn't know anyone who could fix him up with a job as a taxi-driver in London. Neither did I have any dollars to sell. Poland, he insists, must feel like outer space. Did I know that Poland had paid Russia seven million dollars to take the first Pole into space? And why did that first Polish cosmonaut return to earth with bruised wrists? Because – and he pauses to make sure that the bus is listening – every time he tried to pull a lever or touch a button up there, one of the Russians would slap his wrists and shout: 'Don't touch!'

The bus finally stops underneath the Palace of Culture, the giant grey wedding cake which dominates Warsaw's horizon and which my new guide describes as Stalin's visiting card. We get out and join a taxi queue and he wonders out loud how much Poland spends every year on the Palace's upkeep. Further along the skyline, the Lot Airlines Tower stands unfinished but elegant, a tribute to British smoked glass. You can already buy postcards of it in the kiosks, taken from such an angle that you don't notice the cranes or the missing windows left behind when the British company that was building it pulled out, unpaid.

'Tell me,' he nudges me in the ribs, 'why is it that we Poles were never allowed to build our own buildings under Gierek? Why did Gierek's Mafia spend millions of dollars we couldn't afford starting buildings we didn't need?' Someone else in the queue answers him with another question. How do you think Gierek's wife could afford to have a hairdresser in Sweden? He taps his nose several times and rubs his thumb and forefinger together to indicate that dollars flowed under as well as over the counter.

I notice that the cigarettes he's been smoking, which used to be called Sporty, are now called Popularne. He laughs, coughs, and explains that the sportsmen objected. Besides, everything in Poland is now called Popular something or other. 'We have Popular cigarettes, Popular tea, Popular liver sausage, Popular soap powder, Popular theatres and bars. There used to be so many different brands of tea but now you can only buy one so, of course, it's a very Popular brand.'

I suppose I came to Poland in search of signs of history being made, a set of ideals being put into action, some sort of heroism. Warsaw hasn't changed. It is still a town with an identity crisis, grey and unfocused. The Four Sleepers are still dozing, two Russian soldiers and two Poles, they are supposed to be keeping guard around the Monument to Bravery. But anyone who looks soon notices that they appear to be asleep on their feet. The bear pit is still there, the occasional drunk still falls in.

Work is still going on in the Old Town, the heart of Renaissance Warsaw completely destroyed in the war. The Poles have been rebuilding it for decades, brick by brick. To guide them, they used the paintings of Bernardo Bellotto, the nephew of Canaletto, who came here in 1767 and stayed till his death. This is where all the real Polish architectural energy has been spent. Gierek's skyscrapers were left to foreigners, who by all accounts behaved like an invading army and concentrated on getting drunk and finding bed partners. The English, everyone assures me, were as bad as the rest, worse than the Swedes, worse than the French, as bad as the Turks and Irishmen sent by the West Germans.

Marek is twenty-two and a student. I met him originally in London. We had arranged to meet in the cafeteria of Warsaw's Grand Hotel. Sunning themselves in the porch was an unexpected group of young Arabs, in conspicuous American baseball jackets, sunglasses, and Afro haircuts. More young Arabs are sitting around the foyer or propped up against the hotel's columns, chewing gum. Outside the hotel you can see the taxis circling like sharks. Fifty yards away an official taxi queue stretches back towards the hotel. As often happens with Polish taxi queues, it appears to be undergoing some sort of inspection from a swaying drunk.

An arriving taxi disgorges a smart young Arab. He is in such a hurry that he stumbles as he pulls the blonde Polish girl with him into the hotel lift. The few Poles in the foyer bristle, the lift attendant bristles. The taxi driver hadn't bothered to switch off his meter because he hadn't bothered to switch it on. I notice that he is paid in dollars and that he too is chewing gum. A sign in the hotel lobby promises Dinner, Dancing, Striptease – and other attractions – all in English. The lift attendant who sees me reading it needs no prompting. 'And those other attractions cost a lot of money,' he mutters darkly.

The Grand Hotel's cafeteria is dark and depressing. It is some days and many cafés later that I realise that this is not an attempt to create permanent romantic moods but a nation-wide darkness caused by the shortage of light bulbs. Dotted around the café are more parties of young Arabs, most of them with a Polish girl as the centre of attention. The girls all seem to be blonde although the roots of their hair are invariably showing black. The Arab boys drink Coke and the girls sip coffee but my waitress swears she had neither left, so I order tea. 'Are you trying to be clever?' she snaps when I ask for lemon.

Marek isn't sure where all the Arab boys come from. Some he knows are students from Syria, Libya and Iraq on cultural exchanges. Others he thinks are residual Turkish workers from West Germany. 'Over there they earn big money but are treated like shit. So they come over here and we treat them like kings.' Some of them are here six months out of the year. They live in the hotels. Some speak fluent Polish. Some have a 'wife' and kids. *That* is why they all come here. He nods his head towards a pair of teenage girls trying to look older at a nearby table.

Why did I think that the Palestinian, the terrorist, that man who organised the Israeli massacre in Munich, was shot here? What was he doing in Warsaw? He came here for exactly the same reason as the rest of them. The girls giggle and conspire and do their best to ignore the angry stares directed their way by everyone except the Arab boys.

Some sort of deal is being arranged at the next table. I lean over to listen. In broken English, a Pole is trying to tempt a party of slightly older Arabs to leave the hotel and to stay with him. It will be cheaper, more comfortable. They can stay as long as they want. They can have their own key. They can feel as if they are at home. All the time he is casting nervous glances over my shoulder, towards the door. 'Petro-dollars,' spits Marek, loudly enough for the man to hear.

First stop on the new tourist's route of Warsaw are the shops. We walk along Warsaw's 'Oxford Street,' and into a department store. 'The Polish Harrods,' jokes Marek. Much of the shop is roped off and the signposts no longer make sense. Women's lingerie has become Men's Clothing. All they have for sale is a long, very eerie row of gleaming white shirts. And yet the shop is packed.

Marek dips to the front of every queue to see what they are standing for and explains that they don't wait around half a day for nothing. One turns out to be for soap powder, another for ladies' stockings, a third for toilet paper. Back on the street, the crowds bear no relation at all to the empty shelves, to the sad, empty window displays. Everyone seems intent on buying something, somewhere. Marek wants to practise his English, which is unfortunate because every few minutes another disembodied voice whispers, 'Change money?' in my ear.

The grocer's shop which once took up the bottom two floors of a building is now a single counter selling apples, and another which sells tea, sugar and flour. An argument is developing by the second counter. A woman waving a ration card is upset that there isn't any butter left. The shop attendant is not mincing her words either. Come earlier in future, fat legs, come tomorrow. 'But I have a card,' replies the customer, 'so why don't you have any butter? It's those bastards, Solidarity. Those bastards, they've ruined my country.' Nobody in the shop pays her the slightest attention.

'Stage-managed,' mutters Marek with a dismissive wave in the woman's direction. 'She knows perfectly well that you can't buy butter at this time of the day.' He pulls out his own crumpled stack of ration cards and waves one riskily in the air. Did I know how much he could sell it for? It's a vodka card, vodka and sweets.

Vodka, sweets, cigarettes (fifteen packets a month), meat, flour, sugar, butter, petrol, are all rationed. The old people don't remember it being this bad, even during the Occupation. Rumour has it that shoes will be next and so everyone is buying shoes even though the shoe shops are now down to oddments and wellingtons. It doesn't matter if the shoes don't fit – no one appears to be trying them on.

But it is almost impossible to buy a newspaper. You have to be up at six o'clock, and even then you usually have to be content with the *People's Tribune* the official party mouthpiece. And yet Wajda's *Man of Iron* seems to be playing at every cinema in Warsaw, uncensored except for a few moments of the original newsreel material taken at Gdansk in 1970. The film's eye-catching poster, a man's head with a huge iron nut screwed down over the eyes and mouth, is everywhere, the Solidarity logo incorporated ostentatiously into its title. I try to buy a ticket but evening performances for the next three days are sold out. They might be able to do a matinee, no, not tomorrow, but the day after. As I leave the cinema, another disembodied voice whispers in my ear. Did I want to buy a ticket?

Marek hasn't seen *Man of Iron* yet but he has seen *Saturday Night Fever* – four times. It's been playing in two cinemas in Warsaw to packed houses for some time now, along with *Young Frankenstein, Star Wars, Return of the Pink Panther* and *The Last Remake of Beau Geste*. No wonder the West seems to him like a well-stocked amusement arcade, a mirage vibrating on the horizon. That night we go to a discotheque where a troupe of Polish John Travoltas do a dance which they call the disco-polka.

It was a relief to leave Warsaw. Our car tucked itself in behind a beer truck and we followed it all the way to Chopin's birthplace, where it quickly unloaded and fled, leaving the queue to fight it out. And all the way a police patrol car had kept us and the beer truck in its sights. Riding shotgun, laughed Marek's father, as he filled his boot with beer bottles. Strange things have been happening to beer trucks recently. And not just beer trucks.

What happened to all the supplies that he'd heard had been sent to Poland from France, America, England? He didn't know a single person who'd even seen a foreign lorry. And what about the parcels? For God's sake don't send me any parcels, he pleads. They'll only make someone else rich. Everything disappears as soon as it crosses the border and then turns up next week on the black market.

He insists that to see Poland at its worst we must visit the open-air market on the outskirts of Warsaw, the blackest of black markets. He needs something for his car, the inevitable Polish Fiat.

People converge on the market from all directions – like a Saturday morning football crowd. Outside the enclosure itself a man is selling cassettes from the boot of his car while the speakers on the roof blare out Stevie Wonder. Marek joins the cassette queue but soon returns. The blank cassettes are not Japanese. Besides, what he really wants to buy is a pair of jeans, the fashionable 'punky' ones, a yard wide at the thigh and skin tight at the ankles. A friend had phoned him early that morning to say they would be available, West German ones he thinks.

Most of the stalls are no more than blankets spread out and covered with second-hand clothes, cheaply coloured sweaters, plastic handbags. Someone's selling Smiley badges which say 'Smile – Despite Everything'. Someone else is offering a set of tea towels decorated with giant ration card designs. But far and away the longest queue consists mostly of spotty adolescents. On closer inspection, the slides they are holding up to the light and buying eagerly – in between guilty glances over their shoulders – turn out not to be home-made porn at all but re-photographed centrefolds from *Playboy*. The well-thumbed originals are carefully displayed on the counter in see-through plastic bags.

Marek picks up a copy of a magazine which promises inside exclusive pictures of Debbie Harry and Joanna Lumley. But before he can unwrap the plastic it is snatched out of his hand. 'Do you know how much this costs?' snarls the stall-keeper. 'It's for buying, not looking at.' It costs 2500 *zlotys*, or half the average monthly income.

I had had a memorable train journey. A group of soldiers joined the train at Katowice and we spent the whole night playing a drunken game of cards. When one of them ran out of money he took off his boots and slammed them on the table. We'll play for these, he roared. In between hands they taught me a new version of the Polish National Anthem.

There's no meat and there's no cheese, we sang. Even lard has disappeared. Very soon we'll have to eat the complete works of Lenin.

And now it was morning and I found myself in a church, nervously aware of the almost evangelical fervour of this huge Catholic congregation, listening to a sermon on the evils of drink.

The priest finished his sermon and began his announcements. Almost all of them concerned future Solidarity meetings. I remembered the Solidarity window I had seen at Katowice station, a window packed with official Solidarity information, with up-to-date reports on what was being said in Gdansk, with warnings about forged posters bearing the Solidarity logo, with pictures of the visit of the Nobel prize-winning poet, Milosz, to Poland and, finally, with a list of church services for the coming week. This then was the alternative news service, the way to circumnavigate all the official news channels.

After the service, over a frothy beer, a village luminary told me not to be so surprised. Remember that cemetery, he said, and I remembered the cemetery at the back of the church with its gleaming white gravestones and its festive displays of freshly cut flowers. 'Three years ago that cemetery was under a foot of dead brambles and weeds. Then Poland got herself a Pope and we discovered real Catholicism again. We cleaned out the cemetery. We got rid of all the old German graves.'

Walesa and the Pope, he continued, are like that, and his huge hands met in a fearsome grip. Why do you think they tried to kill him? Why? It was a question I was asked many times.

The atmosphere, the tempo of village life, hadn't changed at all since my last visit. You are still more likely to see a horse pulling a plough than a tractor. Quite often you see them both together and know who is the rich farmer and who the poor. The village football pitch is still covered in cow pats, even though grazing has long since been banned there; the cows still come home in the evenings in ones and twos. Chickens and children are everywhere.

There are, however, some new crops, a hemp-like plant with leaves like cannabis, and, most dramatically, tobacco. I had seen it from the train, hanging out to dry round the houses like an Hawaiian grass skirt. I was told it was easy to grow and profitable, but that it was only suitable for cigars.

But even though times are hard, hadn't I noticed that things in the village had improved, hadn't I noticed all the new houses which had been built in the past few years? I could hardly help but notice them for most had been left unfinished when building materials suddenly became scarce. Not just this village, but the whole of Poland seems to be waiting for a plasterer to come and cover up its exposed breeze blocks.

'That over there,' he pointed to a grey, windowless wall, 'can hold 100 pigs. And there are now three or four farmers in the village with over 20 hectares of land. When you were here last nobody could have more than eight hectares. There are a lot of people in this village,' – and he leans over to whisper this in my ear – 'who didn't do badly under Gierek, a lot of people who don't want Solidarity.'

Besides, he lowers his voice even further, things aren't that bad in the villages yet. You can always kill a chicken, there is always milk, eggs, flour. 'But don't tell that to the town people. They've been coming here for too long with their cars, their big money. Now suddenly they want to be friends. Well, too bad!'

The Solidarity office was housed in a second-floor flat, well off the main street. It took me two attempts to find the entrance. Having seen so many factories bedecked in red and white, loudly proclaiming their allegiance to Solidarity, I hadn't expected the district office to be so shy.

The inside seemed to be decorated entirely with posters and notice-boards. Everyone was furiously busy. They were changing the furniture around for the third time, I was told. People kept coming in and out of doors and every new face looked younger than the one before. It felt uncannily like a students' union office.

I joined a short queue waiting to see the man in charge of information. In front of me someone had brought a cassette recorder and was making a copy of a Walesa speech from a master tape. Two schoolboys wanted to see the secretary. Their whole school wanted to join Solidarity. Everyone else seemed to be here to buy badges. 'I tell you they were ripping them off my jacket,' someone is explaining to the man at the desk. 'If you let me have another six hundred I can sell them all.'

'And I tell you,' replies the harassed salesman, 'that I

don't have the key to the store. All you can have is what you see here.'

It turns out that everything was disorganised because he had just got back from a court appearance. Two of them had been caught painting 'Polish Television Lies' on a fence. The worst thing, he shivers, was that he had a whole week's takings in his pocket at the time. But the police hadn't even searched him, otherwise that money would surely have disappeared.

'They were scared,' interrupts Jacek, who works for Solidarity. 'They're scared of us. Just as you lot in England, the Dutch, the rich Belgians are scared. But we're not scared of them. Forty per cent of us – the young ones – will fight. Only the old ones are too scared. They remember the last war.' Anyway, he says, you don't have to worry. The Russians won't come. They'd have to take over all our debts.

His penultimate words to me were a reminder to listen to what President Reagan said, because Reagan was the only one who understood the danger of communism, and finally taking me aside, could I send him four or five albums, preferably Led Zeppelin.

*7 November 1981*                    **Waldemar Januszscak**


# The legacy of Three Mile Island

This morning the massed membership of the House of Representatives' Interior Committee will arrive in Harrisburg, Pennsylvania, to inspect the largest tombstone in America.

That is not the official description of their trip: ostensibly they are going to see progress in the cleaning up of the Three Mile Island nuclear power station on the third anniversary of its infamous accident. But they might just as well lay a couple of wreaths and go home.

It has become more and more plain that the alarm bells which went off in the control room on 28 March 1979 were tolling not only for General Public Utilities, the owners of the plant. The accident, involving loss of coolant, dealt a cataclysmic blow to the whole nuclear power industry in the United States.

The official statistics tell the story. From 1970 to 1975, there were orders for 144 new commercial reactors in America. In the past five years there have been just two orders – and both of them in the first year. Not a single order has been placed since the accident. By the end of 1981, the Nuclear Regulatory Commission had granted three operating licences for new reactors – and one of those was revoked when it emerged that the designer's notion of earthquake-proofing at Diablo Canyon, California, was radically different from the NRC's. One of the other licences was for limited preliminary testing and only the William McGuire plant in North Carolina went into full operation. In contrast, six projects were completely cancelled and forty-four were delayed to the point where their future must be questioned. Of the seventy-eight operating commercial reactors in the country, four have been wholly shut down for safety reasons and one has had its licence suspended. The latest row has centred on Washington State, which has decided – at horrendous cost – to mothball indefinitely three plants under construction.

The row about who is to pay to clean up the Harrisburg mess is still going on and looks likely to rage for the rest of the decade. The total cost is now estimated at about $1000 million. The owners were paid $300 million by their insurers, but most of that has now been spent, and they are busy lobbying Congress to establish that this is a national problem whose costs ought to be borne by the Federal Government. In this age of budget-slashing, there are not many people singing their tune. Nor have their colleagues in the generating industry shown any greater enthusiasm towards a proposal for joint shouldering of the burden. The half million gallons of radioactive water swilling around the reactor building have mostly been pumped out but, as funds run low, the work is being slowed. But this is only a preliminary. There is the building itself to be decontaminated and then the imponderable business of getting to the reactor core. No one knows quite what will be found inside: the original investigation suggested that most of the fuel rods were either wholly melted down or substantially damaged. The $1000 million estimate assumes the damage is no worse than now guessed.

This is in Reactor Number 2: a more chilling story for the industry comes from TMI-1. That had been shut down for refuelling at the time of the accident to TMI-2 and the owners made repeated efforts to get permission to restart it. The NRC finally agreed, but was over-ruled in a court case. No sooner had that happened than it was found that Number 1's steam generator was badly corroded and will need at least a year to repair. It is now known that this problem affects all pressurised water reactors and comes from a hitherto unsuspected chemical reaction between their radioactive core cooling water and the steel piping carrying it. Of the 72 reactors actually working in the United States, 49 are PWR's and face a similar hazard.

But that is far from the end of the story. An undergraduate at Cornell University, John Stephens, has recently come up with a shattering additional finding about this chemical corrosion. He discovered that one of the elements added to strengthen the steel turns into the highly-radioactive Niobium-94, which emits powerful gamma rays and has a half-life of 20,300 years. This means that, when a power station has to be dismantled at the end of its useful life (and that is already occurring in some places) there is a far greater problem about radioactive waste than had been thought. There have been some pretty scaring calculations of the cost of dismantling based on a waste storage period of 30 years. For the average plant, it works out at about $100 million at 1978 prices, and the waste storage accounts for nearly two-thirds of that. What is the price likely to be if the residue has to be kept safe 700 times longer?

*29 March 1982*                                    **Harold Jackson**


# Back to feel-good movies

American audiences and Hollywood studios seem equally eager today to avoid facing reality. Runners may stumble, yet they win their races. Couples may split, yet their love remains alive. Babies are stolen, but they are found. Heroes are killed, they come back to life. Characters may have faults – God knows America isn't perfect – but they never do any real harm, and everything turns out all right in the end. Alcoholism is hilarious, paralysis is a load of laughs. Prostitutes are redeemable. Derelicts don't smell. These days, even downers are uppers. Is the oldster irascible? Team him with a profane little punk and soon they'll be best of friends. Is the hero hideously deformed? He must die, but with a smile on his face. Is the hero a graverobber? Put him in a fedora and call the movie a fantasy. Is the hero a failure, a sneak, a bit senile? The audience will forget all that if you cast Burt Lancaster.

Casting is vital in feel-good movies. In the book from which *Taps* was adapted the leader of the cadets' rebellion was an unsympathetic automaton, but giving the part to Timothy Hutton drew enough teenage girls into the cinemas to make the movie a hit. With decent, respectable Jack Lemmon playing the Nixon-loving businessman whose son goes *Missing* in Pinochet's Chile, the audience knows he'll soon see the light. Musical comedy star Treat Williams made the drug-dealing, extortionist, informing liar he played in *Prince of the City* seem almost heroic.

Hollywood does still make serious, issue-orientated movies, but fewer now than in some recent times. They tend to fare poorly at the box office and many are flawed by feel-goodism. *Pennies From Heaven* cancels its bleak message by out-Berkeleying its 1930s models and by tacking on an it-was-just-a-movie-folks epilogue. *Ragtime* de-emphasises the political critique of Doctorow's book and adds a romantic element.

Ah, romance! *Reds* shows John Reed as a lover first and a revolutionary second; *Rollover's* Kris Kristofferson has adding machines behind his eyeballs but in the end we find he loves Jane Fonda truly; in *Absence of Malice* there may be a misunderstanding between misguided reporter Sally Field and maligned businessman Paul Newman, but they don't let that keep them from going to bed together; the cavemen in *Quest For Fire* express themselves best wielding clubs yet the film ends with the cavemen-in-chief and his girlfriend sitting arm-in-arm, staring calf-eyed at the moon.

Crime movies are also romances: the tougher the gooier. Master criminal James Caan's motivation in *Thief* was to have a wife and kids and live in the suburbs; super-sleuth Burt Reynolds in *Sharky's Machine* seems happiest when filling baddies full of lead, but it turns out that what he really wants is to have a wife and kids and live in the suburbs.

A curious counter-trend is the audience's rejection of movies in which romance is men's and women's only aim in life. Today's active young moderns, the hard-to-pleasers responsible for 95 per cent of American audiences today, seem uninterested in out-and-out boy-meets-girl, boy-loses-girl, boy-finds-girl love stories like *One From The Heart*.

In general, though, Hollywood succeeds when it goes to any length to send people out of the cinemas feeling good. *Shoot The Moon* has a horrifying, violent climax, in which Albert Finney wrecks his ex-wife Diane Keaton's tennis court and gets beaten up by her new boyfriend. Except the movie doesn't end there: it goes on to a freeze-frame of Finney reaching out to Keaton. Tony Richardson's *The Border* is the most blatant current example. The ending originally shot showed disillusioned border patrolman Jack Nicholson wrecking his HQ after discovering that his superiors were murderers and thieves. Universal vetoed this and sent them all back into the desert to shoot a new ending in which our hero retrieves a baby stolen from a Mexican madonna: freeze-frame on their tearful reunion in mid-Rio Grande.

In today's Hollywood, even homosexuals can have happy endings. Mariel Hemingway in *Personal Best* breaks off her long affair with another woman athlete and goes straight with a male water-polo player, yet reaches out at the end to help her former bedmate make the Olympic team. In Francis Veber's script for *Partners*, gay cop John Hurt killed himself at the end, but Paramount decreed that homosexuals today needn't respond to a cruel world so despairingly, so Hurt lives happily ever after. In *Making Love*, Michael Ontkean plays a doctor who discovers he's gay after eight years of marriage to Kate Jackson. He goes off and finds true happiness with a male lawyer but somehow remains in love with Jackson.

Kids and old folks remain an essential element in keeping real life off the American screen. The box office hit of 1982 so far is *On Golden Pond*, with Henry Fonda as an irritable but lovable old curmudgeon who trades four-letter words with his spoiled but lovable step-grandson. At the end Fonda isn't irritable any more and the boy isn't spoiled but both are even more lovable.

In many American movies now, a very old character, usually from Britain or Broadway, is injected to show how sensitive and perceptive the main characters are. Killing off the old codgers adds a few easy weeps to pictures like *Making Love*, in which Wendy Hiller's departure shows how deeply stars Ontkean and Jackson really and truly care.

For three-quarters of *Arthur*, John Gielgud's Oscar-winning performance consists of insults to Dudley Moore. When Gielgud's character turns sickly, his true niceness is revealed and Dud's capacity for deeply honest feelings shines forth. Geraldine Page's death in *I'm Dancing As Fast As I Can* functions to display Jill Clayburgh's capacity for warmth and sympathy.

As for child actors, not since the days of Shirley Temple have they had such mature characters to play. They are far more sensible than their bickering parents in *Shoot The Moon*, a movie that also plays the oldster card by stationing Finney at Keaton's dad's deathbed. Little Christina in *Mommie Dearest* was clever enough to withstand mum's coat-hanger attacks and grow up to get her own back. Neil Simon's two latest collections of one-liners, *Only When I Laugh* and *I Ought To Be In Pictures*, are both about teenage girls who breeze in from nowhere and rescue a long-lost parent from his or her shortcomings.

As usual with rat-smelling expeditions in America, the spoor leads to Madison Avenue. Hollywood's feel-good film cycle is but an echo of happy-face TV ad campaigns like 'Oh, oh, oh, oh, what a feeling – Toyota!' and Rice Krispies' 'It's gonna be a great day!'

Hollywood sells its movies these days like so many Toyota-burgers. '*Making Love* is a love story about a young woman,' Twentieth Century-Fox alleged, '. . . and ultimately a love story with three happy endings.' *Whose Life Is It Anyway?* may be the most extreme example of an ad wagging a dog of a movie: 'In a Boston hospital a love affair ends, a new one begins, and a man learns the true meaning of courage.' I suppose MGM could hardly have sloganned: 'Fast-moving! See the restless quadriplegic' no-holds-barred search for suicide!'

*17 April 1982*                                              **Bart Mills**


# The enigma of Werner H.

Werner Herzog, like a good many other directors equipped to offer something special for the jaded palates of film buffs, has never liked to do anything the easy way. When Lotte Eisner, the mother-figure of the West German cinema, fell ill in Paris, Herzog walked from Munich to her bedside to comfort her. Asked to explain why, he simply said: 'She deserved the trouble.'

Practically all his films have, in the end, deserved the trouble he has lavished upon them. And where Hollywood lavishes money, Herzog puts into them more than a little of his eccentric self. *Fitzcarraldo* is just the latest of the mountain peaks he has climbed – in its case quite literally, with a steamship, 700 extras, and film equipment to keep him company.

The tales behind the making of his movies are, in fact, quite as amazing as the films themselves. He shot *Fata Morgana* in the Sahara, where he contracted bilharzia, and in Central Africa where he was thrown into a rat-infested gaol on suspicion of being a mercenary. For the end sequence of *Heart Of Glass* he took his crew in open boats through stormy seas to the precipitous Skellig Isles off the Atlantic coast of Ireland.

And most people now know that Klaus Kinski, the star of

*Fiszcarraldo*, was only persuaded to go on with Herzog's earlier *Aguirr!*, *Wrath Of God* by the director pointing a gun at him. It seems that Herzog needs to find out just how far he and his actors can go before he makes final decisions about the nature of his movies.

He himself puts it thus: 'If you are a scientist and want to find out about the inner structure of some matter, you will put it under extreme circumstances. People under that sort of pressure give you much more insight about what we are, about our very innermost being.'

Such statements would seem close to pseudery if the films of Herzog did not contain some kind of extra dimension, a magical quality. But they do. The deaf and blind people in *Land Of Silence And Darkness*, the dwarfs in *Even Dwarfs Started Small*, Walter Steiner, the ski-jumper, in *The Great Ecstacy Of Woodcarver Steiner*, and, above all, the enigmatic Bruno S, star of *The Enigma Of Kaspar Hauser* and *Stroszek*, are exceptional characters placed in circumstances by Herzog that underline their qualities.

Herzog has often been accused of exploiting these people for his own purposes, of making them into showcase freaks. Bruno S, for instance, had been abandoned by his prostitute mother at the age of three, had spent twenty-three years in various institutions, and was discovered by Herzog working as a lavatory attendant in Berlin. Sent off, following the triumph of Kaspar Hauser, to Cannes, he seemed so inextricably confused with the part he played that many felt he might never recover from the experience of becoming famous.

Yet Herzog consistently denies that he has ever harmed anybody, and as justly claims that the risks he asks others to take are only the same as those he takes himself. The result is films that can go from the sublime to the ridiculous but which contain within them a mysterious quality, founded on German Romanticism perhaps, but able to engage the imaginations even of those who know nothing about its tenets. Herzog is the antithesis of rational man. Film, he says, 'is not the art of scholars but of illiterates. And film culture is not analysis but agitation of the mind.'

He adds, "I would ask of my audience three things. First, I ask for some sympathy – not much, but as little as there is black under my nail. Second, I ask that people should look straight at my films, without the sophistication that dulls the senses.

'Thirdly, I ask the watcher to remember that you learn more about the shape of a town from its outskirts than from its centre. The same applies to people – you learn more from the marginals than from the ordinary. Besides, there is really no such thing as an "ordinary person." '

*Fitzcarraldo* has been three years in the making after an abortive start when Herzog was caught between opposing Indian factions and once again accused of exploitation, and after Jason Robards and Mick Jagger withdrew from the cast (one through illness, the other because of the delay and his other commitments). It is a typically Herzogian enterprise.

The fact that it achieved for its maker the Best Director prize at Cannes surely gives us leave to hope that the New German cinema has found someone to replace the loss of Rainer Werner Fassbinder. Herzog, though not the same animal at all, has always had as amazing a talent, capable of international recognition. It may now come fully into its own.

*8 July 1982*                                          **Derek Malcolm**


# Godfathers of a children's crusade

OPA TERROR, it says in chalk on the walls of the Berlin underground – Grandad terror! It could mean those old Nazi grandfathers, but the A is enclosed in an O, the anarchist sign, and it's an ironic reference to a strange alliance which has grown up in the theatre workshop or political laboratory which is West Berlin. It's an alliance between certain elders – old anti-Nazi pastors like Bishop Scharf, Dr Albertz, Professor Gollwitzer and other teachers and writers – and the new generation which emerged three years ago with a surrealist political manifesto, the manifesto of Tunix (Berlinerisch for Do Nowt, or Drop Out). This begins like a German fairytale – ' "Come with us", said the donkey. "We'll find something better than death wherever we go" ' – but ends crisply enough: 'We want womething different! And we want it now! Gefalligst! (*If* you would be so kind!)'

For years now, says Ulrich Albrecht, one of the younger elders, people like Heinrich Böll and these others have been trying to disinter and refurbish an alternative, democratic and less materialistic native tradition to set against tightased hysteriprone, Protestant ethic-perverted German authoritarianism. It may not be quite what they expected, but suddenly here are these Tunix people, rejecting with a kind of stroppy pacificism 'the whole Coca-Cola-Karajan culture . . . the dreary asphalt-concrete wastes of the new estates, the gun-toting presence and violence of the police apparatus that destroys our dreams with Peter Stuyvesant and Springer's Bild. . .'

It's a fine and furious document, proposing a general youth evacuation of Germany for the winter, a sort of reverse Children's Crusade: 'We're fed up with it here. The winter's too triste, there's no spring to speak of, it's stifling in summer . . . and the beer tastes flat, like bourgeois morality. They've bossed us around enough, inspecting our ideas, rooms, passports mugs. We're all off to the beach at Tunix, so the police can choke with boredom and bubble-gum, and the special branch get round to protecting the Grundgesetz against themselves for a change.'

And it goes on to dream of empty factories, kindergartens, schools and universities 'the big stores having to sell their trash to each other, while on the empty floor, before the sobbing supervisors, the lone and lonely personnel manager dances the Dying Swan. . . .'

What's left of their 'new form of opposition . . . new ideas for a new struggle' is first an explosion of 'alternative' media concerns, pre-eminent among them in Berlin, a successful *daily* newspaper, the *Tageszeitung*, and the illegal and very popular Radio Alice (in Wonderland) which specialises in hilarious de-mystifying translations for the fans of the 'straight' media's account of the news (so: no need to buy them. . . .).

Then there's a substantial network of small businesses – the usual mixture of handicrafts, repair shops, whole-foods – supported partly by a regular 'tithing' from the oldies, the Paten, or godparents, as they're called, and based on a largish and rather idyllic commune that took over part of the old Nazi UFA film studios at Tempelhol.

Its other legacies are to the peace movement, especially among the young, who oppose its dreams to the black baroque fantasy of the sober-suited arms-race 'realists,' and as one source of ideological justification for the squatters who now occupy far more newspaper space, police resources and political debating time than the number of houses involved seems to warrant.

The practical problem of the squatters is real enough, however. There is a large Turkish immigrant population and a dire shortage of cheap housing; and meanwhile Berlin's peculiar constitutional status and reputation as 'dream city' in the last few years has drawn tens of thousands of out-of-work, draft-dodging young refugees from the rest of the Federal Republic. Add to them an altogether disproportionate Berlin intake of students whose supplementary grants have dwindled through pegging by a coalition government under heavy political pressure to cut welfare costs, and the situation's explosive potential is easily seen.

In fact, it is seen increasingly as a microcosm of the pressures now building up in Germany. The lines are drawn more clearly here, just as the Wall draws its ineluctable line between the two German successor states. On one side, behind the police lines, a growling 'silent majority' and the indignant building societies who want to develop the squatted properties for quite other uses, stands the stocky authoritarian figure of Heinrich Lummer, Senator for Internal Affairs, not the loveliest of the CDU's new breed of politicians.

On the other side of the squatting line are the tatterdemalion ranks of the not so respectable-looking young, many of them still full of serious German idealism, but with an increasing, alienated fringe which is far from pacifist: '*Staat – hau ab!* . . . Clear off, State!' is their ruling motto now. And behind them stand the old priests and teachers and writers and social workers who have moved on from 'tithing' to taking sleeping bags down to the squats and sleeping there by rota, like seventy-five-year-old Professor Gollwitzer and his friends, in the hope of providing some '*anständig*' insurance against police harshness.

'More phantasie,' was one of the calls of the Tunix folk and some of their successors certainly have that. On my last night in Berlin I dined by candlelight in a grim old ruin of a house that stands at right-angles to Potsdammer Strasse behind a patch of waste ground, just across the road from where Klaus Jürgen Rattay was killed after the evictions of September 22.

A series of hand-drawn posters on the fence gave some of its history. Once it had been a Prussian officers' club, where General von Bülow had his Rittersaal. Petty racketeers had taken it over in the early thirties. It survived the last war, and in the fifties 'the first puffs of pot floated out of the Cafe Paradise which had nested in its basement.' Since May, after standing empty for some time, it had been occupied by a couple of 'families' of rather classy young squatters (whose protective 'godparents,' interestingly, turned out to be the printers' chapel of the gentlemanly old Berliner Morgenpost.)

There was a civil young pig-tailed pirate, late of Johns Hopkins, Jakub, a physics student, two law students, several who did fringe social work with kids and among Berlin's dangerously large number of heroin addicts. (There's an almost twenties-style war going on in the city between Turkish and Italian dealers). In all, about a score of them, half of them out of work, and half a dozen still painting and scraping and hammering in the half-light when I arrived; the fine boards of the second floor dining-room had actually been sanded and polished to von Bülow standards.

Jakub's contribution to phantasie was a sign that stuck out along the second-floor balcony. He'd found in a ruined factory a jumble of big neon letters, and wired them up, so that normally across the waste land, among all the rotting commercial kitsch of the 'potse,' there shone out in fine, fat art-deco capitals the legend: *BESETZT* – Occupied.

But the lights were out now. They'd had their electricity from the house around the corner from outside which Rattay had been chased into the road after the eviction there. The water supply had been restored, but only for three weeks. And it was colder than it had been since they moved in.

'Scheisskopf!' roars my tough old ex-Wehrmacht taxi-driver as he swerves close to the flower-banked shrine which, ten days after Rattay's death, is still in place at the spot on the road where he ran under a bus. It's guarded now early on Sunday morning, by a boy wearing a multi-coloured blanket shaped into something like a cope, and a girl holding a red banner with a black star in the middle. 'Shit-heads! The red flag in the streets again!'

Among all the leaflets and posters blaming Lummer and the police for Rattay's death, there are a few others advocating a 'citizens against the Chaoten,' creatures of chaos.

In Bremen there is a newspaper report of a plan to organise an armed citizens vigilante group, and wild talk of backing from 'solid Bremeners, millionaires among them.' 'You've got to remember Berlin's special position,' says my own dangerous driver. 'If our police don't really deal with these layabouts, the Americans will put troops in. Yes! And then the Russians will start to poke their noses in.'

A well-informed source, as they say, told me before I left Berlin that although the city government had agreed to negotiate with the squatters' advisers it was known that dates for further police evictions had already been fixed. And the word from elsewhere on the squatting 'scene' (not from the Potsdammer Strasse) was that their conception of *Nachrüstung*, to borrow the official euphemism for increased armaments, now included petrol bombs as well as cobble stones.

Germany this autumn presents a paradoxical face to the world. For many good and serious people, and not only on the left, this is a time of hope. The 'angst Movement' is

141

shifting old social and political roadblacks and generating an energy of debate that's warming to watch. But the movement's cooler heads know that there is also an angst of the right, always latent in their society. These competing anxieties are beginning to bid each other up inexorably and there are signs that, at the ballot box, the angst of the right is likely to prevail.

*15 October 1981*                                                  **W. L. Webb**


# Europe 'smells like Neville Chamberlain'

In considering the very idea of American isolationism, which only a year or two ago would have seemed incredible but now is not, let me start by quoting the utterances of three great Americans, Presidents Washington and Kennedy, and Secretary of State Haig.

Washington: 'Steer clear of any permanent alliances in any portion of the foreign world.' That was in 1796, in his farewell address. His words were heeded until 1941, when there was no option. The address is still read to the Senate every year on or around Washington's birthday, to a bare quorum.

Kennedy: 'Let every nation know, whether it wish us well or ill, that we shall pay any price, bear any burden, meet any hardship, support any friend, oppose any foe, in order to assure the survival of and success of liberty.' That was in his inaugural address, in 1961. It is splendid, but it is hubris. What followed was the humiliation of Vietnam.

Haig: 'It is inconceivable that I shall be isolated.' He was speaking two weeks ago to reporters about his own position in the administration after William P. Clark, a former chief of staff to Reagan when he was governor of California, was appointed National Defence Adviser with responsibility for the whole foreign policy portfolio and direct access to the president. Poor Haig was rebutting suggestions that the President would therefore have less time for his Secretary of State. It was just another episode in the habitual public bickering that goes on between members of Reagan's administration. Secretary of State Haig and Defence Secretary Weinberger in particular take Montesquieu's concept of checks and balances to hilarious lengths, and hardly bother to conceal their differences.

Haig, in the wider sense, is no isolationist either. He may look fierce when he snarls at reporters who have the impertinence to ask about Poland and El Salvador in the same sentence. He may very well have said – he has after all the gift of the gaffe – that Her Majesty's Principal Secretary of State for Foreign Affairs is a duplicitous bastard. But he is no hawk. He does not want to withdraw into Fortress America, or go it alone. He believes in the Atlantic Alliance, and has said so not only publicly, which might mean nothing, but also privately, when, of course, it has been leaked. There are those in Washington, and not only at Pentagon parties, who go so far as to say this will be his undoing unless matters take a quick turn for the better.

What Haig opposes is a feeling, real enough in some quarters, that Europe can go to Hell, and that NATO is a liability. The American ambassador in Bonn has said, very well, if the 350,000 American troops in Europe are not welcome, they will not stay. Kissinger, in the *New York Times*, has expressed grave doubts about the alliance. That solid newspaper, the *Wall Street Journal*, has said in a leader about Poland that West Germany, showing increasing signs of another mass psychological breakdown, has in effect sided with the Communist generals in their take-over. It has published articles saying the alliance has had its day, and that the US should sever its ties with NATO. One such article, by Hodding Carter III – who is no relation to the former president but was one of his entourage – said NATO was closer to disintegration than at any time since its formation, and included this modest statement: 'The number of nations willing to follow our lead without question can be counted on the fingers of two hands.' The U.S. should be so lucky.

In publishing these articles, the *Journal* is speaking not so much for the bankers and businessmen who are its principal readers, as for the new political far Right. It is also relevant to point out that the *Journal* has its religious idiosyncracies. Every Christmas Eve since 1949 it has published the same, identical, leading article condemning Tiberius Caesar for his enslavement of the subject people of the Roman Empire, presumably as un-American, and extolling Jesus Christ as the light of the world. Well, Tiberius was a bad lot, and Jesus has his following to this day, but is it news?

No, it is not, but the continuing appearance of such an article is important for reasons that I think will be apparent when I report, later in this article, on a morning spent at the Pentagon.

But first, what are the official views that a reporter gets from 'informed sources' – that is to say from people who are in a position to know and who like you to believe that they will speak frankly if you agree not to identify them or, at least, not to attribute anything directly to them?

The British view, expressed in London, Washington, and elsewhere, and expressed with urbanity, ease, and in one instance with the informed feet up on a really handsome desk, is that Reagan is no hawk; that one trouble is that the Americans expect their allies to support them on *every issue*, including El Salvador, which isn't reasonable since no two chaps can agree on everything, and anyway what sort of allies were they to us at Suez; that, deep down, the United States resents that its time as a paramount power was so short, and can't understand why; but, finally, that Schmidt may have been booed in Washington and Haig in Berlin, but that everything will turn out all right in the end.

As for the Americans, the State Department produces soothing talk and opinion polls, one of them nearly two years old, showing no evidence of neo-isolation. Then there is the Pentagon. Pentagon opinions are unattributable, so I shall name no names, but since it's obvious that any reporter would go there I'll describe my visit.

The Pentagon is where the Defence Department lives in Washington, in a complex covering thirty-four acres, said to be the largest office building in the world. I was there just after President Reagan had held a prayer breakfast for General Dozier, the man who said he'd prayed in captivity and that people had prayed for him, and that when you were on the receiving end of so many prayers you sure as Hell knew it. As I entered, I picked up an invitation to another such meeting, organised by the Pentagon Prayer Breakfast Committee, at which music would be provided by the US Navy Sea Chanters.

Then, while I was waiting, I had the good fortune to meet an American reporter, an old hand at covering wars, politics, politicking and the Pentagon, whose views were downright. After Kennedy came out best in the Cuba crisis, he should have gone in and got rid of Castro; since Vietnam the allies had been just a liability; if the Europeans all wanted to become Swedes, then let them; and did I know what Europe smelled like to him these days? It smelled like Neville Chamberlain.

Then into the office of the general, which was decorated with a globe, a flag, and models of an MX missile and a B52 bomber. But first, there was a briefing by a civilian, and a formidable man he was. The United States, he said, really didn't want to paint its allies in too black a tone, but a sense of fair play, inherited after all from Europe, told Americans that the allies were just not sharing the burden. And this was not only a financial burden, but a psychological one. The Nebraska farmer who had a Minuteman taking up twenty of his acres, didn't understand why a Bavarian farmer should object to having a Pershing II in his potato patch.

When the general came in he was not in civilian clothes, as his English counterpart would be, but in uniform, and with a sergeant-major haircut. The superficial resemblance to General Dozier was great. He was all sweet reason. NATO, far from being near the end of its usefulness, had achieved all it had set out to do (which is manifestly true). It was like a family, and there were bound to be strains in any family. And so on.

A third man burst in, boisterously pulling rank on the general by hurrying him up for their lunch date, and cracking a joke about the questions some pinhead from the BBC had asked him, and we all parted in great good humour. I drifted off, strolled along corridors, and had lunch for $1.99 in the

Pentagon cafeteria, which is in itself an experience that tells you to be careful not to think you understand too much or too well, because the United States is a very foreign country. Any country where full colonels and naval captains, in uniform, stand in line with clerks and corporals and carry plastic trays to plastic tables, has to be strange to a European. Because that is equality run crazy.

So I cannot be sure I understand. But I believe the general was saying that NATO may have worked, but that the Europeans had better sit up, take notice, and do more. He probably puts it more bluntly to his fellow officers, saying Gosh darn it, a man can take so much, and if those Europeans spit in a man's face . . . And his colleagues would say, those goldarned so-called allies, they all moan what lousy leaders we are, but won't *let* us lead. I hope that generals at least have their own mess where they can say such things.

I can see that general as a missionary, with an overweening moral purpose. 'We, the people of the free world,' said Reagan, presuming to speak for everyone on the occasion of his television spectacular on Poland, the one where they lit candles. Americans are terribly touchy when their high morality is impugned, and bitterly resentful when they are, as they think, treated as being on the same moral footing as Russia, as when military governments in Poland and El Salvador, the one supported by Russia and the other by the United States, are mentioned together.

Outside, in a Pentagon corridor, I walked past a display of the many flags of the United States throughout its history. Among them was the navy battle jack of 1776, with its emblem of the rattlesnake about to strike, and the legend, 'Don't Tread On Me.' Which is a reminder that America has traditionally been an island power, a sea power. If even Reagan, one day, could find only so much to spend on defence, and it should come to a choice, then troops could be withdrawn from Europe and the United States could perfectly well defend herself, and to a lesser extent her present allies, by the threat of missiles to be fired from ships at sea.

As I left I picked up a few leaflets from a rack. They were not publications of the United States government, but there they were, many of them, on open display, in the equivalent of the Ministry of Defence in Whitehall. One of the pieces of paper was in the form of a cheque on The Bank of Universal Life (Resources Unlimited). It promised to pay to the order of 'Whomsoever believeth' the sum of 'Eternal Life', and was signed by Jesus Christ. We were back to prayer breakfasts, back to a theme I shall touch on again in subsequent articles in this series. There does seem to be a strong lobby holding the view that the principal ally of whose help the United States stands in need is Jesus Christ.

*1 March 1982*                                    **Terry Coleman**


# Against a Second Coming

Jesus Christ will not return to poverty when he comes back to earth – provided that he arranges for the Second Coming to take place within the next eighty years. An insurance policy arranged through Lloyd's of London will pay the Saviour over £300,000 as soon as he proves his identity.

In the meantime, the remote cousins of Mr Ernest Digweed can benefit from the £30,000 which the Portsmouth religious recluse bequeathed to the Messiah in his will.

The Public Trustees' office, a Government department which acts as executor for several thousand wills each year, will shortly be going to the High Court for permission to finalise this somewhat worldly arrangement.

Mr Digweed, who appointed the Public Trustees to be the executors of his will, died four years ago. But his closest relations asked the department to treat Mr Digweed as though he had left no will – so that the legacy earmarked for Jesus could be divided between them. The office has provisionally agreed – but wants to take out an insurance policy in case the intended benficiary returns to collect his money.

Mr Digwood was well aware of just how much interest his lump sum could earn. His will lays down that the money is to be invested to produce a $12\frac{1}{2}$ per cent return. It stipulates that if the Last Judgment takes place within the next twenty-one years, Christ should receive capital and interest – which by then should come to £324,115.90.

Mr Digwood spent some time working out the date of Christ's arrival through a series of calculations based on figures in the Book of Revelation. He expected it to take place before the twenty-one years were up, but his will lays down that should the return be postponed for any reason, the lump sum should be kept for God the Son, although all further interest would be diverted to the state.

Unless the claimant returns, the trust will remain in force for eighty years. Under the sixteenth-century law of perpetuity it would then be dissolved, and the money would go to whoever Mr Digweek's closest relations happened to be at the time.

Rumours in the insurance market are that one big insurer has offered to take the risk at ½ per cent of the total £324,000 – a premium of £1,620.

The biggest worry is going to be identification. The insurers will want to put in tight conditions. Two claimants have already tried and failed to get the money.

*10 December 1981*                                       **Tom Tickell**


## Unequalled temperaments

Arturo Benedetto Michelangeli: the name is known to only a small coterie of concert-goers in this country, yet for them it is synonymous with the ultimate refinement of piano-playing. Mention the name to agents or concert promoters, however, and smiles of scepticism appear. Michelangeli for them means last-minute recital cancellations, sudden flare-ups between the pianist and his colleagues in rehearsals and recording sessions, and unending sagas over the impossible conditions at halls, the unsuitability of particular instruments, the incompetence of piano-tuners and technicians – and so on.

The smiles grow broader when you mention that the London Symphony Orchestra have not only booked Michelangeli to play the Ravel G major piano concerto at two Festival Hall concerts – on Thursday next week and the following Sunday – but have invited Sergiu Celibidache to conduct on both occasions. For Celibidache is almost as famous for his cancellations as Michelangeli, and has controversial ideas about acoustics and interpretation that entail re-positioning players in the orchestra, twice as many rehearsals as most other conductors demand, and other requirements likely to upset the administrative apple-cart.

Already there is a row because he wants the swell-box of the RFH organ closed and the management refuses because they say it will affect drastically the tuning in a period when they have an organ recital scheduled.

To have engaged two such capricious and inflammatory musical autocrats may seem like carelessness. But it could well turn out to be a clever move. For curiously enough, Michelangeli has never cancelled a concert with Celibidache – and they have worked together many times on the Continent.

Michelangeli is, for Celibidache, the greatest pianist ever. And it is regularly Celibidache who succeeds in calming things down when Michelangeli is disturbed or provoked, and who also succeeds in persuading him to play when everyone else's protestations have been rejected. Celibidache is even prolonging his stay in England until an hour or two before Michelangeli's recital on April 13, just in case problems arise.

When Michelangeli arrives tomorrow from Switzerland, he will bring with him two of his Model D Steinways and two technicians: a third technician is on call in the event of a real emergency. Celibidache will already be here, adjusting to the London atmosphere; he has been ill recently, and has cancelled all his engagements up to the first LSO date.

Seven rehearsals are scheduled for their two concerts (the first of which will be shown on BBC-TV). Additionally, Michelangeli has several periods available at the hall when he can be alone with his pianos and technicians: these include the day of his solo recital and the entire day before.

Celibidache, when I visited him earlier this week in his Paris apartment, defended these apparent extravagances quite volubly. For him it is all justified by Michelangeli's special qualities as an artist, about which he rhapsodised at some length. In a nutshell, he feels that Michelangeli better than anyone perceives intuitively the relationships of the various component parts of a work to the totality. This stems from an acute awareness of the possibilities of musical colour – and that in turn derives from a sensitivity to tuning.

The temperature of a hall, sudden draughts, dampness or tiny flaws in the regulation and tuning of the instrument – these can all prevent him from obtaining the perfection of touch and balance that result in exact colouring of chords and phrases. Hence the preparation and last-minute apologies to an already-seated audience (which happened twice in one week when he came to play at the Festival Hall nine years ago): 'My piano is not ready yet.'

Celibidache has worked with Michelangeli for over twenty-five years. At first he didn't understand his peculiarities of phrasing and articulation. But the harder he listened, the more he was convinced. Furthermore, the experience of making music with Michelangeli helped to change his approach to conducting.

'I wasted eight whole years,' he says – referring to his period as chief conductor of the Berlin Philharmonic Orchestra (1945–52), where Furtwängler eventually succeeded him – 'before I decided to give up this music-making which was all at the bottom level, just playing the notes.' Studying with Franco Ferrara, and observing Michelangeli's highly idiosyncratic style of pianism led him to re-formulate his interpretations.

What the pianist seemed to possess by instinct the conductor had to learn. To allow every note to breath and vibrate properly requires both acoustic understanding (hence his objection to an open swell-box at the RFH, which would mean a good third of the orchestral sounds being lost), and also plenty of time. Time, above all: if the detail is to be heard clearly, then tempi have to be slowed down. It's not an approach that endears him to critics who genuflect before the composer's metronome markings or the stopwatch. But it's an aspect of interpretation on which he is unrepentant.

Both artists have spent a lot of time teaching. Michelangeli has given many master-classes and summer schools, often hiring castles in Switzerland or Italy and paying for the travel and upkeep of the students himself. Celibidache runs conducting courses in Mainz. Neither has produced pupils of any eminence.

Celibidache's teaching overlaps into his rehearsals. Thus, he is likely to be followed to London by about 40 students whom he allows into his LSO rehearsals. Michelangeli, by contrast, bans everyone from his rehearsals. Celibidache also hates recording. Michelangeli does a certain amount, though invariably there are eruptions. The latest occurred when he recorded the Ravel G major concerto for DGG. He and the original conductor, the tempestuous Carlos Kleiber, had a fierce argument before they had reached the studio door. Kleiber left and a more placid maestro was found to take over.

Abroad, the two artists have had a mixed reception. Michelangeli came particularly unstuck in Japan, where his tantrums over the state of the pianos led to such sinister threats that eventually he had to be rescued from his hotel room (where he had locked himself in) and taken out of the country under diplomatic protection. Celibidache has also broken off relations with the Japanese since they failed (amongst other things) to fulfil their intention of building him a special concert-hall.

With the LSO, they are likely to be treated with some tolerance, especially by the wind section, who relish being moved into positions where they don't have to fight to be heard and where they can establish a better relationship with the piano. Michelangeli has, in truth, superlative technical skills and in Ravel and Debussy he is nothing short of revelatory. Celibidache, too, in his more deliberate way, can offer fresh insights into this repertoire. Their joint appearance on the London musical scene – and Michelangeli's first since 1973 – should be a matter for rejoicing.

*2 April 1982*                                    **Meirion Bowen**

# Hands of the sick reach for the Pope

John Paul's quarryman face and tender hands dominated a national service for the sick, elderly and dying yesterday afternoon at St George's Cathedral, Southwark.

The event, the biggest of its kind held outside the Lourdes pilgrimage, was the last public occasion of his first day in Britain. It was also the first at which intimate qualities of strength and love were able to emerge clearly from the man who quarried stone as a student.

The service brought a cavalcade of 4000 desperately ailing people on stretchers, in ambulances and on crutches through the streets of the south London borough. Among those who walked the final mile from their coaches were two women in their eighties, bent over sticks and supporting each other as they sang the Lourdes version of Ave Maria, a woman in a wheelchair with the legs of a small child, scores of mentally handicapped people, and a gigantic parade of sick children.

The interior of the cathedral was stripped of furniture so that they could lie or sit under blankets. Sometimes a dozen hands were held out to the Pope as he walked through the nave past each group at the beginning of the service. Their faces opened like flowers as he touched them back on the brows and fingers.

Nine of them – one from each of the diocese's nine areas in southern England – were picked by ballot to be anointed with oil by him, while other priests moved through the rest of the congregation. The eldest of the nine was Mrs Alice Kelly, aged ninety-one. The youngest was in her fifties. Those able to talk said after the service that it had not led them to expect miracle cures. Mrs May Mehan, aged fifty, of Peterborough, who has lost the use of her legs said: 'It's the most wonderful thing of my life. I don't think it will help physically, but it will mentally. I've been to Lourdes fourteen times, so I don't expect too much.' Mrs Peggy Suckveki, of Northampton, whose husband Csevlau had his left leg amputated last year after being paralysed down one side for five years, said: 'He can't talk but you can see how happy he is.'

The Pope's personal force could be seen most pointedly from close to the altar during the anointings. He clasped the hands of his people and looked with concentration into their eyes.

His homily included an 'urgent plea to this nation' not to neglect its sick and elderly. 'Do not push them away from the margins of society. The sick, the elderly, the handicapped and the dying teach us that weakness is a creative part of human living and that suffering can be embraced with no loss of dignity.'

By the end of an event of great intensity, not only the sick but many of the able-bodied in the congregation had to be led out of the cathedral while they recovered from its impact.

*29 May 1982*                                        **John Ezard**

# Papal bull

*The Borgias* (BBC-2) is a spaghetti *Dallas.* There is 'Pop' as he likes to be called ('We are Pop'), two sons who yell at each other a good deal and little Lucy of the disastrous love life. The difference is that while – wail hail – we expect Texans to have trouble with their vowels, it comes as something of a shock to discover that Pop, or Alexander The Sixt, as he prefers to be known, is almost unintelligible. And in *The Borgias* Pop (Adolfo Celi), a sort of explosion in loganberry, looms large.

'We have been cold to St Peter's chair,' he says. 'We cerry the world upon our shoulders like a patient has.' Like a patient has what, we gibber, scrabbling at the screen with demented fingernails, but he spurns us. 'You yelp and squeal like deflower red virgins,' and dismisses us. 'That is owl. Gow naow.'

It was like the memorable English of Ansermet, the Swiss conductor: 'Don't spoke! Don't spoke! If you didn't like it, you went.'

Rome is rife with, according to the Italian element,

romas. These romas are circulated avidly and received with indrawn breath, but I could never quite seem to get the hang of them. 'If Ferranti dies before Christmas, there will be French Lances in our olive groves by spring.' Er . . . 'But will they unseat Roderigo?' W . . . ell. 'If Sforza becomes Pope their brother, the nephew, will boldly strangle his aunt and become Duke of Milan.' That can't be right . . . can it? I have it, however, on the best authority, improbable as it seems, that France and Spain both want to be the Kink of Naples.

The prevalence of romas can be attributed to the fact that anyone delivering a straight message in *The Borgias* is apt to be flung to the floor with an unmuffled oath. A stable-lad, reporting some innocent intelligence from Rome, got a par-for-the-course curse – 'I'll hang you by your neckbone from a harness hook and saddle your wife before your eyes,' while poor old Perotto, having galloped miles to tell Cesare Borgia that his Pop was Pope was received with the unsettling: 'Dogs bark. Asses bray.'

There is little any prudent messenger can add to a remark like that but a nervous nod. Borgia households were notable for what Wodehouse, writing in somewhat similar circumstances in Hollywood, called Nodders. That is, yes-men too terrified to speak.

This pervasive nervousness was evident in the cast. Those with something to say shouted, and nodders with no lines bumped into things. An extra, required only to push a chamber pot through a hatch, contrived, I noticed with some sympathy, to bang it both on the way in and on the way out. You would think, in a £2½ million production, they could have re-shot that.

This ten-part tale of treason, simony, heresy, corruption, murder, incest, extravagant expenditure and aggravated assault on the English language is a co-production with Italy and Australia. Or an unholy alliance, as the BBC calls it, on the cover of *Radio Times*.

The Pope made frequent references in the first episode to boos. Borgia boos and papal boos. And well he might.

*15 October 1981*                                    **Nancy Banks-Smith**

# Where a dream began

Here is a little literary quiz. See if you can identify the author of these wistful lines:

> *Dreaming 'bout a pile of money*
> *dreaming 'bout wedding rings*
> *when you're saving with Burnley Building Society*
> *that's where your dreams begin.*

I will give you a clue. It is an early work, set to a simple melody composed by Ronnie Bond and issued in 1978 on a single entitled 'The Best Dreams Begin with B'. Still not got it? Very well then. It is Salman Rushdie, winner of the 1982 Booker Prize for his novel, *Midnight's Children.*

Matthew Diamond, of Woodford Green, is the sneak who has sent this record in. He comments: 'The words only begin to make sense when one sees the song as a metaphor for the newly independent India trying to establish its own identity and sense of unity, an aspect that pervades all Rushdie's work.' Professor Colin McCabe, please note.

A Burnley spokesman tells me – not without a certain pride – that the above verse was but a fragment of the canon works Rushdie penned while a copy writer for Ayer Barker. 'How about this?' said the spokesman: 'Better Save than Sorry.' Another pithy Rushdie gobbet from the same period, as you no doubt spotted.

*5 May 1982*                                          **Alan Rusbridger**


# Dreams of violence

Novels set in Venice tend for some reason to be sinister, as if there might be something about the place itself that confounds expectations of ordinary decency. Mr McEwan's new book\* bears little resemblance to Mann or Henry James or

\* *The Comfort of Strangers*

indeed anybody else, though his opening situation reminds one of John Bowen's *The Birdcage*, and a character called Robert performs a gratuitously evil act, like Robert in Muriel Spark's *Territorial Rights*. One important difference is that McEwan never names the city; it is grand, squalid, and touristy, but not even St Mark's is identified by name, and the dust jacket, from a Turner watercolour containing gondolas, canals, and St Mark's, but very hazily, was clearly an inspired choice.

Two lovers, rather upper-class package tourists, are in this anonymous town, doing some of the sightseeing incumbent upon them but existing in that state of dissociation sometimes experienced in foreign cities; unable to manage maps, they are always losing their way, and feel most at home in bed.

As always, McEwan manages his own idiom with remarkable grace and inventiveness; his characters are at home in their dreams, and so is he. Detail is rich but oblique. There is a suspicious insistence on a feminist theme; feminist posters and heated arguments are counterpoised against the man next door, singing in his shower the duet from *The Magic Flute*: Mann und Weib, und Weib und Mann . . . But the point is not politics. In a deeper, more dreamlike way, the book speaks of the mutual sadistic exploitation of the sexes.

Brilliant little marginal notes (a man taking a photograph, an extraordinary bed in a shop window, a swimming adventure at the unnamed Lido) soften the focus of the tale, which begins to move when Colin and Mary are taken up by a stranger called Robert (Venetian, but denied an Italian name). By degrees they are embroiled in the fantasies of Robert and his wife Caroline (Canadian), who is already crippled by her husband's sexual attentions. Each of these two has an inset narrative, describing their lives to date.

That McEwan can write doesn't need saying. But one's admiration for this book is mixed with apprehension, lest he never break out of his obsessive representations of obsession. The dream is of violence. Colin, struck without warning by Robert, writhes on the floor and gasps for breath.

His being complicit in the act makes him rather like

McEwan's readers, subject to unexpected blows in the stomach, or elegant razor strokes; at the mercy of the author, who may or may not want us to think of sex as a pathological relation between strangers, may or may not want us to draw an old-fashioned line between what is real and what fantasy, what relevant and what not.

We don't collaborate in the decisions; we admire the control, the deliberate building of a climax which is to violence as Turner's picture is to Venice. And as we applaud, we may be hoping McEwan will discover a country in which we are not necessarily such strangers, and he less of a Robert.

*8 October 1981*                                             **Frank Kermode**


# Watching brief

Wimbledon's No. 2 and No. 3 courts are divided only by a steeply raked grandstand pyramid. When there is a lull on one court spectators at the top of either stand can lean over the dividing wall and take in play on the other.

Yesterday, simultaneously, Martina Navratilova was on Court Two, Christine Lloyd was on Court Three – and across the concourse, in the cockpit itself, was the astonishing Billie Jean King. Of a sudden the Centre Court exploded.

Immediately Mrs Lloyd netted an easy cross-court volley in her match against Barbara Potter. At almost the same moment, would you believe, Miss Navratilova fluffed a backhand return against Joanne Russell. They were two of their rare mistakes in the hour. The news had engulfed them too and they knew that their women's game had been ignited once more by its very founder, the bow-legged brave in the glinting granny glasses.

Aside from that passing swirl which prefaces great dramas in store, both the first and second seeds yesterday moved comfortably – perhaps a little too comfortably in these new circumstances – into their semifinals.

'Hey, c'mon!' said Mrs Lloyd crossly to herself when she let slip her only game in the second set. The few points she lost on account of Miss Potter's youthful power she would say 'Yep!' and nod an appreciation across the net to her opponent. She left the court smiling and sweetly signing a string of autographs – and off she went to a remarkable eleventh successive Wimbledon singles semi-final.

Over the crowded pyramid, however, it was very much a team effort. Sterner stuff, which makes you feel that really there can only be one result in Saturday's final.

Accidentally (promise!) I sat next to Miss Navratilova's 'seconds.' I could not resist furtive glances as Renee Richards made copious, amazing notes on a loose piece of paper torn from a school exercise book. Every shot she logged and every point. Minute and zany hieroglyphics the like of which would have made Sir Mortimer Wheeler twiddle his moustache with one hand and get out his magnifying glass with the other. Stuff like an Arabic Bill Frindall scoring a century by Botham in Dubai.

The grey-haired – with a tiny trim of ginger – Renee herself made the code up. Next to her is the clean-limbed, bouncy redhead who translates it into words for the handsome passionate, superb sportsgirl out there.

Renee is the 'brain' coach; Nancy Lieberman, former basketball player, is the buddy who is the 'brawn' coach, the cheerleader.

Renee writes on: 'Right on!' says the pretty red-head, scarcely audible, but her eyes show that the player picks up the signals . . . 'way to go!' or 'pick yourself up, girl.'

One time, as another clinically outrageous pass stirs the tramline chalk, Nancy shouts 'Oh, shot!' at exactly the same time as the passed and despairing Miss Russell says 'Oh shit!'

And, at the end, across the court from the umpire's chair, Martina secretly and fleetingly throws her team of two the most beautiful of Slavic smiles – and bobs a tiny, scarcely noticeable curtsey.

*1 July 1982*                                              **Frank Keating**

# A country diary: Keswick

There is as I write a pair of magpies on the birch outside this window outlined against the fells. They came in the wintry weather to the shelter of the spruces and now they are seldom away, seldom apart. At present one, watched intently by the other, is prising something out of a cache between the birch trunk and an ivy stem. Both have lately taken to hiding treasure in there and this looks like a chop bone – doubtless well-ripened. Magpies have, here, in the past robbed bird's nests, killed nestlings and been generally villainous – but how to get rid of them? They, like foxes, have to live and too, like foxes, can provoke a love-hate relationship. My liking began long ago with a parentless young one who, hand-reared, grew strong and thievish. Its favourite game was to sail silently down from the wood to tweak any sleeping cat's tail and be off. It happily went wild in spring. Two years ago a pair settled here and then I appealed for help. Eventually a man came, smelling strongly of something like Stockholm tar. He came in, took his ancient cap off and sat on it, then saw the 'pies in the garden and, grinning cheerfully, damned all vermin and all naturalists (me?) who might protect them. He went down to the spruces alone and stood there, visible but un-moving, for almost twenty minutes, seemingly lost in contemplation. When he had gone he left nothing behind, nothing to see – but the magpies went too. Was it something in his very presence spelled danger? Are magpies really prescient? He may be needed again shortly.

*15 February 1982*                                        **Enid J. Wilson**


# A frozen world in Llanerfyl

I measured the snow depth today – the flat, average, un-drifted depth on our place. It was 2ft 9in. In the drifts, where the wind took it from the fields and sculptured it in the lanes, it is immeasurable.

The pregnant ewes are buried where they have sheltered, under the hedges and walls and in the gullies. Maybe next month we shall know how many have died.

Our smallholding is in the valley bottom, where the wide, fast salmon river is frozen almost across. Twenty yards of water have been reduced to two, and that gap will probably close tonight.

But we are lucky. The council sent a snow plough along our single-track lane yesterday, a priority journey so that the meal lorry could get through to a neighbour with 47,000 poultry in his two huge broiler houses. I don't know whether it arrived. My neighbour's phone is out of order now. The lines have collapsed with the weight of ice.

Across the lane, another neighbour has worked out an ingenious cross-country route – over his own fields and those of three other farms – to take silage by tractor to his 200 sheep on a plot of land he owns a mile away. The lanes are impassable. I met him yesterday. 'The ewes mill around so much when I'm feeding them it's impossible to count, but there's a lot fewer than 200,' he said. We saw him because we took advantage of the part clearance of our lane to walk to the village, first digging a narrow channel for 200 yards along our private approach road. My wife pulled a funny face as I photographed her breaking through the last bit of a 5ft drift. And then it took us more than an hour to walk the one mile to the village shop, where stocks already are running low. In the shop, one farmer told us he had driven his Land-Rover that morning until he could go no further, then he had tried to walk, dragging the fodder for his hill sheep. He had to give up because he was on his hands and knees. And he has no idea where the sheep are.

Our village headmistress – senior of a staff of two – was there also, having tried to see that everything was all right in the school. She withdrew when she found 5ft drifts in the playground. Goodness knows when the children will return.

I spoke this morning by telephone to a friend lower down the valley, a dairyman milking seventy Friesians. Milking, but not selling. Outside the village, we have not seen the milkman since Friday because he cannot get beyond the main road. My friend has not seen the milk tanker for the same reason. He tried to cut his way out and buried his tractor in a drift. It is still there, blocking his farm road. Three days' milk has been poured away so far. It is a total loss for him.

And ours is only a pocket, not particularly remote, in a vast area of snow and painful cold, and frozen pipes and frozen men and frozen animals. We walk in trenches, cut through the snow to the cow-house and the poultry and the ponies and to the sheep on a wind-cleared patch.

Old Evan, who is over eighty and lives in the nearest cottage to us, says it is the worst winter than he can remember, worse even than 1947 and 1963. No doubt we shall talk about this year too for many winters to come.

I can hardly believe it! Trevor Roberts, Trevor the Post, has just called with our mail, struggling down our lane on foot having struggled up to Goetre Farm a mile over the fields.

We gave him a coffee, and off he went to struggle on to Rhosgallth Farm. He deserves the MBE.

*13 January 1982*                                    **George Hawthorne**


# 21 years a-growing

When I joined this paper, it was decided to amaze the captive traveller on the tube with posters of me supposedly sitting in a carriage with Ena Sharples, Richard Nixon and other regular users of London Transport. It boiled down to a day in a siding in Neasden in November shooting this thing. The man playing Richard Nixon felt unable to give his all unless he could mould his nose nearer to the heart's desire with mortician's wax. No one volunteered to go and dig up, so to speak, a mortician. A nice woman in a hairnet said she was just back from a health farm and rather pluming herself on her figure and glamour when she was cast as Ena Sharples.

All this, I imagine, had much the same effect on the *Guardian*'s circulation as a coronary. It is no use arguing with an advertiser's conception of a campaign but, as it happens, I didn't and I don't watch politicians or *Coronation Street* much. Politicians because who does? And *Coronation Street* because I come from a pub in Queen Victoria Street indistinguishable from the Rover's Return and rovers rarely return except for marriage, funerals and similar family collisions.

Yesterday *Coronation Street* was 21 years old and marked the occasion with five such celebrations: Annie Walker's Silver Wedding on Monday, Stan and Hilda's Second Honeymoon on Tuesday, the Silver Jubilee Celebrations last night, Rita and Len's wedding tonight and Christmas ten years ago on Friday.

The choice might have been more varied. A compulsion to dress up as Queen Elizabeth/Victoria/Boadicea/Britannia overcomes the street regularly and did so twice here. Then all characters in long running serials are extraordinarily lucky in competitions, effortlessly winning wonderful weekends in the lap of luxury. And did so twice. The most evocative was certainly the first which was shot in black and white and, from the way everybody was acting their socks off, live.

Ena Sharples was still appearing then with a puff of sulphur in the corner shop and thumping the ungodly with some vim. 'Martha and Wilf's mother fell out at Lily's wedding and they haven't spoken since,' she said with satisfaction adding, without pause for breath, 'Half a pound of lard.' Passing by a natural progression of thought from weddings to wakes, she remarked that Mr Sharples had died in 1937 from a wet mac, having marched in the rain to improve the lot of the workers. 'Did he improve the lot of the workers?' asked Minnie Caldwell. 'Not mine he didn't,' said Ena ungratefully. 'I've never stopped working since.' 'Like poor Bertha Harris,' sighed the gentle Minnie. 'Her husband didn't leave her anything.'

'He left her plenty when he was alive,' snapped Ena, adding darkly that Mr Sharples was no plaster saint but he had his principles.

Enter No Piaster Saint. Twenty years ago Elsie Tanner looked more like the Big Dipper than anything natural. Pat Phoenix was not only a wonderful couple of stones overweight for television, she seemed magically to move when she was standing still. Her little black dress, borrowed from a shop without the formality of asking first, disposed of the popular fallacy that you can't get a quart into a pint pot. 'One good sneeze and it'll be on the floor,' glowered Ena from the snug (Snugs being an all-female redoubt are, I suppose, illegal now.) 'Oo, you are awful, Elsie,' goggled her friend and Elsie was that all right. Len Fairclough wore the look of a man whose tie is caught in a mangle. You couldn't take your *eyes* off her.

Annie Walker, her cut-glass vowels shaming the pint pots, was trying to rise above this unsavoury turn of events by hitting every aitch on the head with a hammer, scattering aspirates like holy water.

That was a tremendous trinity of earthy goddesses, Ena and Elsie and Annie. Ena started to smile and eventually, like the Cheshire Cat, disappeared. Elsie grew respectable. You will scarcely credit it but, when a man makes a pass at her in tonight's special, she slays him with her noble birth. Is this the girl that every brush salesman used to dream would open the door? Annie's still in there pursuing her twenty-one-year attempt to raise the tone of the neighbourhood. And, judging by this week's animated discussion of how to cure chilblains by soaking your feet in a chamberpot, failing.

The new star in the street is certainly Hilda Ogden, the scrawny driving force behind that immoveable object, Stan Ogden. Hilda is a blot on the landscape who is determined to better herself, by becoming a blot on some other landscape. Even now she is making improbable plans to move to a new housing estate. I bet folding money that several firm offers for the Ogdens bijou period residence, No. 13 Coronation Street, which offers considerable scope for the do-it-yourself enthusiast, are already in the post to Granada.

As it happens Granada are knocking down Coronation Street but only so they can build a more substantial set. I suppose that up till now they were afraid that it might not catch on.

*10 December 1981*                        **Nancy Banks-Smith**

# Irving's back

When day breaks after a heavy snowfall, Manhattan wakes up to the clanging of shovels on sidewalks and the splatter of salt on newly cleared and shiny concrete. By 11 o'clock, as luminous snowbanks line the roads, the neighbourhood creeps out to inspect the wonder left behind by the dark night.

There is nothing like a good snowfall to make a New Yorker feel pleased with life. Nothing cheers like the thought of all those wheels turning helplessly out in the suburbs, that land of watered lawns and summer pools. Here in the white, hushed city, everything the heart desires is but a shuffle away along those sidewalks which shopkeepers and doormen are required by law to keep spanking clean.

It is the moment for settling old scores. Gruff restaurateurs and stuck-up brown-stone owners may find the slightest streak of ice left before their building to be an excuse for an outraged phone call to the necessary authority. It is amazing how people somehow sniff their way through the labyrinth of City Hall to find exactly the right place for a complaint.

New Yorkers love to call down the wrath of the law. When a roof-tank water pipe freezes in an apartment building, half the tenants are bribing the staff to carry buckets of water for them to and from the basement supply while the other half are phoning their lawyers to see whether they can withhold rent and sue besides.

For all that they are supposed to be 'crisis-orientated' and boast of living under perilous conditions, New Yorkers actually fall apart under the slightest strain that has not been planned for. It is only to be expected, perhaps. How much pressure can be withstood by those who swallow Vitamin C and B Complex stress pills just to manage the everyday routine?

The interruption to the building's water supply has been revealing indeed. It has not, after all, been that terrible. True enough, at such moments there's not much to be done about a dish-washer, washing machine, Jacuzzi fitment or massage shower head. The art of bucket flushing took a while to master although health club freaks have been crowing about not having to bother. ('Thank heavens for muscle control'). But the rides to the basement are snug and, by way of compensation, the super has turned on the heat at night.

Talk in the elevator, however, has been mutinous. Some have deputed lawyers to research the possibility of suing on the grounds that men are not working through the night in the driving blizzard on the roof. ('If you pay, you can get anyone to do anything,' is the New York gospel.)

Some tenants, of course, have simply vanished. 'How can I be expected to live like this?' whimpered more than one faintheart, as if a frozen pipe was a personal betrayal by the landlord. 'How can this happen to me?' cried other egomaniacs, most of them on their way out to hotels. Some have adopted hardship costumes, wandering around in battle fatigues and voluminous scarves. Others have had the vapours, trailing down to the basement in dressing gowns all day as if life itself has frozen. This latter approach has been encouraged by the super. Unloved at the best of times, he has known not to show his face too often. When he has, it has been conspicuously covered in thick bristle, as though Mrs Super has not been boiling water like everyone else.

And amid all the carryings-on, histrionics, and mutterings at the Front, it took a while for the real news to get around – that Irving had reappeared at the corner stationery store. In the years to come, when survivors of the neighbourhood look back, they will surely remember the particular smell and feel of Irving and Henry's Park Stationery.

On the wet mornings when brown cardboard goes down to protect the smudgy grey and black floor and the air is thick with the smell of damp coats and scarves, there is always someone in need of some curious-sized envelope or type of refill that only the owners can find amid the jumble on the 400 or so shelves lining the walls.

Here, amid the candies, papers, books, cards, toys, pads, and dusty Halloween masks, Irving and Henry have stood and bickered and scurried together for twenty-two years. Irving is thin now; he sports a succession of jaunty hats instead of the long silver hair he lost with chemotherapy. Henry watches the shops. His sons, one a teacher, another a psychiatrist, come in on Saturdays more to show love than to help.

Henry, brusque and suspicious, has a sadder, gentler air. His eyes follow Irving with affection behind his thick glasses. 'What can I tell you?' says Henry, taking the change from the old cash register. 'What can I tell you?' echoes Irving, reaching for some special prize high on the wall.

They come here from the water crisis to buy papers and cigarettes before going to breakfast next door. They bring their woes to Henry and Irving as they have for so long. What can no water mean to Irving, back for an hour or two just to be with Henry? What can it mean to his partner who came through concentration camps in Europe to build a new life for his family and with his friend?

*23 January 1982*                    **Linda Blandford**


# Heir to the painter's gatehouse

I must be the first *Guardian* man to live in the Street of the Prophets. Not, as it happens, the first foreign correspondent. Arthur Koestler lived down the hill at No. 29 from 1927 to 1929 when he was covering the Middle East from Jerusalem for the *Neue Freie Presse* of Vienna.

The house, he wrote in *Arrow in the Blue*, was five minutes from the Via Dolorosa and another five from the Mosque of Omar, where for a shilling you were shown the Archangel Gabriel's fingerprint on the rock. ' I have never lived at such close quarters with divinity,' he complained, 'and never further removed from it.'

Prophets was one of the first streets, as distinct from cluster suburbs, built outside the city walls in the second half of the 19th century. Today it climbs from the jumble of Arab wholesalers, water melon stalls and taxi ranks opposite the Damascus Gate to Davidka Square, with its monument to the home-made drainpipe mortar which helped the Israelis to hold the New City in the 1948 war.

166

It was, and remains, a cosmopolitan street, the home of Jews, Muslims, and Christians, of consuls and bishops and doctors, a street of schools, convents and hospitals. Writers, painters and architects lived here. So, near enough, did Eliezer Ben-Yehuda, the stubborn visionary who revived Hebrew as a spoken language. Kaiser Wilhelm camped here when he visited Jerusalem in 1898, and here Theodor Herzl solicited his aid in creating a Jewish State.

Bertha Vester, who came to the city as a child with the founders of the American Colony, then a Christian missionary community, now a hotel of soporific charm, remembered the unpaved Street of the Prophets in the eighteen eighties as 'the back road' (it runs parallel to Jaffa Road, the main route to the north and, in those days, to Europe). 'The back road,' she wrote in *Our Jerusalem*, 'was muddy or dusty according to the season of the year.'

Edwin Sherman Wallace, the United States consul at the end of the century, recorded: 'Here are the finest residences. Many of the Turkish officials and families of high social and financial standing among the Muslims consider this a desirable location. The European population generally has followed them.

'On the highest part of the ridge stands the consulate of our own great nation and when the Stars and Stripes are floating they can be seen from nearly every point of the city.'

We live on the same cool, if less fashionable, ridge in the courtyard of a house built in 1876 by William Holman Hunt. It is less a yard than a big unruly garden, part Mediterranean, part desert, a wilderness of pines and pomegranates, of giant cactus, prickly pear, bay leaves, loquats, bitter almonds, figs, cypress and bamboo, all surrounded by an eight-foot stone wall against the ravages of bedouin marauders.

Our house was the gate-keeper's lodge. The oldest part – a thick-walled, double-vaulted living room – was once the whole building. If you look closely at the ceiling, you can see the traces of a dividing wall. The wooden floor – a rarity in this city of stone and tiles – is printed with a shallow notch where a connecting door used to bolt. Jerusalem makes archaeologists of us all.

Holman Hunt, the most consistent if hardly the most gifted of the Pre-Raphaelites, paid three extended working visits to the Holy Land between 1854 and 1893 (as commemorated by a stone bench carved in English and Greek outside the Mar Elias monastery on the watershed between Jerusalem and Bethlehem). Most of his religious works were painted here on location (The Scapegoat by the Dead Sea, the Temple pictures with Sephardic Jews recruited in the Old City to serve as models).

He built the Prophets Street house, with a large room suitable for a studio, on the second of these trips, by which time his canvases were fetching four and five figures in guineas. He worked there on The Triumph of the Innocents, which Ruskin celebrated as 'the greatest religious picture of our time.' It was, he wrote, 'a flight into Egypt, but treated with an originality, power and artistic quality of design hitherto unapproached by him.' The Walker Gallery in Liverpool bought it for 3500 guineas when the sovereign was still a sovereign.

Jesus and Mary were the hardest parts for Hunt to cast. The Jews, the British consul James Finn noted, were 'very sensitive on matters of religion.' They were worried that the picture would be placed in a church and become an object of prayer, a graven image. According to Finn, 'it was not possible to get a portrait of a woman for a likeness of the Virgin Mary, even for a lot of money.' Mrs Vester, however, remembered meeting 'a converted Jewish girl whose waving golden hair he had copied for the Christ.'

Hunt's biographer, A. C. Gissing, tells us that he took possession of the newly-built house and worked on The Triumph of the Innocents 'until the rainy season set in, when such was the nature of the tiled roof and such the character of the workmen, that water streamed into the room and collected in puddles all over the floor, so that his picture had to be protected by tarpaulins and work came to a standstill until the necessary steps were taken to render the chamber proof against the drenching rains.'

A century later, we all know the feeling. I typed my own first despatches from the Street of the Prophets in sou'wester and wellington boots for much the same reason. And, by the way, when *did* the damp course come to the Promised Land?

When the Triumph was finished, Hunt locked the house and left it unoccupied for fifteen years. When he brought his family back in 1893, so many other buildings had mushroomed around it that, 'it was with difficulty that we could recognise our own house.' On that last visit he worked on The Miracle of the Holy Fire, a painting of the wild Greek Easter ceremony in the Holy Sepulchre. 'In the end,' he wrote, 'we packed up such furniture as moth and thieves had kindly left us in our house, and abandoned it and Syria (sic) for ever.'

But that was not quite his final link. In February, 1896, Hunt published an appeal for the 'resettlement of the Jews in Palestine,' calling on all Englishmen to support his programme. 'The Jews,' he wrote, a week before Herzl's first English version of *The Jewish State* appeared in the *Jewish Chronicle*, 'need a proper national metropolis and a representative spokesman.'

The Arabs, Hunt suggested, would serve as the soldiers and policemen (this was later amended to 'hewers of wood and drawers of water'). Unlike Herzl, whom he denounced as 'utopian and not practical', Hunt advocated a State independent of the Turkish Sultan. Palestine, he predicted, would become 'a centre of peace, security and stability.' So much for prophecy.

After Hunt's departure the Prophets Street house passed into the hands of the Russian Orthodox Church, which had planted its flag in Jerusalem after the Crimean War with a massive compound a couple of hundred yards down the hill. 'Modern buildings,' scolded the Rev. Dr J. L. Porter, President of Queen's College, Belfast and pioneer travel writer, 'of questionable taste. The Russian church, and the convents and hospices, . . . look like factories'. Western criticism was tainted. The Russians exploited their confessional links with the Greek Orthodox to buy land. The Greeks were Ottoman citizens and thus enjoyed privileges denied to the Catholics and Protestants.

For sixty years, from 1918, our courtyard was governed

for the Church by Dr Helena Kagan, a formidable Russian Jewess who was Jerusalem's first paediatrician. She continued practising from Holman Hunt's studio until her death at ninety-two. Every child in the city seems to have been her patient. It makes directions easy. 'Dr Kagan's house,' you say. They smile and tell you anecdotes. How, for instance, she saved the children of Jerusalem by introducing cow's milk (she kept the beast in the courtyard); her musician husband who left her to found the Budapest Quartet.

After the First World War she brought a Russian friend, Rachel Bluvstein, to live in a small, undistinguished house between ours and hers. To Israelis she is known simply as 'Rachel', or at most 'Rachel the Poet'. She was the laureate of the Second Aliya, the first Zionist pioneers of the 20th century, and was suffering from consumption. Rachel's exchange of love poems with Zalman Shazar, Israel's third President, is part of the national folklore. A book of her poems is laid reverently by her grave near the Sea of Galilee – and invariably stolen, one hopes just as reverently.

Rachel has put us on the tourist map. Groups of Israelis, schoolchildren, soldiers, youth clubs, kibbutzniks in sensible shoes, troop into the courtyard to see the poet's house and the pear tree, long dead and smothered in ivy, which she immortalised as the blossoming 'conspiracy of spring'.

We are still the gatehouse. The pilgrims knock on our door and ask coyly what we know about the history of the place. After twelve months here I deliver a well-rehearsed answer in my classroom Hebrew. The youngsters tick off the pear tree, the rock-hewn water cisterns (now used by the Defence Ministry as emergency fuel tanks in case Jewish Jerusalem ever has to relive the 1948 siege), the famous English painter's house. Their teachers and their sergeants will be reassured that the day was well spent.

The courtyard is at once private and public. We are in the centre of town, yet we turn our backs on the traffic, rejoicing in the greenery, the scent of honeysuckle and jasmin, the resin of hundred-year-old pines. But the street comes to us, unbidden and without a by-your-leave.

Anonymous scavengers pick anything worth recycling

from the dustbins (moth-eaten sweaters, wornout shoes, bits of old transistor). Arab market women deposit mysterious, but so far unsinister, bundles behind the gatepost. Yeshiva students and elderly gentlemen pee discreetly in a corner. Lovers moon in the shadows. Tramps kip in the sun (one is said to have spent a whole summer here, camping benignly under an old fig tree and complaining only when somebody beat him to Mrs Bran's Jerusalem Post at six in the morning). Despite the cross over the gate, we are a secular court yard. Six families and not a skullcap or crucifix among us. But the religions of Jerusalem impinge. Ethiopian and Episcopalean churches within belfry range, the muezzins of al Aqsa audible before dawn, the ghetto of Mea Shearim a stone's throw to the east.

'The whole unholy history of the city,' Koestler lamented in his haven down the hill, 'is an illustration of the destructive power of faith, the failure of man's attempts to come to terms with God, and the resulting unpleasantness of the union of the mortal and the divine.' Amen.

*10 April 1982*                                    **Eric Silver**


# Spike having kittens

The idea, you see, was to talk to Spike Milligan about this painting he's done. 'Never mind about that,' he said. 'This is much more interesting. Somebody has just put three new-born kittens on my doorstep. I can't tell you the majesty of a kitten accepting milk from a dropper. It should be compulsory therapy for all politicians.'

As for the painting, I said. 'This box just appeared on the doorstep,' said Spike. 'I didn't advertise for kittens. I advertised for a Rolls-Royce. Somebody rang the doorbell and we rushed out. I thought these kittens couldn't have rung the doorbell. Then suddenly I realised these are my brothers and sisters.'

I gather it's got a funny title, I said. 'Are you English?' he asked me. 'You can take something for it: Sanatogen.' And so on. The point is that he has painted this painting, which is called Infra-Pelvis and which has just been accepted by the Royal Academy. 'They passed it,' he said. 'At 28 miles per hour. It must have been a blur.' As far as I can gather it is in wax and ink. I wish I could tell you more. 'My father was a journalist,' said Spike. 'How does one get a job on the *Guardian*?'

You see my problem?

*11 May 1982*                                                **Alan Rusbridger**


# The guilt in the fearful symmetry

John Berger thinks that Zoos are a disappointment because the animals trapped in the cages don't match up to the ones trapped in our minds. Tigers don't ripple as they seem to do when they're selling petrol. Chimpanzees smell of something other than freshly brewed tea. Polar bears have buttocks caked in excreta and they prefer gory meat to glacier mints. Berger respects Gilles Aillaud's paintings because they show the zoo as it is and not as we'd like it to be.

A python lies next to an old heating pipe and you can't help but notice the likeness. A pair of porcupines come sniffing around a drain. Staring across a maze of partitions you see a blob of grey in the distance. The title identifies it as a hippo. Aillaud's paintings are always on their toes, peering round corners and having difficulty seeing. His animals are the sort that refuse to come out of their lairs, the sort that you can't quite make out because of the reflections on the glass, the sort that only show you the bits of themselves that won't fit under a log. And by dealing in a snap-shot reality, by plucking the display feathers from his animals, Aillaud has succeeded in producing a series of paintings which are every bit as sanitised and dull as the zoo interiors they poke around in. Here is convincing, albeit accidental proof of why artists have usually refused to treat their animals as animals. Art's Garden of Eden is full of humanised animals representing our hopes, feelings, fears and doubts. The evil snake, the dove of peace, the courageous lion, the imperious eagle, the adulterous monkey and the hardworking ox, they have stepped straight off the ark and into the dictionary of symbols.

The ICA is trying vigorously to fan away these mists. Four different species of artist make four very different contributions to the effort. If Gilles Aillaud is a vulture, slowly, drily, cynically stripping animal myths down to the bone, Duncan Smith is a magpie. Flitting from place to place, from era to era, he has assembled a fascinating collection of zoological bits and pieces, a zoo scrapbook.

In the middle of the first room sits a stuffed panda, Chi Chi, carefully sifting through a pile of bamboo shoots. The walls around Chi Chi are covered in old engravings, fading photographs, posters, cuttings from which you too can build a clear image of the composite zoo animal.

In 1969 three new arrivals appeared at Chessington Zoo. Duncan Smith has included a photograph of them in his catalogue of zoo highlights. Visitors can be seen peering keenly into a cage at the three somewhat bedraggled specimens of homo sapiens (Caucasian), one adult female and two adult males – one of whom was the performance artist Stuart Brisley. This photograph is the best illustration of an argument which rages all over this display; just who is doing the watching in these zoos, us or the animals?

The zoo animal's gaze is a recurring focus in the photographs and drawings. John Berger writes about it in his catalogue introduction. Is it, as Berger claims, a blind gaze? Do zoo animals have eyes which are 'immunised to encounter', or do they have eyes full of sadness, loneliness and pathos as the poets would have you believe? Of course not. All you can see when you look into the liquid brown eyes of the okapi is a reflection of your own guilt. Duncan Smith has included a poem by Stuart Brisley in which Brisley admits to seeing exactly the same guilt when he looks into the eyes of down and outs.

The third artist, John Stalin, some sort of kookaburra I feel, asks the question in another way. In a moment of comic inspiration he went to Madame Tussaud's and photographed

173

their model of Barbara Cartland. What a splendid old bird this is, with its flamingo pink feathers, its puffed out chest and lively eyes ringed in black.

This exhibition throws such titbits to the visitor like a zoo keeper feeding the sea-lions. Drawings by Henri Gaudier-Brzeska, a live parrot in one cage compared with a set of zoo toys in identical colours in another; a Jak cartoon here, an Esso advert there. It is Kerry Trengove who answers the call for one work of art to draw together all the mysterious fears and feelings encouraged by the show and to supply the exhibition with a masterpiece.

Voices in the House of the Dead is an installation inspired by a recent visit the artist made to Mauritius, the former home of the dodo. Mauritius still has eleven unique species of bird, eight of which are on the verge of extinction. The island has the rarest birds, trees and plants in the world. Kerry Trengove's installation is a sort of shrine to this flickering candle of an island, originally known as the Island of Paradise and now called 'the floating mausoleum'.

You enter through a low Romanesque arch and walk out into a small, stooped space, half chapel, half cave. All over the walls the artist has drawn a breathtaking collection of animal fragments in a style popularised on cave walls 40,000 years ago in the first hunting pictures. Birds, fish, fruit bats, men, women, the images crowd your eyes. It feels like some secret and holy place where generation after generation of artist has come to record their visions of the animals.

The silence of the shrine is ploughed by the taped voices of the zoologists and botanists the artist met in Mauritius. Their voices float in and out of focus . . . 'It was a pilgrimage if you like, it was a symbolic species. Here we are on the island of the dodo which became extinct about 300 years ago, and here we have the Kestrel right on the very brink of extinction . . . and it seemed to me that I had to come and see it just as one would go to visit a very famous work of art'. . . . 'There is one plant that was discovered in 1960, a Paendanus, a sort of palm tree. He stumbled across this plant; there is only a female left. It has a beautiful orange flower which blooms in November. But this plant has no male partner. . . .'

And as the voices of the island's peculiarly wistful breed of scientist float by so more species appear on the television screen, embedded in the wall like an aquarium. Exotic fish swim by. A black kite circles the screen. For one-sixtieth of a second you catch sight of one of the fifteen or so surviving Mauritius kestrels. Beautifully choreographed, this full colour animal ballet on the TV screen adds another layer to the sadness.

This is an installation which drives all thoughts of zoos out of your mind, an installation which soaks your senses and emotions, an installation which opens the door of your cage and pushes you right out into the animal kingdom. Cold, lonely dangerous, this is no place for homo sapiens.

*9 June 1982*                                   **Waldemar Januszczak**


# Vive la concierge!

The post girl has been welcomed, the poodle calmed, a visitor sent on his way. Lucée Pelegrin retains the art of doing several things at once and not getting in a fluster about any of them. It is a skill expected of a Paris concierge.

Madame Pelegrin, who is forty-eight and Spanish, lives off central Paris' Boulevard Haussmann, looking out on a plant-filled courtyard. She is a fortunate member of the city's 80,000-strong concierge contingent. Not for her and her husband the accommodation which exists in some quarters: rooms which are little better than cupboards, or riddled with damp. The Pelegrins have a good-sized living room and bedroom, as well as the concierge's 'loge' or office. The plumbing is modern and the electronic code on the street door a 'boon' – it keeps out the tramps.

She has to look after a baronial building. There is carved stone, wood panelling and marble. She says, 'Four stair-cases, each of six storeys and all carpeted, plus very big windows' (her husband helps with the cleaning). There are thirty-five tenants including two shops, a printer, and lawyers' offices. And they all get looked after. She puts out the dustbins at 6 a.m., distributes the post three times during the day, takes in parcels, lets in the meter reader (and the tenants themselves when they forget their keys), and does a thousand other little things. How can the English survive the 'catastrophe' of living in flats without concierges, she asks?

She thinks the pay is rather low. Her nationally negotiated conditions involve working hours of 7 till 11 in the morning (she has to be up earlier in this quarter) and 2 till 8 in the evening. Weekends are free from Saturday mid-day. She can have holidays of a month, provided she can find a replacement, and she receives a bonus of a month's pay at Christmas. Her salary works out at about £250 net a month. (The national minimum wage is around £300 a month, average earnings £430).

But at least she is not having to compete for accommodation in Paris's appalling overcrowded housing market, where even students find themselves having to pay over £100 a month.

Then there's the gossip, the traditional perk of the concierge. She looks me straight in the eye to deny it, when by happy chance a Spanish friend drops in for a chat. 'Well, tenants expect us to know what is going on.' They both laugh.

The old style concierge of French folklore is alive and well. You see them fluttering around the churches at mass time, or out in the afternoon, taking in the sun and bad news. They are mostly old, in their checked pinafores, or widow's weeds, and woolly socks. They impose rules which one dare not ignore: don't touch the glass, don't come in with dirty feet, don't expect any service from me without a tip.

Unlike Madame Pelegrin, who will one day go back to her dream flat in Burgos, they need a hold over their tenants. It is their one compensation for miserable accommodation and pay – I was told that the very old may get as little as £50 a month. It is their one defence against those who are tempted to translate the word concierge literally – it comes from the Latin 'servus', slave.

Those who follow on from these Simenon characters are even more vulnerable. The modern concierge hierarchy in

Paris is now largely immigrant, descending in status from Spanish and Portuguese (the most numerous) to Yugoslavs, Turks and, at the bottom, Moroccans, Algerians and Tunisians.

In our quartier there is an intelligent, extraordinarily capable Moroccan concierge handicapped in public esteem by her race and her three children. 'Why should I be deprived of them?' she said to me once. 'Would you be deprived of yours?' The family has had to live in two dark, damp rooms, the children constantly ill with bronchitis.

There is no question of according her the conditions laid down in the national convention. So she has taken on numerous cleaning jobs to supplement the unskilled labourer earnings of her husband and what she has been getting as concierge. Only recently, after six years in the neighbourhood, have people spoken up for her and helped her get a decent 'loge.'

The roots of the institution go deep. In a city largely given over to apartment living, landlords need someone to look after their property, tenants like someone reliable on the spot, and the lodgings draw applicants in ever greater numbers as the city gets redeveloped. Modern building design provides for concierge accommodation with families in mind.

Fewer than 10 per cent of concierges are unionised, making it difficult to improve conditions rapidly, let alone force employers to respect those already in existence. Even so people want the job of concierge. *L'Echo des Concierges*, the amazingly sober paper which, according to its title page, was founded for their defence and information, has columns of 'loge wanted' ads.

Increasingly the French themselves are looking for these jobs. That seems ultimately the significant social change: that the French now think that the job can be defined in terms of service rather than slavery, and that men will increasingly take on the job. Some concierge jobs may be cut out in the smaller buildings, or the business areas, and replaced by contract cleaning services and the electronically coded bell. But elsewhere, or so it is said in our quartier, there are family or national clans keeping their hands on the best 'loges'.

As a resident in Paris one can have no regrets that the job is becoming more civilised. But there is a fond hope that the best lines may remain. An example is the story of the famous French concierge who ruled our quartier till recently, the young Italian girl tenant and the policeman on point duty. After much persuasion the girl had given him a midnight rendezvous. But at the appointed time the old lady was out of her room before the street door had even had time to squeak. 'Look, I am a policeman.' stuttered the young man. 'I am the policeman here,' came the reply.

*2 July 1982*                                                    **Anne Corbett**


# Robert the good

As the dreamy caress of the sun licked the last dew from the neat panes and fine red brick of the episcopal seat, a dishevelled white motor car bumped to a halt beside the shrine of culture on the little city's north side. The theatre was engirdled by the gentle viridigenous slopes of a grassy rise. Its temporary atmosphere, however, seemed to portend a slide to ruination only marginally interrupted.

A man, no longer young, leapt from the driving seat and pressed urgently towards the office where attended the object of his manifest concern. Behind a pair of unpainted swing doors, with his back to the naked plaster-board of a corridor in an incompleted suite, sat a personage to rival the Bishop himself. He did not rise. Weariness from jetlag prevented it, and a slight mature distaste for meetings with the press. An elderly plumpish acolyte effected introductions, her hair aflame with an unnatural glow. 'I hope you'll be all right here,' she added. 'There's a bottle of wine, and if you need anything else. . . .'

The eminence beheld his interlocutor. The hand Sir Robert extended to shake could have been kissed, or rather the ring which was worth coveting. As he shifted, a range of bracelets moved tactfully across his right wrist. The skin of his face was smooth and tight, his silver-white hair an aureole, his eyes popping slightly with the nervous excitement of a King Charles spaniel.

'My father asked me to say,' the interview began, 'that he has never forgotten your *Fanny By Gaslight* on radio in 1947.' 'That's right,' Sir Robert mused. 'I did it with Gwen Ffrancon-Davies.' He seemed to look back an infinite distance over a marathon career whose tortuous route included reminiscence of much, much more than one wireless thriller.

'No, no, no. I live here. Last year I was four months in New York, three months in Australia . . . I lose track. I love Australia. Of course, I am Australian.' It all started with sheep and cattle on the border of South Australia and Victoria. 'That Sam Helpmann's son should want to be a ballet dancer was quite unbelievable. He was a very well-known figure in the stock and station world.'

But Sam, a good father, had penetrated to Anna Pavlova's dressing-room – and may, Sir Robert hinted, have penetrated further. 'She liked big handsome men, you know.' Since both his father and Pavlova died without explaining, nobody will ever know how Robert Helpmann at fourteen got to start his dancing lessons on the very best footing.

In America he had just done one musical, *Colette*, with Diana Rigg, and here he was, a sprightly though temporarily sedate seventy-three, into another. '*Colette* should have been charming, but typical of America. . . . You know, they sacked the director, sacked the choreographer, so two million went down the drain. Diana and I came out of it marvellously because we got all the press.

'The American theatre is mad. There was a scene in the dressing-room of a provincial French music hall, and I wore a dressing-gown that cost $3500. Well, I mean, you could have gone to Woolworths and bought one that would have been more effective. My role was Jacques, which was a sort of composite picture of Jean Cocteau and all the odd people that surrounded her.'

The men in her life?

'Er . . . well, the men . . . the men question-mark.' It had been a well-written part for Helpmann, though the little dancing it required he had done with an air of studied dis-

taste. It had had its touching moments, but the director. . . .
Witnesses were produced, good solid professional authentic
opinion, that the director of *Colette* simply couldn't do it.
And Helpmann had turned down Cardinal Pirelli, in *Valmouth*, because of *Colette*.

'And then the night they decided to close *Colette* in Denver,
they heard about it here and rang me with the invitation
again. So I came back via Australia because I had to see
Kenneth Rowell's designs for Gounod's *Romeo and Juliet*
which I'm directing in Australia next year. No I never saw
*Valmouth*. I've just been directing an opera in Australia –
Handel's *Alcina*, which everybody thought would be a
disaster.

'Well, it was an enormous success; Joan Sutherland hid
behind my skirts because she didn't think it would go. Well,
anyway, now she's going into it. After my Romeo I shall be
putting the Dame into Alcuna. Romeo is in the Concert Hall
of the Sydney Opera House. It's a biggy. And then I'm re-
viving The Display for the Australian Ballet's 21st birthday,
the first ballet I did which made a great success for them,
about a lyre-bird displaying'.

He had read Firbank, all Firbank, he noted, finally turning
to the matter in hand, because Constant Lambert had known
him, and Constant had been a great friend of the Sitwells and
all that set. 'I was mad about Firbank's books.' But wasn't
*Valmouth*, which opens on Wednesday, quite tame and respectable by modern standards?

'Oh, I don't know. They've put some lines back. She says:
"Have you been at headquarters lately? I've heard of Cynthia
Agate's audience with the Pope." And Pirelli says: "Oh yes,
she kissed his toe, and then went on to do much, much more."
That was cut out by the Lord Chamberlain before.

'What the audience will make of it I don't know. Everyone
says it was before its time. I think it's before its time now.
Of course it's incomprehensible to me. I sit there and think,
"What are you doing?" But I'm having a lovely time. I'm
absolutely mad about it. I've only got about fourteen lines,
but one very good number. It's called The Cathedral of
Clemenza, sort of phony flamenco'.

That raises, prompted the interviewer, memories of Hermione Gingold's Liaisons. Sir Robert lit up – not his cigarette which he holds elegantly and occasionally caresses between his lips: 'I do this to stop smoking,' he explained, 'and somebody immediately comes up and lights it for me, which is not at all what I require.' His eyes brightened with a mixture of hope and envy at Gingold's apparent immortality. A few months previously, he said, he did a talk show in America with her. 'She's just unbelievable. She's eighty-five, you know. Beautiful young men trailing round with her as always. Bright as a button. Of course I was in two reviews with her – Swinging The Gate at the Ambassadors during the war.'

John Dexter is directing *Valmouth*. 'I knew him when I did Nekrassov at the Court in the early sixties, when he was stage director there. But *Valmouth*'s a very difficult play. It doesn't mean anything. Nobody has any connection at all. It's rather like Gertrude Stein. You think there's no plot, and then gradually, as the nonsensical lines somehow come together, you realise that this is a picture of the absolutely absurd life in England when Firbank was alive, when people used to dress up and go to Lyons Corner House and fake wedding parties and lunacy. High-class lunacy. Upper-class lunacy.'

How did he like the novel arena stage and bare concrete of Chichester's theatre, which is totally alien to the extraordinarily extraordinary baroque of Pirelli's Clemenza? 'Well, I'm a boxes and gold leaf and red velvet boy myself.'

*14 May 1982*                                    **Tom Sutcliffe**

# School tied

As I read these reminiscences* I kept thinking of Eamonn Andrews smiling his crooked smile. 'Gambler, cricketer, soldier, classicist, composer of manly romances *par excellence*, Simon Raven, this is *your* life.'

\*Shadows on the Grass

And out in the wings there'd be Lieutenant-Colonel Killock and William Rees Mogg and Nikkai Urandi and the Right Honourable James Prior and P. B. H. May. 'At St Dunstan's preparatory school you are introduced to the man you afterwards describe as the finest natural schoolmaster you ever met.' Forward steps Colonel Killock, who fancied the young Raven no end and kept a harem of little boys in a tent among the pine trees.

Whether or not that was the beginning of the homosexual trail for Mr Raven, he certainly made profitable use of the lessons learnt on the colonel's knee when eventually he arrived at Charterhouse. In between times he played cricket and when he wasn't dwelling on his chances with the wicket-keeper he played it extremely well. P. B. H. May was at Charterhouse and so was the last but one editor of *The Times*, brimming with schoolboy drollery.

'Sacked from Charterhouse, you join the army and renew your acquaintanceship with your old school friend, James Prior.' Indeed he does. The two chums play endless cricket in India and carry on about a dreadful fellow whose wife had an Old Carthusian blazer run up for him when in fact there is no such thing as an Old Carthusian blazer. And so on.

Prior vomits all over a crowd of soldiers, and Raven is reminded of how on a First Eleven outing from school he urinated out of a train window on to a loitering porter. Then Nikkai Urandi, who figures in the Raven years at Cambridge, tells of Samuel Uziele the groundsman's apprentice at the Gold Coast Cricket Club, who urinated on his stepmother in order to delight her. One way or another there's quite a lot of vomiting and urinating.

Otherwise, the book deftly makes its point: all being chaps together is at its best when the Old School Tie is still wagging away. Simon Raven has made an art of being outrageous and if his dislike of prudery seems almost to have become obsessional it certainly hasn't affected his style. Neither cricket nor Charterhouse may be quite as elegant as once they were but Mr Raven and his prose have lost none of their felicitous gusto.

*29 April 1982*                                       **William Trevor**

# Cherchez la femme – quick!

Five dusky seaside sparrows are spending their last days in a geriatric ward in Gainesville, Florida, each with a pension of over 9000 dollars. American taxpayers have already showered them with gifts of land, food, and security guards worth millions of dollars.

The dusky, a small brown bird about the size of a robin and streaked with black and a bit of yellow, has the unfortunate title of rarest bird in the world. There are six individuals left – five in captivity at the Florida Game and Freshwater Fish Commission research labs in Gainesville – and one in the wild. All are male.

Clearly the sparrow does not have a promising future. Even in better days it was given a pretty rough time, distinctly lacking the glamour of a condor or whale. It is a drab and secretive little bird which dislikes having people around. In fact you would hardly know it was there, unobtrusively munching spiders and crickets on the ground – duskies positively detest trees – and you would certainly find it a hard animal to identify with or envy.

And that, basically, is its problem. Birds like the bald eagle get plenty of attention. Societies are formed for their protection, extensive breeding programmes are developed for their propagation – even the US national symbol provides a bit of free advertising. But the dusky is a different kettle of fish altogether. Prospects are not nearly so rosy for a one ounce brown ball of fluff that doesn't like people. Even some of the people entrusted with its safekeeping have been unable to muster much feeling for the bird.

The dusky is one of nine sub-species or races of seaside sparrow, known in the scientific world as *Ammospiza maritima nigrescens*. All nine are native to Florida and all are on the decline.

It was first described in 1872 by Charles Maynard, living in the St Johns marsh west of Titusville, Florida. Years later a substantial number of birds were located on Merritt Island south-east of Titusville. Mosquito control killed off most of those by 1950, and the St Johns marsh population continued declining until there were only 4000 birds left in the early 1960s. Then a four-lane expressway was pushed through the marsh. Housing developments, drainage, ditches, pasture improvement and enormous uncontrolled fires destroyed still more habitat. In the past, when fires were set by ranchers to manage the pasture for cattle, duskies could seek refuge in any of the nearby savannas. Those savannas are now the housing developments and highways. By 1968 only 900 pairs remained. Biologists had been warning for years that the dusky's habitat was being destroyed. By this time the species had been put on the US Endangered Species list – though suitable habitat management would have been a far better solution. Its plummet into oblivion was happening frighteningly fast.

Then a survey in 1979 revealed that only thirteen males were left. No females have been seen since 1975 when the last sightings of nests and fledglings were made.

It was last year that a warrant for the capture of the last remaining six was issued – wanted alive and singing. The US Fish and Wildlife Service decided that their management emphasis would be on 'captive safe maintenance.' In other words, they can proudly announce that the dusky seaside sparrow will soon join the handful of vertebrates which have become extinct since the Endangered Species Act was passed in 1973. It is clear that to hold the animals in captivity – and to do nothing with them – is futile.

But there is an alternative – albeit a race against the clock. Although the age of the birds is not known precisely, it is highly likely that the species will be extinct within three years if we just sit back and watch. Since duskies have a life expectancy of nine years, and since the last female was observed in 1975, the ones alive today are probably at least six years old. Which doesn't give them long.

Colonies may well remain undiscovered in the Florida marshes, so it is just possible that a female or two has been overlooked. Certainly, they are difficult to spot in the field because they don't sing. Efforts to locate a female are being continued, but the chances of success are slim.

But no, a much more feasible plan has been suggested. All seaside sparrows inhabit similar coastal marshes, from Massachusetts, to Texas, and, although all the populations are separate, they are genetically intercompatible. So, as a last-ditch attempt to save the species, why not cross male duskies with females of the closely related Scott's seaside sparrow, which is not endangered? By back-crossing the offspring with the surviving males for six generations it is mathematically possible to produce a 98.4 per cent reconstituted dusky. If this is successful and the dusky gene pool is preserved, the birds could be reintroduced back into the St Johns marshes.

The feasibility of both captive breeding and subspecies crossing of seaside sparrows has been successfully demonstrated.

Three hybrid dusky/Scott's have already been produced. And the people at the Gainesville pens have been developing handling techniques for seaside sparrows for years.

But there is one problem. The US Fish and Wildlife Service lawyers say that, legally, a 98.4 per cent dusky isn't a dusky. Therefore it would not be an endangered species and, since they operate under strict laws, would not be eligible for federal support under the Endangered Species Act. Unfortunately, the misconceived legal definition of a species is different from the biological definition. There is no such thing as a pure sub-species – or even species for that matter – because there is a tremendous amount of variation within the groups as well as between them.

The Florida State Museum in Gainesville recently offered to sponsor the breeding project, so that no federal funds would have to be involved. But still the US Fish and Wildlife Service say no with their legal quibbling, and in fear of setting a precedent. They seem to forget that extinction is a precedent-setting event that lasts forever.

In the meantime, there has been a sort of compromise, which has received unanimous support. A programme to develop techniques to collect and freeze semen from the male duskies for storage in a sperm bank has been accepted. But the physiologist working on possible techniques estimates that it will take three years to develop the complicated procedure.

Meanwhile, time ticks by. Already, hopes for the future range from pessimistic to despair. The single male in the wild was last seen on 20 June 1980, in St Johns marsh. Whatever happens, the dusky should have served as a messenger, about the kind of environmental degradation that is leading to the extinction of species.

*29 October 1981*                                     **Mark Carwardine**


## Rose, thou art sick

There was a time in England when cricketers assumed that the summer would end with Yorkshire winning the County Championship, a Yorkshire batsman at the top of the averages, and four Yorkshiremen blanco-ing their boots in anticipation of the MCC's winter tour. And today, throughout the county, men who have barely heard of William Cobbett and the backward glance long to recall that golden age of undisputed supremacy, the years between the wars before controversy and commercialism ruined county cricket and when Yorkshire were champions at the end of twelve of the twenty peaceful seasons.

For those two dominant decades they took Neville Cardus seriously south of the Trent, when he reported that amateur Test selectors at Headingley had left Jack Hobbs out of the England team because, with eleven Yorkshire men available, 'they could not find room for him.' They took the story seriously in Yorkshire too.

I was brought up by exiles from Nottingham who used to pretend that Larwood and Voce, not Bill Bowes, destroyed the Australians during the 1932 'bodyline' series. But I breathed the idea of Yorkshire invincibility with the Sheffield air. And in 1946, when the championship came home again, I assumed that the Second World War had merely been a brief interruption in Yorkshire's unassailable superiority.

In that year I began to understand the antagonism that

surrounded Yorkshire cricket and Yorkshire life. One day, on autumn holiday in Morecambe, my father pursued the evening paper with unusual impatience. As always, he turned first to the 'stop press' cricket scores. But, uniquely in my experience (for he was a man of remorseless reticence), the news made him leap in the air with joy. It was an expression of Nottingham's delight that Hampshire had beaten the new champions. Insensitive to my feelings, he turned to assorted Lancastrians who were hanging about the promenade and proclaimed 'at least they've lost one.'

It was another thirteen years before I began to understand why what George Orwell called 'the cult of Northernness' so enraged the South. In 1959, nervous and best-suited, I attended the annual general meeting of the Yorkshire County Cricket Club with the express intention of causing trouble. J. H. Wardle had just been sacked 'for disciplinary reasons.' The arbitrary destruction of his career seemed as stupid as it was callous. For Yorkshire had ended the season eleventh in the championship, almost the worst result this century. As I prepared to make my irresistible denunciation, the President, one T. L. Taylor, called the assembled members to order. 'Welcome,' he said, 'to this meeting of the Champion County. For we know that we are always the champions, whichever team tops the table.'

As the applause died down, I realised that my fellow members really did believe that fate had denied them a success which was rightfully theirs. After the sweet years of almost continuous victory, defeat was bewildering as well as bitter. And the knowledge that the humble and meek beyond the county's border rejoiced to see the mighty put down from their seats, made the humiliation all the more difficult to endure. In the years of continual success, all the problems that rumbled under the surface of Yorkshire could be ignored. When the cheering died down, the sounds of disagreement could be muffled no longer. Indeed, they grew louder and louder as they were augmented by the anguished cries of men unfamiliar with failure. Once Yorkshire started to lose, trouble had a permanent place in the team.

The decline was inevitable once the old men of Lord's

decided to pursue the missing millions by making first-class cricketers play village cricket and allowing counties to entice crowds and ready-made stars from Karachi, Canberra, and Kingston, Jamaica. Yorkshire refused to move with the times and only adjusted to 'limited overs' cricket after the upheaval that sent Brian Close to Somerset. When other clubs engaged 'overseas players,' Yorkshire did not adjust at all.

Yorkshire's years of success were the bridging passage in English cricket which linked the glory of the Edwardian game with the age of falling gates, impatient spectators and players who expect a living wage and a measure of respect from county committees. In Edwardian England, cricket was a players' game that the public was allowed to watch. In the seventies it became a spectator sport, with increasingly self-confident paying customers. If the Yorkshire fans had only wanted victory, there would have been no dispute between them and the county establishment. But they wanted a hero of their own and the feeling that they were part of the club which they followed. The Yorkshire committee was prepared for neither innovation.

Traditionally, Yorkshire has always been the most auto-cratic of the cricket counties. Every schoolboy batsman knows of Lord Hawke's prayer that a professional would never captain England. But Hawke was not Yorkshire's greatest authoritarian. That accolade belongs to Brian Sellers, county captain during the halcyon nineteen thirties and chairman of the cricket committee during the post-war renaissance. If J. B. Priestley had re-written Henry IV Part I with a single character who embodied the hubris of Hotspur, the courage of Prince Hal and Falstaff's lack of interest in the needs of others, the Bruddersford Amateur Dramatic Society would have typecast Brian Sellers for the part. He could not play cricket. But because he captained teams that included Herbert Sutcliffe, Len Hutton, Percy Holmes, Bill Bowes, Hedley Verity, Arthur Mitchell, G. G. Macaulay and Arthur Wood, he was inclined to win championships. He attributed his side's success to leadership and discipline – qualities which the committees of the seventies gladly accepted as a substitute for talent on the field and high morale amongst the players.

'A Yorkshireman in the South,' wrote Orwell, 'will always take care to let you know that he regards you as an inferior . . . he has grit, he is grim, dour, plucky, warmhearted, and democratic.' With one important exception that was, for years, the way in which the Yorkshire committee saw itself. The only characteristic on Orwell's list which they would have rejected as inaccurate and unfair is 'democratic.' In an age when the professional cricketer was first emancipated and then made into a media star the omission was crucial. Now the old order has changed. But the changes came too late to stop the civil war – not least because the rebels in the dressingrooms, the dissidents in the members' enclosure and the paying public in the cheap seats and on the uncovered terrace, found a hero round whom they could rally – Geoffrey Boycott, great outsider as well as great opener, the star who still speaks for 'us' because he is persecuted by 'them,' the only batsman in the history of the noblest game to be greeted on his return from abroad by a mob of admiring skinheads.

Only the most extreme and irrational of Boycott admirers and detractors see the conflicts within the club entirely in terms of his extraordinary personality and his phenomenal performance. But the bloodiest battles of the civil war have been fought around him and there is no doubt that the complexities of his character have increased the polarisation of the feuding factions. He has become a rallying point because in his way he is, like Archie MacLaren during cricket's long Edwardian afternoon, 'the spirit of the age.' The description 'great accumulator' is a journeyman's title that evokes attributes which ought to be more attractive to the partisan than to the purist. Yet he draws the crowds and enjoys the cheers at Hove as well as Headingley, Basingstoke as well as Bradford. He has nothing in common with the classical heroes. Their superiority was supposed to be effortless. His success is the result of obsessive application. They brushed aside praise. He openly rejoices at his fame and fortune. Fry, Woolley, and Ranjitsinghji battled with style and grace. Boycott pushes singles and dabs down on the offside. The crowds who cheer when he approaches their part of the boundary no doubt long to see Victor Trumper jumping out to drive. But they identify with 'Sir Geoffrey' prodding his forward defensive stroke.

In spite of the possession of some impeccably reactionary opinions, he has become the anti-hero who fights against cricket's establishment. That reputation has been enhanced by the behaviour of the Yorkshire cricket authorities and the exploitation by sporting journalists of Boycott's love of popular esteem. The Committee (brutal, insensitive, and idiotic in turn) and the newspapers (always taking 'Sir Geoffrey's' part) have combined to win him allies and strengthen his conviction in the righteousness of the introverted cause. He has worked hard for applause and become the first populist cricketer in sporting history. 'As long as *Yorkshire Post, Manchester Guardian,* and British nation' are behind him, he enjoys what passes, in a turbulent mind, for contentment.

One English colleague wondered how Len Hutton would have reacted to Michael Parkinson's open idolatry. No doubt he would have treated the third impostor just the same as triumph and disaster. But Hutton did not have the Parkinsons of the modern world to contend with. Boycott does. And so do the Yorkshire committee.

There is still no clear indication that the committee have begun to realise either the determination of its opposition or the strength of the critics' conviction that the sins of the last three years are too serious to be forgiven. The dissentients claim to be concerned with the good management of the club. But when in a week or two the 'in-depth inquiry' into Yorkshire's future is published, it will be Geoffrey Boycott's next contract and previous treatment – not the standard of coaching or the economy of concentrating all first team matches in Leeds – that excites the members and attracts the headlines. There is still blood to flow from four old wounds – Illingworth's appointment as manager, Boycott's removal from the captaincy, the confrontation between those two hard men at Scarborough last September, and the awful aftermath of their head-on collision.

Illingworth's appointment should have been a sign of grace, an indication of the committee's understanding that the age of the amateur cricket manager was over. However, they bungled the whole operation. Their approach to Illingworth (then still a registered player with Leicester) was kept secret from the county which employed him. As the surreptitious negotiations were not divulged to most of the cricket committee, Boycott, then Yorkshire's captain, was not consulted about the appointment until the decision was made. Perhaps he found out before the meeting. But he was not *told*. His supporters, mirroring the complexes of their hero, claimed that they had exposed a conspiracy. A year later, when he lost the captaincy, the eight years of failure were forgotten and his dismissal was put down to an Illingworth vendetta. Since he was sacked in the week of his mother's death, the combination of callousness and incompetence that piled grief on grief converted enemies into friends overnight. Suddenly he embodied all the old heroes who had been lost to the county because of the arrogance of men with waistcoats and watch-chains.

Boycott's detractors talk as if trouble only began in the dressingroom when the balding bespectacled youth from Fitzwilliam played his first game. In fact, Willie Watson left the county for Leicester and his best years back in 1957. Brian Bolus only played for England after he had found security in Nottingham. Brian Close was given twenty-four hours to change his attitude to one-day cricket, and ten minutes to decide if he would resign or be sacked. Raymond Illingworth became captain of Leicester and England because 'anyone who prefers a three-year contract with another county to one season with us is better out.' And Fred Trueman, now the establishment's paragon, advertising caravans on television, arriving at Test Matches in his Rolls-Royce, and denouncing dissidents on the radio, was sent home from Yorkshire matches for indiscipline.

If all Yorkshire cricketers were like John Hampshire – supremely gifted, supremely loyal, and supremely self-effacing – the county chaiman's lot would be a happy one, and constabulary duty would be unknown to the secretary.

Events of last year's Scarborough Festival proved, once more, that those who hope for such a blessing hope in vain. On 8 September Geoffrey Boycott complained, during a television interview, about being left out of Yorkshire's one-day game. The next morning he was suspended for behaviour that was a clear breach of the Test and County Cricket Board rules. Inevitably the incident was interpreted as 'Boycott versus Illingworth.' Behind the scenes the drama was being both encouraged and played out by two institutions that are central to the Boycott saga, the *Yorkshire Evening Post* and the Yorkshire Reform Group.

The Reform Group was founded in the seventh lean year of Boycott's eight-year captaincy. But when he was deposed, it became, or allowed itself to appear as, the 'GB Fan Club,' with its most quoted adherents returning obsessively to the need to sack the manager and re-engage the opening batsman. It basks in the warmth of Boycott's popularity. Its real leader, Detective Sergeant Fielden, has won election to the Yorkshire committee with 74.7 per cent of the votes cast in the 88.8 per cent poll of Doncaster members. He is anxious to be conciliatory. But he is determined that Boycott's contract will be renewed. And he remains a profound critic of the old guard – 'not what they do but the way they do it.'

Ray Illingworth's crime sheet now includes the charge that he intentionally heightened the Scarborough humiliation by publicly suspending the player when he arrived at the ground. 'As they had breakfast in the same room' the allegation runs, 'he could have done it in the hotel.' That complaint is typical of the more sophisticated criticisms made about the committee. Boycott's behaviour grows daily more difficult to justify and the Headingley hierarchy is beginning to benefit from the suspicion that no one can live in peace with England's most prolific run-scorer. So complaints increasingly concentrate on the style rather than the substance of decisions. The Reform Group has made a tactical retreat but it now occupies a formidable fall-back position.

Conscious of the need to appear responsible and constructive critics, the Reform Group denies all involvement in the scenes that followed the September suspension. Fielden says that he told officials who asked for his aid in calming the demonstrators and clearing the pitch that, since they were unknown to him, there was no help he could offer. Others insist that he apologised for the behaviour of associated 'hot-heads' and that he collected signatures for the 'sack Illingworth' petition at the pavilion door. John Hampshire has a clear view of the Reform Group's general character. 'They have done untold harm to Yorkshire: enough to crucify us.' The 'us' is sadly inappropriate. Hampshire found the Scarborough scenes literally intolerable and left the Yorkshire battlefield to end his cricketing career in Derbyshire peace.

He may not be the last to go. Illingworth's decision to make the uncapped Neil Hartley stand-in captain caused great offence to older and better players, and Chris Old talks publicly about his uncertain future. But the real turmoil is the result of gregarious men being forced to share hours of each summer day with a colleague who they think disdains their company.

Ten years ago, when Boycott broke his arm in Australia, Len Hutton (who had lost four inches of bone after a wartime fracture) suggested that a visit to the surgeon who had saved his career might help his successor's confidence and morale. After the consultation, Sir Leonard received a polite note of thanks. It bore no address or telephone number but ended with the helpful information that the convalescent could be reached through the Yorkshire County Cricket Club. Today's players have a second complaint to add to the allegation of lonely self-obsession. Middle order batsmen, following an opener who scores at twelve runs an hour, must hit out, get out, and sacrifice their averages. And Boycott has a quality which is worse than selfishness. For twenty years he has been an incomparably better batsman than those who follow him. Envy is not unknown, even in cricket.

The players' criticisms are so openly expressed that it is difficult to understand how a week before the Scarborough incident, John Callaghan of the *Yorkshire Evening Post* could write that Boycott was the players' choice for captain.

Callaghan says that the article was based on 'impressions gained during the year.' It so infuriated the players from whom the impressions were gained that they conducted two polls amongst themselves – one to test the Callaghan view of the captaincy, the other to determine if Boycott was even welcome in the side. A substantial majority wanted him neither as skipper nor member of the crew. On Tuesday, 20 September, the Yorkshire committee decided to publish the result of the poll, partly because they assumed 'the newspaper would get a biased version' and partly because 'Geoffrey seemed always to win on points'. Ironically the action of one of Boycott's favourite journalists probably precipitated the end of the 'great accumulator's' career. Typically most of the criticism for the whole unhappy episode was heaped on the committee.

There are those who say that the chairman, M. J. Crawford, felt that publication was improper. But he stubbornly refuses to confirm a story which, if it turned out to be true, would help him (and the club) through some of the difficult days ahead. His silence is, of course, the reaction of a wholly honourable man determined to do what is right by his own exacting standards, whatever unjust criticism results. But it is also the silence of a chairman who is only speaking to his peers. He is going to do what is right by the old standards of old Yorkshire. And that county cricket club has gone for ever.

It can never be recreated. Perhaps Don Brennan, who is as ruthless in his criticism of Boycott as he was behind the wicket, is right, and there would be no peace in the county whilst 'Sir Geoffrey' remains in, but not really part of, the team. Perhaps Syd Fielden, of the Reform Group, correctly diagnoses one problem when he says that the coaching must be improved and natural talent encouraged. But the crisis goes much deeper than that. Yorkshire is suffering from the death throes of its old supremacy. It will not prosper until its members accept that they support, what is now just another cricket county, distinguished from its rivals only by the refusal to import mercenaries to fight alongside local volunteers. When Yorkshire is reconciled to its new status it will win the championship again – perhaps once in a decade, not twelve times in twenty glorious summers.

*16 January 1982*                                    **Roy Hattersley**


# A bit humpety

A stupendous, power-crazed innings by Botham electrified Indore yesterday. Indeed his 122 lit up the whole legend.

It took 55 balls and 55 minutes. It included 16 fours, 7 sixes, 3 twos, 10 singles and only 19 dot balls off which he failed to score – and 11 of those in the first 3 overs when he was playing himself in. The Central Zone fielders were reduced to shambles. He went from 50 to his century in 19 balls and, before he was caught, at deep midwicket, the previous 4 deliveries had gone 6-6-4-4. Gatting turned the knife with a sparkling century of his own.

Botham arrived at the wicket at 87 for three to join Gatting, who had not scored and had managed 3 when Botham reached his century. England had made heavy weather of things and in fact there was a whiff of fury in the air. Cook had been given out to a questionable catch and Fletcher, having angrily joined in the resulting kerfuffle, was immediately caught at midwicket, obviously still seething at the decision against Cook.

The Somerset celebrant of swipe strode in looking none too pleased. He'd had supper the night before with Cook, one of his particular buddies, who, as everyone knew, was playing for his place here. For once, I noticed, Botham didn't cheerily swing his arms as he bristled in, his now curly long, gingery locks twining round the edges of his floppy white sunhat. He doesn't trust Indian barbers and isn't going to cut it till home.

He played himself in with narrow-eyed and untypically heavy menace. The night before, in throwaway forecast, he had promised 'a bit of humpety in the morning.' Cook's dismissal determined him on it.

This was an hour great-grandchildren will gape over – Botham at Indore. It has the same ring already as Jessop at Hastings and Harrogate, Fender at Northampton or Gimblett at Frome.

You name it, Botham hit it. Even, like WG used to do, his blocks were going for four. Twice he tried two of his patented reverse sweeps. Four, both times – for the last man a captain wants for Botham is a third man.

In all the glorious, galumphing mayhem, as always with Botham, there were one or two quite mesmerisingly wondrous strokes; this time, the ball after celebrating his 50 (34 minutes, 28 balls). With a forearm heave over midwicket, he stepped inside a delivery curving in on leg stump and bludgeoned it in a soaring arc high over the long-off boundary.

You feel even Hammond wouldn't have attempted that shot in a first-class match. Then, after scoring his first two to take him to 61, he pre-determined a sweep but, as he genuflected, the ball dropped shorter than he expected and still on one knee, he adjusted to send the battered red apple soaring high over the mid-wicket line. The century came with a genuine sweep for four (50 minutes, 48 balls, 14 fours, 5 sixes).

When, five minutes later, he walked in to tumult from the disappointingly small crowd of 10,000, he received cheery garlands of oranges. Grinning again, he met those too full on the meat of the bat: Gatting had given all possible strikes to his marauding friend. Of the 55 balls, Botham had needed, the stand of 137 only needed 75.

Once Botham had departed, Gatting himself cut loose. By now, of course, the bowlers were shellshocked; and what's another mortar or two then? Gatting's sprightly manner took full toll, and there was no end to the merrymaking until the shadows lengthened and the umpires called a halt, with England 367 for five, Gatting on 108.

The innings, has probably saved Gatting's Test place. It was wretched luck on Cook, who batted doughtily and well in only his second knock in the middle for a month. He mistimed a hook and shortish midwicket, diving, scooped it up and claimed the catch at the second grab. Fletcher was so upset at the decision that he lost concentration and left at once, livid. That would have been the story of the day, I'm afraid, except that Botham was next man in.

*23 January 1982*                                   **Frank Keating**


# Horowitz

Saturday's audience, which included half the famous pianists in London, rose to its feet to acclaim Horowitz before he had played a note. Under such circumstances the performer has not only to meet the challenge of the music but to satisfy the expectations of an audience screwed up to fever pitch.

The first thing was to dispel the fever, very neatly done with a first group of Scarlatti sonatas. The most intriguing thing about these pointed and polished interpretations was the way in which Horowitz as it were orchestrated the music for piano, anachronistically but so persuasively, using rhetorical devices not available to the harpsichord. These were skilled translations which gave much pleasure once prejudices against Scarlatti on the piano were laid aside.

On his first temporary retirement in 1936, Horowitz remarked that he needed time to think, one couldn't go through life playing octaves. In a Chopin group, octaves and other pyrotechnical passages were brought off in commanding style, but it was his powers as musical narrator that most astonished and delighted. Horowitz leads us along his particular road, imposing a personal view of the music, painting in the strongest, clearest and most diverse colours so that his own vision is projected in crystal-clear form.

The range of tone colours often forced one to seek orchestral analogies. But the threatening clouded bases in the B minor Scherzo fitted into no recognisable class of orchestral or pianistic sounds. And how does Horowitz make us experience the start of the A minor Mazurka as if none of us knew where the music was going next? Equally out of the ordinary was the return to the main theme of the B minor

Scherzo, the moment of escape from the hypnotic influence of the melodic figure of the second section, bringing a moment of revelation to which all that had gone before seemed to have been tending.

Liszt's Second Ballade also evoked thought of ideal orchestras, as Liszt perhaps intended, pedal being used to produce strange overlapping sonorities and illusions of sostenuto which are special to Horowitz. This grand and theatrical work was followed by the third Consolation played with self-effacing artfulness.

A generous encore group included Schumann's Träumerei. If Horowitz's version was transcribed into musical notation we would hold up our hands in horror, but somehow the enormously long upbeats, the sudden pianos and commas at the ends of phrases, do in the end contribute to a fresh and consistent view of the music. Apart from one hiccup in Scarlatti and a few blurred details in Chopin, Horowitz played like a young virtuoso at the height of his powers.

*31 May 1982*                                   **Hugo Cole**


# Ron the one hand . . .

Today in the light of last night's match in Helsinki and Wednesday night's in Reykjavik, the England team manager Mr Ron Greenwood will be whittling down his original World Cup squad of forty to a final twenty-two, from whom his first choice of 11 for the opening match in Spain will be selected. After many months of experimentation, the pattern of the side is now clear. The goal-keeper is likely to be Shilton, the first choice of many commentators, unless it is Clemence, who was recalled last night to replace Shilton after Shilton had replaced Clemence for the matches with Holland and Scotland. In defence, Thompson of Liverpool seems likely to be partnered by Butcher of Ipswich, though Butcher was omitted against Finland last night in favour of Martin of

West Ham. (Alternatively, some good judges think Osman, also of Ipswich, might yet form a club partnership with Butcher at Thompson's expense, always assuming that there is to be no reprieve for Watson of Stoke City.) In midfield, Robson, Brooking and Wilkins (unless Wilkins is to be allotted the libero role in which he was used with some success earlier in the season) would seem to be strong contenders, though a place may yet be found for Hoddle, who came admirably through what was considered a crucial test in the Reykjavik game, or possibly for Rix, who did well when he came on as substitute for Devonshire in the Holland match but was somewhat surprisingly excluded for the game with Scotland, when McDermott was instead used as substitute.

Up front, Mariner, although called off in favour of Francis against Scotland, now seems a likely choice, especially after Wednesday's injury to Regis, who had previously been running neck and neck with Withe as a possible alternative. If Keegan plays, Mr Greenwood may find it difficult to acommodate Woodcock, who more than justified his recall for the match against Holland before being dropped for the match with Scotland, in which Coppell of Manchester United was recalled – though many still hope that room might be found for the exciting young Aston Villa winger, Morley, who played alongside Withe and Regis in Reykjavik until Regis's replacement by Goddard. After the publication of today's list of twenty-two, Mr Greenwood's range of choice will obviously be narrower than before. Indeed, if we have understood the advice kindly given us yesterday by the Mathematical Institute in Oxford there are only just over 705,000 permutations by which a team of 11 players can be picked from a squad of 22, and since several would involve playing Keegan in goal and Clemence, Shilton and Corrigan as strikers there is some exponential reason to believe that Mr Greenwood may already have discarded them. But certainly there is much food for thought here for England's manager, as he prepares for his final and most crucial process of team selection before retiring to make way for Brian Clough of Nottingham Forest, Jackie Charlton of Sheffield

Wednesday, Malcolm Allison of Sporting Lisbon or possibly Roger Penrose, Rouse Ball Professor of Mathematics at the University of Oxford.

*4 June 1982*                                                    **Leader**


# Going to the dogs

Little girls of ten or so, a vet told me, arrive at his surgery carrying great, suppurating moggies which are flexing their fifty claws and using filthy languages. The little girls tap their noses fondly and tell them not to be big sillies whereupon the big sillies roll over, purring fit to loosen the plaster, and everyone comes out from under their chairs. This virginal power, which was once said to subdue unicorns, seems to vanish quite at puberty except in the case of Barbara Woodhouse, who is forever twelve. Slight, soprano, fearless and bossy as a mass meeting of the CBI.

*Barbara Woodhouse Goes to Beverly Hills* (Yorkshire), where dogs are fun furs, was not at all a bad idea. 'Lots of people rent them,' said Wilfrid Hyde White ironically. 'The house, the children, the dogs. If a dog makes a mess they change it for one that doesn't.' Husbands likewise, of course. But a natural gem like Barbara Woodhouse does not need to be fussily set, it detracts from her own radiance. I will not believe that she wrote the script herself. 'Tinsel town . . . Tippi Hedren, Hitchcock's favourite icy blonde . . . the immortal TV series *Bonanza*.' It takes a long apprenticeship walking behind bulls with a bucket to perfect that sort of style. And I could have done without some of the more prominent poached eggs in the old asylum, the dog astrologers, cosmetic dentists, couturiers. That is Alan Whicker country.

Just the stars and Barbara would have been lovely. There she was with her jumper rucking up at the back in the well-loved way and Zsa Zsa Gabor in a little thing of purple and crimson chiffon who was describing the start of an ill-omened marriage ('My Scottie bit him on my wedding night') and the end of a passionate affair ('I lost the love of my life, Genghis Khan'). 'This little chap?' asked Barbara, describing all too exactly a photograph of a hairy grasshopper.

'I give them a good old bang,' said Barbara briskly. 'Bang. Bang. Bang.' So, indeed, does Zsa Zsa but she seemed uncharacteristically lost for words.

Wilfrid Hyde White began a polished anecdote about his dog Roman who 'doesn't know about lifting his leg and sits like a bitch.' 'Doctored,' said Barbara briskly. 'That accounts for it.' 'Is that so?' said Hyde White unhappily, then suddenly, like a baby whose dummy has been spectacularly snatched, 'You spoilt my story!'

'After I lost my husband,' said Dorothy Lamour, 'my step-son came in with Cocoa.' Cocoa is a Scottie. I think a bloodhound would have been more practical. On the other hand, if you lose your dog you send for Sherlock Bones, the dog detective. There was a most affecting reunion – by happy chance the TV team was on the spot – between Anne Lockwood and her wandering dog, Cameo. 'Cameo! You are home!' cried Miss Lockwood vibrantly. 'Oh thank you, thank you for bringing her home to me!' Who is Anne Lockwood? Shower that woman with scripts, nominate her for an Oscar, cast her in *Come Back Little Sheba*.

William Shatner of *Star Trek* turned out to be a burbler: 'We bought him with love and the desire to fulfil his macho personality.' Shatner's macho Doberman rolled over and waved his paws about. 'Stand up!' said Barbara Woodhouse. Dog and man stood to attention. 'You are a big man to him,' she directed Shatner. 'Walk away with head up. Confident. He is going to stay.' He stayed. '*Now* cuddle him.' Shatner cuddled him as who would not.

Yorkshire's cameraman was called Barker, so appropriately that one wondered if he was not chosen for his name alone but when Tippi Hendren's forty lions and tigers poured towards him at the lope and it came to the crunch (though one hopes it didn't literally come to that) he stood like Custer or Casabianca. Good boy, bang, bang, bang.

*31 December 1981*                     **Nancy Banks-Smith**

# Falkland factoring

Is there a correlation between the Falkland Islands and the money supply? Quite probably; after all Lord Kaldor and his colleagues at Cambridge succeeded in correlating monetary growth with the incidence of cholera in West Central Scotland and the coming of Christmas. I see no reason, therefore, why the Falklands Factor (FF) should not be added to the government's list of economic indicators. It might even manage to devise a Medium Term Falklands Strategy (MTFS).

How shall we define FF? The Prime Minister attempted to do so at Cheltenham Race Course last Saturday and where better to rally the nation to a new sense of unity and purpose. FF, by the narrower measure (FF3), is the knowledge that 'we can do it,' that 'we haven't lost the ability.' It is 'the spirit of the South Atlantic – the real spirit of Britain.'

This, she said, caused shipyards to adapt ships ahead of time and dockyards to perform refits faster than anyone had thought possible. If we could do it in war why couldn't we do it in peace? And, she went on, 'Just look at the Task Force as an object lesson. Every man had his own task to do and did it superbly. . . . By working together each was able to do more than his best. As a team they raised the average to the level of the best and by each doing his utmost together they achieved the impossible.' Try that at British Leyland.

Later in this same astonishing speech, she proposed a broader measure for FF (FF1) which incorporated the 'new mood of realism in Britain.' In this she included the realisation that it was no good printing money to accommodate inflation. The Government had abjured such a disreputable way of proceeding and, increasingly, the nation wouldn't stand for it. People were now confident enough to face the facts of life. 'The battle of the South Atlantic was not won by ignoring the dangers or denying the risks.' (Ergo, the Falklands were recaptured as a result of the government's control of the money supply). And, with a final flourish of logic, she added: 'And that's why the railway strike won't do!'

While Mrs Thatcher was at Cheltenham the Chancellor was at Cambridge, and where better to deliver a long dull lecture on his economic policy? Sir Geoffrey gave two explanations of FF. First, he said, it had increased confidence in our ability to see difficult decisions through. By this he presumably meant that the winning of the war would assist him in meeting his monetary targets. Secondly, he said, turning to the supply side, events in the South Atlantic had 'graphically demonstrated the supreme importance of individual heroism and personal endeavour, of people – not institutions – working together against enormous odds to turn humiliation into victory.'

Note the careful parenthesis '*not institutions.*' It was the soldiers and sailors who won the war, not their nationalised industries – the Army and the Navy. Sir Geoffrey, presumably, would favour the privatisation of the armed forces. As it is, his vision is of enterprising mercenaries, driven forward by the incentive of their pay packets and prepared to lay down their lives for the PSBR. The Battle of the South Atlantic was won not on the playing fields of Eton but on the enterprise zone of the Isle of Dogs.

At Cheltenham the Prime Minister quoted Churchill. He usually springs to mind with the mention of war. Churchill said: 'We must find the means and the method of working together not only in times of war, and mortal anguish, but in times of peace, with all its bewilderments and clamour and clatter of tongues.'

She might just as well have quoted Harold Wilson who said (on December 12, 1964): 'I believe that our people will respond to this challenge because our history shows that they misjudge us who underrate our ability to move, and to move decisively, when the need arises. They misjudged our temper after Dunkirk, but we so mobilised our talent and untapped strength that apparent defeat was turned into a great victory. I believe that the spirit of Dunkirk will once again carry us through to success.'

There is probably no post-war Prime Minister who had

not at some time or another invoked the Dunkirk spirit. Why improvisation in extremis should be regarded as the talent required for economic success is a mystery. I suppose the reason is that for most of the post-war period we have felt our back to be against the economic wall. That, perhaps, is why we go on thinking and talking about the war, watching films and reading books about it, more than any other nation in the world. The Falklands war brought back some of those folk memories, became part of the nostalgia cult which distracts us from the present and the future.

The war was a Golden Age in which nobody went on strike, and everyone was cheerful and sang in the shelters and made cups of tea for each other. In fact, a lot of people went on strike and fiddled and showed Howe-like enterprise in the Black Market; and, contrary to the myth, morale became very low during the blitz, about as low as on Thatcher-blitzed Merseyside today. Nevertheless, there was during the war a greater social discipline and a stronger sense of national cohesion because there was a sense of national purpose. The problem with peace is that it offers no equivalent of 'winning the war.'

Wars in this century have produced social progress through collective action. People's wars can only be fought if they are given some social as well as military purpose. In the last war the State intervened to insist on fair shares; war production was planned and price control was the essential pillar of the Home Front. When the attempt was made to extend the national unity of the war into the peace it was done by massive social reform – secondary education for all, universal welfare benefits, a National Health Service. There would have been no way the war could have been won, or the economy reconstructed afterwards, in the spirit of Thatcherism.

There might be some relevance to the 'Falklands Factor' if there were today some purpose beyond the subjection of the nation to market forces. It is not easy to take patriotic pride in three million unemployed, declining industries, rundown public services, and a deteriorating urban environment. The power of the State scored a brilliant feat of arms in the South Atlantic but what does the State do at home but malignly neglect the economy and condition of the people?

FF is not going to create jobs for three million unemployed and the Government has no policy for doing so. It has no policy for economic growth, no policy for improving public services, investing in the public sector, or alleviating the condition of the poor and needy. To be sure, combatting inflation is a necessary task and breaking the hold of restrictive trade unionism is a necessary condition for industrial growth: but the patriotic spirit, which the war has supposedly aroused, cannot be harnessed to such nebulous and negativist goals as this Government puts forward.

As patriotism in time of war requires the State to exercise its power, so it does in time of peace. If Mrs Thatcher wishes to cash 'the spirit of the South Atlantic' she will need to set the nation a task worthy of uniting around. It is not difficult to imagine the broad outlines of a Plan for National Recovery which would be consistent with Tory principles. The power of the State would be used to promote new industries and to invest in public services; social policy would be approached in a spirit of generosity and fairness; indeed, rather than invoking the spirit of war it might invoke the spirit of Churchill's successful peacetime administration.

Mrs Thatcher's government came in pledged to arrest and reverse the nation's decline. It was the first government to admit to the condition and to dare to use the word. Three years on, the Chancellor in his Cambridge lecture referred grandly to 'our programme to reverse Britain's decline.' But the government has no such programme, only a belief in market forces now supplemented by the mystical FF.

In so far as decline is a moral condition, a taste of victory may do something for the national morale. But the relative decline of the British economy, and the absolute decline of British power and influence, are due not to moral lassitude but to cumulative errors, neglects and shortcomings spread over a hundred years or more. Indeed, when the history books are written the war in the Falklands is unlikely to be seen as marking the moment of national regeneration but rather as a footnote to a fatal chapter of strategic over-extension, one of the chief causes of the long decline.

Moral revivalism is no substitute for policy. FF is not the elixir of growth. The 'real spirit of Britain' may be 'the spirit of the South Atlantic' but the real Britain is a stagnating economy, still rising unemployment and a depleted and uncompetitive manufacturing industry. The Prime Minister's race course vapourisings show an earnest wish to enlist the patriotic spirit of the nation in the arrest of its decline but they show also that she has not the slightest notion of how to go about it.

*7 July 1982*                                          **Peter Jenkins**


## Ode here, what can the matter be?

'Flexible minds got together and rejigged their perception – and came up with the answer. If this had been offered to us in the first place, we would not be here now.' Lord Victor Matthews.

*When flexible minds get together*
*A re-jigged perception takes place*
*Questions become 'how' not 'whether,'*
*And answers flow forth at a pace.*
*Great ships sail an ocean of subsidy.*
*Grim governments reach for their purse.*
*When rejigged perceptions move flexibly*
*The borrowing requirement gets worse.*

*Oh jig me a flexed reperception,*
*Oh flex me a jiggery poke,*
*Hard talking, no hint of deception.*
*A story of plain business folk.*

*When malleable minds meet contextually*
*Then changing dynamics can come.*
*Cash limits perform ineffectually,*
*To the tune of a rather large sum.*

*Say boo to the yards of Korea,*
*Say nuts to the nips of Japan,*
*If there's public opinion to fear here,*
*Those who never could, suddenly can.*

*Oh context me a chap who is malleable,*
*Oh give my dynamic a change,*
*Straight dealing is always most valuable,*
*A story of price, in my range.*

*When politics is the purveyor,*
*With patriots tied to the stake,*
*Then here's your Atlantic Conveyor,*
*Forget all the profit you make.*
*Those things that might have been easy,*
*Add a tear, and they suddenly are,*
*With a government queasy and squeezey*
*Pursued by the Express and Star.*

*'The train about to depart from*
*Platform Six is for British Rail*
*to boast about on the Today*
*Programme, World at One,*
*PM, BBC and ITN News,*
*The Nine O'Clock News, News*
*at Ten, The World Tonight,*
*Newsnight . . .'*

*9th July, 1982*

*Oh jig me a flexible roster,*
*Oh flex me a deal that is vague.*
*A story for counting the cost. A*
*Quotation to rival Al Haig.*

31 July 1982                                              **Leader**


# MPs bore for Canada reserves

The Commons was formally asked yesterday to repatriate
the Canadian Constitution, or rather to patriate since, like
a Brixton-born black, it has never actually been home. It is
as British as you, me or Mr Enoch Powell.

You may feel that, what with inflation and the ASLEF
dispute, it is a little late in the day for the Westminster
Parliament to be devoting valuable time to giving Canada
its independence, all 3,851,801 square miles of it.

Perhaps you even thought it was independent already or
as independent as a country can be that close to the United
States. Or even that a one-line bill saying: 'It's all yours'
would suffice to dispose of the residual constitutional rights
in the British North America Act (1867), the fourteen amending acts, not forgetting the Statute of Westminster (1931).

Alas, as a number of MPs were indecently eager to point
out yesterday, life is rarely that simple. It may be a rum constitutional business, but it is an even rummer political one.
Exotic figures like Mr Trudeau, Quebec's Rene Levesque
and the Red Indians of Canada – some of whom were stalking
the bill in the gallery yesterday – have to be considered.

But there was a human side to yesterday's drama, or
rather to the lack of drama for like all great historic occasions
– Magna Carta or the SDP's Kensington convention – it
was shatteringly dull. At the centre of the interest were a
number of decidedly unexotic characters who hung around
the building looking for trouble.

These were Westminster's doughtiest proceduralists,
worthy MPs without whose vigilance we would all sleep less

soundly. Names like Powell, Walker-Smith, Maxwell-Hyslop, English and Sir Bernard Braine, the Tory Island Specialist who was yesterday tackling his largest-ever land mass.

These men do the dangerous work at the legislative coalface. There is flexible rostering and the dust is awful. They have to wear special protective clothing: the black three-piece suit. The trouble with these legendary figures is that they are at their happiest when being exceptionally boring.

Yesterday they were having a really good time. Cabot may have discovered Canada in 1497 but for them it is still a virgin continent, rich in untapped possibility for conquest.

At the start of the debate there was a flurry of activity as they started hacking their way through the forest with various technical inquiries.

Mr Michael English, the Labour MP, made a promising start by repeatedly interrupting Mr Atkins on a point which was lost on almost everyone except Mr English (a really exclusive point), but he tired after a while. Mr Enoch Powell made a menacing inquiry early on. He asked if the Government's reluctance to amend the bill extended to deletions. Unlike the others, Mr Powell's meaning is usually all too clear. He wanted to delete the whole constitutional code.

But yesterday's prize was easily carried off by Sir Derek Walker-Smith, QC, the former Health Minister who approached the bill with what he said was dedication but 'a natural reluctance' – of which he showed no sign.

Sir Derek was splendidly pompous and systematically incomprehensible. It was a grand sight. At seventy-one he cannot be far from retirement. We may well have been watching Walker-Smith's Last Stand with strong overtones of Mr Justice Cocklecarrot's last case for Sir Derek peppered his speech with learned references, Latin tags and quotation from Burke, Clausewitz and Sir Ivor Jennings.

As MPs glazed over it became clear that Sir Derek was refusing to support the bill until the Canadian courts had sorted out Quebec's latest action. So that was it! Walker-Smith defending Quebec from the English.

It was too much for Mr Jonathan Aitken, the great-nephew of Lord Beaverbrook, who attempted to scale the Heights of Abraham and capture Sir Derek. Like Wolfe before him, he succeeded only with some difficulty by muttering loudly: 'You've got it wrong.' Sir Derek disagreed.

*18 February 1982*                                   **Michael White**


# A little fling

*Dear Mary*

Starting at college again has brought Jane out in a new rash of non-specific irritability. Coming home, she walked in on me saying to Josh, *poor* Mrs Thatcher. Immediately, her face went critical. Poor? she said, why poor? Jane, I said, Mrs T's only son Mark is lost in the desert, that's why poor, and she's been crying about it. I don't believe it, said Jane. What do you mean, you don't believe it? I said. It says so on the news. I could feel myself getting all hot under the collar, I don't know why. Jane, how can you *not* believe that a woman and a mother gets upset and cries when her only son is lost in the desert? I just don't, said Jane.

So then we had a long boring wrangle, with me saying of *course* Mrs T. was crying, *naturally* she was crying and Jane saying huh and yeah and in a pig's eye. Really, I was confounded. And then Jane says she's only doing it to win the next election, like those Hollywood stars who are always getting lost and things and then they pop up with their pictures in the papers and everyone says aaah. Jane, I said, how can you *be* so cynical, how can you . . . but we had to stop there because Josh came out from under his papers and said would we mind taking our high-level political discussion elsewhere because he had papers to go through.

Two days later, Jane slaps a newspaper in front of me and says there, what did I tell you? I know, Jane, I said. He's been found and very nice too. But listen, says Jane and she reads out Mark saying 'We were not lost. We knew where we were, although we weren't where we were supposed to be.' Jane, I said, it's no good knowing where you are, in the

Sahara, if nobody else knows where you are. You can't sit around in the sand saying I know where I am to the vultures, can you? Well, *he* did, said Jane and we were into another long boring wrangle. Mary, I'm all for young people having a healthy disrespect for politicians but to deny them all human feeling *and* accuse them of manipulating yours. Well. The trouble with Jane is, she simply doesn't know how to argue, either. She doesn't know the *rules*. Then, of course, I got your letter saying Mrs T. wasn't crying and it was all a plot to take our attention off the rail strike. Oh *Mary*.

To change the subject quickly, I had a little fling this week. V. embarrassing, really. My tiny swain Carruthers phoned and said would I like to have lunch with him and I'd said yes before I'd thought at all, it just popped out. I mean, I'm happy to have lunch with anyone from Carruthers up – and from Carruthers there's a long way up. So, after I'd scrabbled in the cupboard trying to find a skirt and asked Mrs Next-Door to come in and laugh at the baby, there was Carruthers at the door, looking ever so dapper in an elfin suit and a weeny anorak. And, Mary, you won't like this, over the Steaks Diane in this quite posh restaurant, Carruthers said I love you.

It was terrible. I didn't think I'd heard him right and I said what? and he said I love you again. At which, a piece of Steak Diane got itself stuck in my throat and I coughed and spluttered and Carruthers punched me in the diaphragm because he'd read that Colour Supplement where it said that's what you do and my eyes streamed and this dreadful Mafia-figure in a dark suit came over and asked us to leave. Obviously thought we were having some ghastly marital hulla-balloo. Like me saying, dear, there's something I've got to tell you, we're hopelessly incompatible because you only come up to my elbow.

I didn't tell Josh. I mean, I didn't *not* tell him, I just didn't tell him. You can't go around telling your husband that his wife has been told she is loved by half a male person, can you? I'm still quite amazed, myself. If there were only two of Carruthers, one on top of the other, I might be a bit thrilled. When I got home, Ben was there, sent home from games because of the snow and reading some magazine. Look, Mum, he said, there's this whole lot of men and women advertising here about wanting to meet and describing themselves and that but, Mum, why do they say at the bottom 'Object Matrimony'? Like, if they object to matrimony, why do they advertise? So I explained that one and he said, oh, and then he said, Mum, why do they say 'Looks unimportant'? Why do they want people who look unimportant? Honestly, Mary, that child makes my back flare up. OK, so he can finally read, but what good's that if he can't make any sense of the words? Or was he having me on? I don't like to ask in case he wasn't.

And to add to my burdens, Josh said this morning that the papers he'd been going through were actually Tom's manuscript of the *Flasher's Guide to Feminism* and, Martha, it's good you know, really very droll, ha ha. Ho ho, I said to the baby, highly risible, I'm sure. But then he went off and left a large package on the kitchen table for me to post, with the address of a Famous Publisher on it. That's his way of making sure that I'm involved, an accessory after the fact. So I can't say, afterwards, nothing to do with me because he'll say but Martha, you posted it. So I didn't. I took it upstairs and stuck it under hundreds of pairs of laddered tights in my laddered-tights drawer. We'll see.

Mother has ushered herself into my life again, via the phone. She said, Martha, I was deeply hurt when you put the receiver down on me and some people would find such behaviour impossible to forgive but I am a Christian woman and I am prepared to forgive and forget. Never mind forgiving me, just forget me, I nearly said. But didn't.

Yours trapped in the family's bosom,

*Martha*

*20 January 1982*                              **Jill Tweedie**

# Don't say bra, say bust bodice

Dame Emmeline wore X-ray pince-nez capable of lasering through the regulation blouse to the contraband bust bodice and the beating heart beneath.

Ros and I had cut two bust bodices, the official term for bras, from the blackout, having read with admiration the chapter in *Gone With The Wind* where Scarlett O'Hara cannibalises the curtains. It did not, in the thrill of the idea, occur to us that, when the light was switched on, two illuminated busts would signal cheerily to Hitler's hordes. Dame Emmeline, whose oration On the Occasion of Two Gels being seen Eating Chips in Keswick, is still spoken of in the same breath as Cato on Catiline, spat on her hands and delivered herself at some length On Giving Comfort and Support to the Enemy.

Two small and suggestible juniors, with no busts at all, burst into passionate tears.

Dame Emmeline herself sported that undivided bust, swathed in maroon marocain, popularised by Queen Mary. On that prominence the pince-nez, starting wildly from their perch at some transgression, would come to rest. Whereas Queen Mary resembled the Jungfrau, a glittering cataract of white, Dame Emmeline looked more Helvellyn, cloud capped with flying wisps of grey. I used to think she was God in drag.

She was said to have evacuated the school overnight from Brighton to Keswick with a Baedecker in one hand and a bible in the other. And, eventually, back again. The school believed in perpetual motion and the mountaineer who climbs 'because it is there' would have felt at home with us. We were ringed with the things and on every half-holiday, it seemed, scrambled up some damn crag, leg sinews snapping like guitar strings.

Dame Emmeline in the school magazine: 'On a perfect October day, forty-three girls climbed Great Gable, sixteen climbed Scafell Pike, seventy-nine climbed Helvellyn, sixteen bicycled to the Langdales (46 miles), seven walked all round Derwentwater. I was obliged to go to London.'

I was obliged to climb Helvellyn and I remember it well for, sitting down on that scythe-sharp ridge to eat my packed lunch, I dropped my pork pie. It bounded away down the slope, giving little leaps of delight as it hit the ground. A peculiarly solid pie, it seemed to lose no crumb or crust until it skipped from sight.

My very sould was stirred as with an egg beater. Despite rationed food (one bun for breakfast on Dalton Days), I was extravagantly fat. This, however, was hidden by the djibbah, an enveloping garment spotted by the founder somewhere east of Suez and shrewdly adopted to disguise the growing girl at all points.

In lacrosse I was generally put in goal on the theory that I filled it more than most and attackers would go easy on someone in glasses. This was wholly fallacious. They came in like Apache and as the cries of the supporters grew louder – 'G squared D, No. 3' (Grit, guts, and determination, No. 3 House) – I shut my eyes behind my shatterproof specs, and breathed in. This not only helped to fill the space available it also stopped me screaming. 'Played No. 3' says my diary. 'Lost 15–1.'

This monotonous document shows me as indistinguishable from a toad beneath the harrow. If toads moulted. There seems to have been no hour of the day or night when I was not losing something vital to the smooth running of the school, and approval of the staff.

MON: Unpacked. Can't find fountain pen. Very unhappy about it. Prunes and junket.

TUES: Haven't found pen. Bike not arrived. Lost? Snowing.

WED: Found bike, lost 'crosse stick. Felt bitter against God.

THURS: Found 'crosse, lost brolly. Thunderstorm.

FRI: Amy shared fish paste and everyone got diarrho. Minnie (a teacher) said she nearly polished them orl orf.

SAT: Broke my watch that had just been mended for 10s 6d. Wrote bitter poem: 'Rattle window! Blare O Wind! Flail your branches broken free! Though the world be washed away what concerns it me.'

SUN: Rained, snowed, and hailed all the way to church. Terrible man from the United Society of Christian Literature shouted at us. Blew all the way back. Rice pudding decorated with chocolate and cream. Lost laundry book.

MON: Nasty letter from Mummy about pen. Needlework. Seem to have lost stuff for petticoat. Ruth got tooth-ache. Had her rissole.

TUES: Invasion started. Hip, hip. Listened to King G. on the wireless. He talked about the power of prayer. O God help me find my gym shoes.

Forty years on I feel the first stirring of sympathy for those brisk and capable women who daily said I must have taken leave of my senses. My senses, my gym shoes, my laundry book, and my bike. I seem to have survived that whole term somehow without a pen.

In the conservatory which had been converted into a laboratory and dripped despondently, I sat under my umbrella (when not lost) and considered the life cycle of the spirogyra, no less damp and desperate than my own. The spirogyra's lot seemed, indeed, the more blessed of the two. It hadn't lost its gym shoes, it wasn't racked with unrequited love for the history mistress and it wasn't going to be sent out of dancing because it couldn't do the foxtrot.

Deep depressions, in every sense, pursued me to Brighton where, when the wind shrieked, the call of 'Storm clorths, gels!' rang out, summoning all hands to stuff wodges of cloth against the windows lest the school sink. As the Navy had occupied the school during the war, it seemed only appropriate.

'It will be some years before our buildings can entirely recover – if indeed they ever can – from their prolonged occupation by a Number of Men' said Dame Emmeline sombrely. 'For some time there will be many strange erections in the grounds.' But in this, for once, Dame Emmeline was wrong.

*17 May 1982*                                **Nancy Banks-Smith**

# Feeling foreign up the sporran

Mr Roy Jenkins, SDP candidate at the Glasgow Hillhead by-election, has been sharply criticised for attempting to use the ancient Scottish word '*hoddendoon*', which means frustrated, in a constituency speech. It has even been suggested that this is not the sort of word Mr Jenkins habitually uses, and that he has deliberately smuggled it into his vocabulary to ingratiate himself.

*'Ours is a very open marriage. At the moment Harriet is protesting against Tory politics and the state of the Labour party by having a torrid affair with an SDP candidate.'*

*30th March, 1982*

Though Mr Jenkins has not replied publicly to these charges he is said by usually reliable sources to be feeling extremely ramfeezled by them and even to have been driven at times into a state of loundering kippage. The allegations, Mr Jenkins is believed to have told friends, amount to nothing less than a humgruffianly humdudgeon, designed to create the maximum possible mixter-maxter of argle-bargle, flyte and collieshangie.

Mr Jenkins is understood to attribute the circulation of such calumnies to 'a rickle of camstairy clishmaclavers, gilpylike gaberlunzies and murgeoning rinthereouts' in rival political parties. In a speech to be delivered in Hillhead later this week, he is expected to describe the allegations as 'simply the flaffing, fuffing and flichtering of fozy fikes.' And he will advise Hillhead voters not to attach so much as a firlot, forpit or mutchkin of credence to such 'gumple-foisted and wanchancy' attempts to beflum the people of Hillhead.

Reports that Mr Jenkins had been overheard expressing the hope that 'the de'il might nirl the noops' of those guilty of such miscalling, and even that they might be smitten with the braxy, were authoritatively discounted yesterday. And late last night an SDP spokesman said accounts of Mr Jenkins's resentment should not be exaggerated. 'Candidly,' he added, 'he disnae give a plack about it, Jimmy.'

(Sassanach readers seeking elucidation are referred to *Chambers Twentieth Century Dictionary*, Edinburgh, £8.95, though in view of its definition of the word Jenkins – 'a society reporter; a toady' – this may not be much used by the SDP.)

*19 January 1982*                                              **Leader**


# Socialism in one city

It is a mild irony that the man who declined an invitation to the Royal Wedding on the grounds that he hadn't been elected to go to weddings but to run the buses, has now been told by the Lords that he can't do that either. But really, London buses are not Ken Livingstone's biggest trouble. His trouble is a belief, lovely to behold, in the goodness of human nature. He is a syndicalist utopian. He is trying to run London as if it were New Lanark or New Harmony, and look what happened to them.

He was born in 1945 in South London, the son of a Scots merchant seaman and a music-hall dancer. His father went to sea as a boy. In the war, his ship was torpedoed on one of the Murmansk convoys and he was adrift for two days on a wintry, Arctic sea. He recovered after six months and was working as a scene shifter at the Streatham Empire when he met an acrobatic dancer who was doing the round of the halls with Donald Peers. She never had a speaking part. They married and, though Livingstone senior went to sea again as a trawlerman and was away for long stretches, it was a happy marriage. Ken Livingstone's father is now dead, but his mother still lives in London.

He was brought up on the Tulse Hill estate, went to comprehensive school and at the age of eleven – already fascinated by politics – was arguing that if Nasser and Eden wanted to fight at Suez they should each get into a tank and have it out, without embroiling the rest of us. This, of course, says Livingstone, was before he was aware of the full nature of the evil British conspiracy. Having said this, he sits back amused and waits for you to take the bait. He is an agreeable, clubbable man, though he may regard my saying so as a libel.

He has a reputation for devouring political biography but denies this. Mostly he reads science fiction. 'My favourite author,' he says, 'is Ursula Le Guin, who wrote an incredibly powerful book called *The Dispossessed* in which she created a society created on anarchist lines. The anarchist section of this world has left an intensely capitalist world and gone to live on the rather barren moon and share the work collectively, and so on.'

That appealed to him politically? Syndicalism? 'Syndicalism,' he agreed. 'The work is shared and everybody spends a month doing the drudgery work but even in a world which has been *created* along anarchist lines there is still the natural tendency for people, by ability, to have power concentrated around them. And she explores that theme, without coming to a conclusion.'

But had he come to a conclusion? This world, he said sadly, was leadership-orientated.

Yes, indeed, and wasn't he leader of the Greater London Council? 'The least powerful leader the GLC has ever had.'

Come on: surely he and Herbert Morrison of the old LCC were the only two leaders whose names were even known. Names being known, he said, was different from power. The

GLC was now run by the Labour Group, which met every Monday; he had an influence but not a dominant one.

To return to his younger days, what had happened after he left school at seventeen? 'I was sent for training in China, in subversion.'

Naturally. But after that, what had he done in the eight years or so before he went for teacher training? Well, he said, at school he had been a difficult child, undisciplined. He got four O-levels, but then left half-way through the sixth form. Although it was a comprehensive school it was run by a man who had been deputy headmaster at Dulwich College and they still had to wear caps and so on.

He left to get a job and although he was interested in politics his main interest since the second form had been in natural history and animals. So he went to the Royal Marsden Hospital to work in the animal house. He did try to get taken on at the London Zoo as a keeper in the reptile house, but they only took on staff in March.

Why reptiles? 'You've got some 2800 different species of frog and toad, and the diversity, and the way they've adapted, is really quite remarkable. They don't attract the same attention as primates do, or herd animals.'

Mr Livingstone's interest in the political activities of advanced primates came to its first fruit in the late Fifties and Sixties, the time of Pope John XXIII, and John F. Kennedy, and Wilson, his great white hope; but some died, some were assassinated, and others were an appalling flop.

'When Wilson was elected in 1964 I remember trembling with excitement because I believed his government would eliminate poverty. If you were born in 1945 you had no experience of what could go wrong with a Labour government. . . . My generation went through school and grew up looking at the Conservatives as a joke. All these grouse-hunting, tweedy, old gentlemen who were clearly incapable of running anything. We assumed that the abrasive, aggressive Wilsonites were actually going to be better.'

Would he ever again tremble at the return of any political party, of any complexion, and think it was going to put the world to rights? 'No. People have to do it themselves. And you can't hinge it all on a small group doing it for you. I think there *are* people you could take great enthusiasm in getting elected. It would be a tremendous boost if Benn could be elected Prime Minister. That I think would give people a tremendous amount of hope.'

Ah, yes.

'Socialism,' Mr Livingstone continued, 'means people having day-to-day control over their own lives. The move towards socialism means the same movement as there was among Solidarity. It was a reaction against bureaucracy, and powerlessness, and helplessness.'

But then he took his analogy one step too far. 'Bureaucracy is inherently anti-socialist. Witness this place.' (We were talking in his room at County Hall.) And he went on to liken the County Hall bureaucracy to a blood stream from which the Labour administration, like an antigen, was being rejected all the time.

Except, I suggested, that his officers had to come to him and say, 'Yes, Minister.'

'They do. They also come and say, "We think this might not be legal." '

Pity they hadn't said that about the buses. 'Well, nobody believed the law said what the Lords now tell us it means.'

We were to return to buses later, but for the moment went back to his beginnings in local government. In 1973, when he was just about to complete three years of teacher training, he was first elected to the GLC. He qualified as a teacher, but from then on devoted himself full-time to politics. He had been a member of Lambeth Council since 1971. In 1978 he stood unsuccessfully as a Parliamentary candidate in Hampstead.

But the turning point was May this year. He had a safe GLC seat in Hackney but chose to fight a marginal in Paddington. Why? He said he had been eight years in opposition, four in opposition to the old Labour party, and four to the Conservatives. He wanted to do something productive, and making faces at the Tories from the back benches wasn't. If Labour won Paddington they would probably win the council, and he wanted to be sure he was there if they won, but not if they lost. If they lost, he might have become a Labour agent.

As it happens he was lucky. A few months later and the SDP would have snapped up the seat anyway.

Why, when once he was re-elected, and Leader, had he made wild statements about gay rights, and the IRA, and the police, and so on? 'What's wild?' he says, and admits no wildness. These issues have been so much chewed over that I stuck to one, which is his belief that the left could be rounded up in an afternoon and sent to the gas chambers. Had he said *that*? Did he believe it?

'Yes. Look what's happened in Poland, overnight, two days, the whole of the Solidarity activists have disappeared into Labour camps. Many will be killed.'

My clear understanding, and I was sure his too, had been that we were talking about England. Did he believe the left could disappear into gas chambers here?

'No,' he said, apparently changing his answer; but then he went on to say that there was the potential for a military or police takeover here because half the police were trained to use arms and because the army, thanks to Northern Ireland, had the most sophisticated grasp of civilian control of any army in the world. 'They aren't,' he said, 'able to completely crush the IRA, but if we got into general upheaval and disorder on the streets, and the army chose to step in. . . .'

Chose? Of its own free will? 'Of its own free will, because it believed perhaps that we were degenerating into chaos, and that it couldn't rely on Parliament to continue to govern.'

He then put forward the following possibilities. Suppose that Mrs Thatcher continued to fail, was succeeded first by an SDP–Liberal government, and after eighteen months of that by terrible disillusionment. Suppose that then Britain swung either to the far right or to the radical left. If it were to the left, there would be many in the army who would, in good faith, have grave doubts about allowing Labour to take power.

How many generals, or other British officers, did he know, who were likely to behave like that? 'I would guess, and it is only a guess, that within the military the overwhelming political view is a Conservative view.'

I said I had asked how many officers he knew. 'I don't know any at all. . . . The left and the military don't have good links.'

From this statement of views by Mr Livingstone, which demonstrates a complete incomprehension, the more dangerous because he honestly believes what he says, and which reveals a fundamental ignorance from which his parliamentary colleagues, who have met a general or two, really ought to deliver him, I fled to the safety of GLC infighting.

In October the Conservatives brought a censure motion against Mr Livingstone, condemning his conduct as leader. The council meeting was in the afternoon. The Labour group had been sitting all day beforehand and it was obvious there had been a deal. The Labour members had told Livingstone, look, stick to the manifesto, don't say these things that get into the papers, and in return you can stay leader and we will support you. Was that true?

'It's a misreading,' said Mr Livingstone, choosing that word carefully. 'I think the press, in the week or two weeks before that, had gone so over the top that they drove the Labour group into a united stance, and the group closed ranks, because even the people who would want to change me couldn't be seen to change me under that sort of press campaign. 'We came out with something that everybody was quite happy to go home with. I took no part in the whole proceedings.'

And that is as frank a political statement as ever was made, and three cheers for any man who can make it, and with that we passed on to his splendid attempt to run the buses and bring fares down to what people could pay.

On Mr Livingstone's office door there are warnings against Fire, Flood, and Bombs, but none against the House of Lords. But the Labour group had obviously taken legal advice before cutting fares? Yes, he said, before the promise was put in the manifesto. (That was before he was leader.)

And they obviously believed they had the discretion to do it? 'Yes.'

So when did it first appear that they might be in trouble? At first, he said, they had taken Bromley Council's action as a political gambit to get a bit of publicity, but shortly before the first hearing, in the High Court, the council's chief solicitor came in. Livingstone said: 'Oh well, could be a bit difficult.' That was the first warning.

Then? 'Once we'd won in the High Court we felt quite encouraged but our lawyers always warned us that if we went to appeal to Denning we'd be bound to lose, Denning would find it irresistible.'

But Mr Livingstone said that, after the GLC lost in the Court of Appeal, the Labour group were stunned to lose in the Lords on the principle of the right to subsidise. They thought they might lose on a technicality, or on the amount of the subsidy, but not on the principle.

'And in a sense,' said Mr Livingstone, 'the Law Lords have saved Heseltine (Environment Secretary), because he can't get through the legislation he wants to get control over councils but the Law Lords' judgment makes it unnecessary, because it shifts the whole balance of every decision in local government, massively, against expenditure. It takes us back to the Twenties. Since the Second World War, both parties have accepted that local government is there to provide a substantial part of the services of the welfare state. Now the Law Lords have affirmed, in straight language, that our primary duty is to the relationship [like that] between directors of a company and shareholders. It's to make the least expenditure and the best profit: services are secondary. Now that changes the whole attitude of local government since I was born.'

So he was in a hell of a mess? Well, he said, let's see how public opinion developed before 21 March, when the fares would have to go up; let's see to what extent there was pressure on Tory MPs to go along with the Labour call for amending legislation.

Mr Livingstone was mighty cool about all this. He says it's not his way to have screaming fits. At public meetings people come up to him and say: 'You're so reasonable: I can't understand it.' But people didn't want to be yelled at and harangued. He said this was the reason for Mr Benn's big success; he didn't go in for demagogy. It was an imposition to talk to people as if they were at a Nuremburg rally.

I recurred to the censure debate, where the standard of debate, with few exceptions on either side, was dismal. Livingstone was told he was the worst thing to happen to London since the Plague, that he bore the mark of Cain, and so on. But one substantial point made by the Conservatives was that Mr Livingstone's true ambitions lay over the river, in the Commons. Was that so?

Mr Livingstone gave a discursive answer. That lunch time, just before we met, he had gone to the council estate at Tulse Hill where he had been brought up as a kid, to play Santa Claus. He had left the estate when he was twelve and there was nothing there. Now the GLC had at least got them an adventure playground. So working with the GLC could be rewarding. If the council had the policy and spending independence of a German regional parliament, or of New York City, it would be a far *more* rewarding place to work than in central government. He wanted a shift of power to local councils.

To which I replied that, having seen the GLC at play, under both parties, I could only say God forbid. 'Um. If you had real power here you'd attract people of real calibre.'

Yes, but what were *his* ambitions? He said he had no game plan for the future. He was also a member of Camden Council, and was one of the borough councillors coming before the High Court in May. They were being surcharged for paying manual workers £60 a week minimum wage. If he lost, he would be out of elective politics for five years anyway.

The minimum wage he said, would be another great cause; it depended which judge you came before; everyone told him he was bound to win, but they'd said that about the buses too.

Besides, he said, apparently wishing to confess all, Labour might not win the next general election. No one knew what could happen in politics. Suppose twenty-five Tory MPs lost their marbles and joined the SDP, that would be Mrs Thatcher's majority gone and there would be an immediate general election. Or some lunatic might get into the House with a bomb and blow himself and fifty MPs to pieces.

But yes, he said, if I was asking him if he'd like to be an MP one day (which, yes, I was) then the answer was: 'I do.'

I had not expected this religious form of words, and it sounded rather striking. He would then, he said, aim to change the Labour Party, along with the likes of Mr Benn and Mr Scargill, into a force worthy of government.

Syndicalism then showed itself again, Mr Livingstone saying he would want each factory run by its own workers, and each school by the parents and teachers.

Chaos, I said. 'No, no, no. Concentrations of power produce chaos.'

But surely few people could run anything? He said everyone was capable, given the chance, and that there was, for instance, nothing special about him.

Rot. 'No, seriously. . . . That potential's there in everybody.'

In support of this argument, Mr Livingstone cited the class he and his wife Christine used to take at the Elephant and Castle. They used to take the kids to France. Many of the children could hardly read a line, but he used to teach them chess, and after two or three days, some of them could wipe the floor with him. Most of those children had gone on to dead-end jobs, or unemployment, or petty crime, and yet they had a grasp, an intelligence, and a rich ability which English education didn't develop. It didn't give them confidence. 'I mean,' said Mr Livingstone, 'the reason I didn't join the Labour Party until I was twenty-three was that working-class kids do not go out and join things they don't know. They become involved when you take them to it. My confidence came in my twenties, and not my teens, and that's the classic pattern for working-class kids.'

Then, preaching what he calls his Reformism, Mr Livingstone began to talk about ending the waste of a consumer society, even on packaging goods, and about directing investment and imposing exchange controls. I wondered how he proposed to achieve all this without the strong central government which he'd been damning throughout much of the interview. He had at one point said Lenin would be happy in the present centralist Conservative Party.

Wouldn't the strong central government that his Reformism required be dangerous? He explained that at the same time he would dramatically increase the powers of local councils, giving them the right to raise income taxes, control over the police, and run the health service. That, he said, was pure Reformism. In a good year, with money around, the SDP and the Liberals would go along with most of that.

We had got, somehow and ineffably, to the SDP. 'The sort of people who read the *Guardian*,' said Mr Livingstone, 'are scared now because they've been believing all the crap they've been reading about this wicked, intolerant Labour Party.'

But it did tend to be intolerant? 'The Labour Party's incredibly *tolerant*. How many people have been de-selected? The Labour Party puts up with the most appalling characters as MPs and councillors year after year after year.'

He thought that Labour was now being seen as more firmly on the left, and new members were flooding in. He mentioned Press manipulation in favour of the SDP, of which he is convinced.

'Undoubtedly,' he said, 'Shirley Williams is a wonderful person and if she was your next-door neighbour she'd feed your cat and water your roses while you were away. Unfortunately she'd a lousy administrator. Even if they do get in, it will be a pretty devastatingly bad government.'

Then Mr Livingstone came to the happy conclusion that once the SDP had failed, *Guardian* readers would go back to a genuinely socialist Labour Party. In the fervour of this expectation, he had plainly forgotten the military coup which had earlier figured so largely in his scheme of things, but for his own safety I feel I should add a note, especially for the eyes of the General Officer Commanding, London District, that Mr Livingstone had also remarked, apropos of coups, that if there were one tomorrow he would be quite happy, if spared, to go off and do natural history somewhere on the south coast.

*21 December 1981*                    **Terry Coleman**


# The Manhattan weekend

At about five o'clock on a Friday afternoon, it is possible to sense a little something in the air. Those for whom days flow seamlessly into one another will stop in the street and look around, wondering whether the wind has dropped or whether some other climactic diversion is responsible for this feeling of change.

Slowly the clues stand out. George the Florist has buckets of roses on special. Harvey the Cleaner is packed with customers collecting chinos and down jackets. Tomasita, in the Puerto Rican–Chinese laundry, is taking in mounds of shirts for medium starch. The TV guide is the news vendors' hot item. A line had formed by the bank's outdoor cash machine. So there it is: it must be the weekend.

Every city has its own special atmosphere when the week's work is done and the days of gentle rest approach. In New York the weekend is not so much longed for as tumbled across as if by accident. Perhaps because this is a place where so many are out of work or resting, the overwhelming feeling is one of disappointment: two days in which no one will call or return calls.

Perhaps because so many here are lonely, there is a sense of depression. Ahead lie three nights of prime-time TV, *The Incredible Hulk*, *Loveboat* and *Fantasy Island*. On weekends, psychotherapists are not available (there is a Manhattan condition known as Saturday anxiety); maids and nannies expect time off; children are out of school. For some it is a reminder that there are no demands; for others it is a time to complain bitterly that there are so many.

What New Yorkers really want out of a weekend is two days in bed with nurturing – checking into a hospital, for instance, would be ideal. So there is much going away on impulse to hotels where others clean the room and go out in the cold for the Sunday *New York Times*. At this time of the year a lot is made of needing to see the Fall leaves in the country. Doubtless Connecticut is magnificent right now in its plump vermillion and yellow plumage, but so too is Central Park.

For those who cannot afford some cheap rural inn or converted baronial spread in upstate New York, there are substitutes. The answering machine is one: 'I'm sorry but we are not accepting calls right now. Perhaps you would leave your name and number and we'll get back to you,' is a common weekend greeting.

And then there is the croissant. The croissant is Manhattan's national dish. It has everything, this flakey piece of pastry. Forbidden calories suggest a riot of freedom for those who all week are accustomed to biting on something thin, hard and ungiving in keeping with the lives they lead. In bedrooms given over to filing cabinets, video machines and metal storage units, the croissant brings dreams of sun-dappled attic rooms in Paris, lovers and romance.

There is no tradition of the weekend joint of beef in Manhattan, of the honest potato and gravy steaming in the jug. There is only this croissant, warm, illusory and oozing butter, suggesting the endless breakfast and a day lost in a haze of orange juice or bloody Marys. With greasy thumb prints on the Lanz of Salzburg flannel nightdress. The croissant is a Me food – to each her own, nothing to share and no one else to demand the best bits.

The weekend is the time for relationships, which is what New Yorkers experience in place of friends. It is a curious contradiction that Americans, known the world over as the friendliest of souls, have a problem with friendship. The casual give and take, the continuity over time and change become too complicated for those accustomed to shedding lives like skin. Relationships are easy: they exist out of time and place in the depths of the inner Me and the new You.

Those engaged in them do not make demands like, 'Will you have my children for the day?' or 'May I borrow your car?' They indulge in intense talk and a chemistry that allows fantasies to bloom and then, fortunately, wither, so that new relationships may be engaged upon with all the mystery of the unknown. Relationships mean being loved and appreciated and sharing an ashtray of low-tar menthol cigarette butts. Friendship means making an effort reserved usually for those who might be needed later for passing on work or a better job. The office ethic ('I like you until you get fired') permeates a culture that understands best the expression: 'I'll scratch your back if you'll scratch mine.'

So the weekend is a time when those who are alone wish that they were not and when those surrounded by others talk wistfully of Being Alone. And in the play-grounds in the park the results of this dichotomy are there in all their confusion. These are father's days on the swings and slides when those with visitation rights try to recapture the familiarity of daily life.

Voices are too loud, encouragement too hearty, the newest Marx motorbikes stand out for the bribes they are. On the side benches sit the newest relationships, trying not to look bored or resentful and wondering whether croissants and chemistry were really meant to lead to this. But Monday will come around, telephones will ring again, and everyone will soon be back on hold.

*17 October 1981*                              **Linda Blandford**


# Claud Cockburn, the knockabout Marxist

When I heard of Claud Cockburn's death it seemed scarcely credible; he survived so many illnesses and other hazards that he had come to seem indestructible.

In the past we have often talked about dying; as in so many other matters, he was con and I was pro, he being fond of insisting that he proposed living to be 100 as his father almost had, and I equally insistent that I looked forward keenly to leaving this life, though with the prospect of continuing an existence elsewhere and on other terms.

Thus it is ironical that I should be writing his obituary rather than the other way round. But then everything to do with Cockburn has a way of turning out to be ironical – he, a Communist who never once visited Communism's Holy Land, the USSR, but who spoke always nostalgically of the USA, and decidedly preferred millionaires to commissars, and P. G. Wodehouse to Karl Marx; an agnostic who felt more at home among the superstitious Irish than the ideollogues of the London School of Economics, and sat more comfortably in the columns of the sedate *Irish Times* than of *Pravda* or *Tribune* or – dare I say it? – the *Guardian*.

Cockburn was, in fact, a revolutionary with little or nothing of the theorist in him. It was action, not ideas, that appealed to him; he was all for kicking over the apple-cart, but with no more than a vague concern as to how the apples fell. In this he was the exact opposite of Orwell, who was always preoccupied with the end and little concerned with the means.

Thus in the Spanish Civil War Orwell lambasted the Catalonian Stalinists for their ruthless suppression of all other brands of Communist, whereas Cockburn having embraced the Republican side, just wanted it to win by fair means or foul, in the same sort of way that if there ever had been a revolt of the animals as envisaged in Orwell's *Animal Farm*, he would almost certainly have joined them against the humans.

I first met Cockburn personally some thirty years ago when I was editor of *Punch*. He was then living in Youghal, near Cork, in the Irish Republic, where he had withdrawn when he broke with the Communists and left the *Daily Worker* – as it then was – not, as far as I know, for any particular reason; just because in a general way he could no longer go along with them.

There could scarcely have been any doctrinal difficulties; I remember Cockburn telling me how when the Communist Party line switched from supporting the 1939–45 war as being anti-Fascist to condemning it as being imperialist, he was writing leaders in the *Daily Worker* and managed to switch over from one position to the other without any heart-searching or embarrassment.

Cockburn went to Berkhamsted School at the same time as Graham Greene, whose father was headmaster. On his mother's side he was related to Evelyn Waugh; his father was in the Consular Service, *en poste* in Korea when his son Claud was born.

After Oxford – Keble College – and some travelling, Cockburn joined the staff of *The Times*, and in 1929 he was sent to New York and Washington, where he served under a famous correspondent, Sir Wilmott Lewis.

He worked comfortably with Sir Wilmott – a Ramsay MacDonald knight – and in reminiscing about him built up one of his best comic creations.

Ten years later when I was Washington correspondent of the *Daily Telegraph*, Sir Wilmott was still going strong. How precisely Cockburn came to, as it were, walk straight out of *The Times* and into the *Daily Worker*, is something that, to the best of my knowledge, has never been convincingly recounted – certainly not in the three versions of his most readable and entertaining autobiography.

Was it some sort of Damascus Road, or, better, Farringdon Road, quasi-mystical experience, or the consequence of much rumination and argumentation, or, as I tend to believe, just an impulse, appealing because it was bound to disconcert those, as the Book of Common Prayer puts it, set in authority over us – a favourite pastime?

Whatever the explanation, it happened, and Cockburn became thenceforth notorious as the opposite of a mole – an avowed Communist and promoter of revolution on classic Marxist terms.

To his great joy and pride at roughly the same time his sometime friend and colleague, sometimes known as Otto Katz, confessed before being executed that he had worked as a spy for Colonel Cockburn, head of British Secret Intelligence, and Senator McCarthy included Cockburn in his list of the world's most dangerous Reds.

His most notable journalistic achievement was to bring out his own paper, *The Week*, a cyclostyled three sheets which circulated during the Neville Chamberlain appeasement period, and included among its readers such distinguished personages as President Roosevelt and Lord Mountbatten.

An excellent and detailed account of this venture has been written by his wife, Patricia (*The Years of the Week*), a lady of great charm and intelligence whom he had the good sense to marry after some other matrimonial ventures, and who has loved and cherished him over the years.

It was in the course of editing *The Week* that Cockburn developed his notion of news as being, like beauty, in the eye of the beholder rather than an independent factual entity, and years later, long after *The Week*'s demise, found in *Private Eye* an organ for continuing to apply this theory.

He was one of the *Eye*'s original contributors, and continued up to the day of his death contributing regularly to it. His three sons, lapped as they were from their earliest years in journalism at its liveliest and most audacious, are all practitioners.

Some rapscalion of an Irish priest is bound to say a requiem Mass for him, to which, with many memories of happy times spent together, I venture to add my own: 'God rest his soul.'

*16 December 1981*                    **Malcolm Muggeridge**


# Epic at the Lyric

Listen, you have heard of the plight of our theatres and how the dearth of monies brought grief to its folk. Then at high summer's hour there came an acting-man, Julian Glover, begging no more than to tell the doings of Anglo-Saxon poem, Beowulf, alone without others.

Little did he ask for stage set, beyond ale-cup, jug and wood-made table. His sword was on the chair, wooden-hangings held high above him. Lights glittered. Then at first-night he leapt, lavish with his word-hoard to the stage-place, white-shirted, and modern of trousers. The ancient poem was in his heart.

He spoke: 'We have heard of the thrivings of the throne kings.' People wondered if they would tire of such word-shapes – would boredom beat in their brains, or horrors hold them? He told of a hero and Grendel, the monster from the Moorland, whose eating ended the lives of men he munched in the Mead Hall, Heorot. Beowulf, a dreadnought, plunged down the swan road, deep (the stage-light blue-hued) for battle and not bloodied, battered him dead.

It is for me to say how Glover gave tongue to this. Bold of voice, smirking at the ways of fate, he stood tree-tall, roared as Beowulf, quavered as Wulfgar the Herald. He moved much, knocked a stool to the mead floor to show the might of Grendel about to gobble a thane. Exceeding strong he was.

Then, in snatches, he spoke in Anglo-Saxon sound. People thought to admire his mind, packed with words, and how John David, maker of scene-sights, sent him sombre into darkness and out again to light of day.

It is fitting to ask that a man should so pass good time in theatre-place, unpack a word-feast of such sort?

Glover dared much. He gave ancient grief and glories, life to dead words. Yet I bewail the way of things, that an acting-place should be a bastion for such as this. Amongst deeds of dare-do this was good. Elsewhere let such happen. In theatres not.

*20 July 1982*                                    **Nicholas de Jongh**

## The roar of the greasepaint

Recognisable at fifty paces: the Rembrandt nose, the barrel trunk. The voice is unmistakeable even farther off, a rich blare of gold klaxon. Leo McKern is the actor as character, the irascible made flesh, and quite a lot of it.

He welcomed us to the Richmond Theatre, where he had never played before, singing the praises of the old Theatre Royal in Brighton, where he had played many times. 'Ah, the sound in that theatre....'

He made it seem like a large Stradivarius, parked down in Sussex. For two weeks there, and then in Richmond, he had been playing in Frank Gilroy's *The Housekeeper*, which arrives at the Apollo next week.

'It's great to make them laugh – and it's great to stop them. That's marvellous!' He rolled his good eye. 'Course when you've got an idiot audience in a play like this, they like it when half-way through the first act suddenly they can laugh, and nod and whisper "Ah, it's a comedy!" But then there's a very solid second act, so you've got to control their laughter.'

How? 'With an expression, by pausing, by a change in the tone of voice. It's different every night. That's why I never sign a contract for more than six months. You exhaust the part, you become incapable of giving good performances.

'Not like Edith Evans. She never changed her performances – not one iota. And she didn't like it if anyone else did. The slightest difference in a pause or intonation when you gave her a cue and there would be *notes* next morning.'

McKern was last seen commonly in *The French Lieutenant's Woman*, where he played the doctor who advises Jeremy Irons about the curious lady of the Cobb. He is not comfortable on 'that bloody merry-go-round called the international film industry. I find films very stressful.

'You have little or no rehearsal time unless it's a very big film, and the take they decide to use may not be the best from your point of view, though it is from the director's. I suppose now I could ask to do it again, and there is no doubt they would.' He looked intently, to be sure the significance was not lost: to be able to ask for another take is a mark of status.

Still, he enjoyed filming the Fowles novel, he said, and waved the book away. 'A film can't do what a writer's style does. Any adaptation of a novel, even a very good novel, even Dostoevsky is bound to end up as a story with a beginning, a middle and an end. You can't convert a writer's style into a visual image. It's like trying to paint the Seventh Symphony.'

He still expresses some exasperation at the way the part he played in the original production of Robert Bolt's *A Man For All Seasons* – the Common Man – was dropped from the film because it was a non-realistic device the cinema could not cope with. He played Thomas Cromwell instead.

He was so frustrated by a year spent on the West Coast of Ireland making *Ryan's Daughter* – mostly waiting for the weather, a notorious non-arriver in that part of the world –

that he upped sticks, family and Volkswagen and drove back to his native Australia for a couple of years.

As a lad there, he was an engineering apprentice until an accident damaged his left eye, which after three years of unsuccessful treatment had to be removed. Odd jobs till he was conscripted, aged twenty, into the army and dumped in a Sydney barracks as a clerk. Bored, he joined an amateur theatre group for something to do in the evenings. The traditional route to the professional stage at that time in Australia was through the amateur ranks.

McKern came to England in 1946, got an Arts Council tour a couple of years later, with a niche as M. Simon in Miles Malleson's translation of *The Miser*. When the production was taken into the Old Vic season, he went with it. That brought him under the eye of one of the crucial figures in the McKern career, Tyrone Guthrie.

One of the special things about Guthrie, McKern said, 'was that he handled crowds in an extraordinary way that no one else seemed able to do. He was very adventurous, one of the early experimental directors, before Brook and the directors' director. His sensitivity and receptivity were vital. Not an actor's director by any manner of means. He hired people for parts because he knew what those actors could do – that's 50 per cent of a film director's job, and that's rather the way he worked.'

He was with Guthrie at the Vic again in 1962 – Subtle in *The Alchemist*, a stocky Iago, *Peer Gynt*. ('Never meant it to be a play, you know, Ibsen. Hated it, hated it. He said it had been written as a poem, not a play, and from an actor's point of view he was right, in four hours, you have about four minutes' off stage, apart from the two intervals.)

'We opened the new Nottingham Playhouse with *Coriolanus* – I played Menenius – and Guthrie set it in the French Empire period. "I'm so bored," he said, "with seeing lots of actors rushing around in *sheets*." But throughout that play, every aspect was enlarged by that setting. The Roman mob became the French Revolution. Coriolanus, the Man of Pride, in plumes and gold cuirasse.'

For a moment, he seemed borne up on a great glittering

balloon of memory, his actor's voice caressing the pride and the plumes and the exquisite bright curves of the word 'cuirasse'.

'And values, it enhanced the values. Now, well, directors perhaps emphasise one aspect of a classic play – and that's fine, he would have gone along with that. He always said there was no such thing as a definitive production or a definitive performance.'

Nevertheless, McKern has defined one role, at least, for the watching public – *Rumpole of the Bailey*. With his court-room histrionics, his tavern manners, his chambers chorus, Rumpole is a kind of legal Falstaff, and McKern could still be playing him if it were not for his fear of being trapped in unending series.

But there is still something eternally Rumpolesque about some aspects of him. At one point he produced a definition of acting that he had prepared over the years: 'Acting is a passionately private indulgence which one hopes will be noticed.' Whereas with some character actors the real man seems colourless, the character far away in the property wardrobe, McKern seems to carry it around with him, like his two packs of Henri Winterman small cigars, his lighter, the key to his dressing room.

'I'm sixty-one now, I've been on a diet for four weeks – lost half a stone so far. I have been up to sixteen stone, you know. I'd like to get down to fourteen. Much fitter then, feel much better.

'I indulge myself, I smoke, I drink. I have a couple of glasses of red wine in the pub after the show, and then I go home and finish the rest of – oh, a bottle, I suppose. And I sleep well. It's good for your digestion, your gut and your bowel.

'You know, I have the blood pressure of a man of twenty-five. Whenever a doctor takes it, he doesn't believe it, he has to take it again.' He gave that intent look again. He was clearly very proud of his blood pressure.

*20 February 1982*                    **Hugh Hebert**

# Noble vision of King Lear

Adrian Noble's production of *King Lear* marks the finest directorial debut we have seen on the main Stratford stage since Trevor Nunn astonished us with *Revenger's Tragedy*. In its emphasis on the spiritual education of Lear and Gloucester it is perfectly traditional. But what is startling is Mr Noble's stress on the wild, grotesque, Absurdist comedy that accompanies the process of moral enlightenment.

The opening scenes tell us we are in for something remarkable. Bob Crowley's set, the courtyard of some gaunt, grey castle with inquisitive faces appearing at high, eye-like windows, suggests a metaphysical Colditz. On Lear's throne the Grock-like Fool and Cordelia sit facing each other, with their necks at opposite ends of a taut halter, as if lunacy and virtue were inseparable. And as Michael Gambon's Lear enters, arrayed in gold, to awesome music you see he is a figure as wedded to power as an Eisenstein potentate.

What follows is a delirious descent into a world of barbarism in which farce and tragedy are umbilically linked. Mr Gambon, thunder-voiced, leaves us in no doubt as to Lear's cruelty as he takes a riding crop to Goneril, a 'degenerate bastard', and as he issues his curse of sterility with malevolent relish. He is a tyrant patriarch clearly in need of redemption. But Mr Noble's originality lies in seeing Lear and the Fool as a spiritual double act descending into the pit in a mood of desperate vaudeville.

We have had in the past old Fools, young Fools, sad Fools, cruel Fools; but no Fool quite like that of Antony Sher. With his red nose, coxcomb, patch trousers, violin case and deformed, heavily booted feet, he is a strange mix of Grock, Little Titch, Beckett's Didi and Max Wall. But above all he is Lear's alter-ego: the visible mark of his insanity, His Master's Voice as he perches on his lap like a ventriloquist's doll, the conscience of the King who, when he cries 'I am a fool – thou art nothing,' echoes the very zero gesture Lear himself has earlier made. When Lear finally stabs him in the hovel through a pillow case in insane fury, it is exactly as if he is killing off the capricious, wild, uncontrolled part of his own nature.

It is a brilliant notion: Lear and Fool as two sides of the same coin. And it is dazzlingly executed by both Gambon and Sher. My only reservation is that Mr Noble, blessed with a strong governing idea, clouds it with an excess of pictorial invention in the central themes. Thus the storm scene is played with Lear, a black-booted Captain Ahab, and the Fool perched atop some vast swaying crow's nest that looms out of eddying smoke. And what with Poor Tom emerging from an underground hovel like a mad jack-in-the-box, spintering the stage floor, and with the hovel itself filled with swirling feathers, you almost lose sight of what Mr Noble is after. It is always thrilling to see a young director exploring the visual possibilities of theatre: but at times less might mean more.

However, even if Mr Noble slightly overloads us with images of moral anarchy and confusion, his production acquires a steely stoic strength in the last two acts. The Dover Heath scene, with Gambon's Lear roving his kingdom with a slapstick, has an inevitable pathos.

But what is fascinating is Noble's insistent stress of un-redeemed cruelty: Edgar slays Oswald by breaking his back with a staff, and the fraternal duel between Edgar and Edmund is a bare-chested, bloody, unchivalric combat that ends with Edmund's head being dumped in water. Even at the last the characters look out into the future in a spirit of sceptical uncertainty.

It adds up to an overpowering portrait of a tough, crazed, cruel, irrational world; Albion gone mad. Although this makes Gambon a public rather than a domestic Lear, his performance has the strength of a rock and limitless capacity for fury: he doesn't often rend the heart but he certainly chills the blood.

I was also taken by Jenny Agutter's Regan, lethally removing a silver brooch from her hair for the blinding of Gloucester, by Jonathan Hyde's Edgar, poleaxed by the recognition of his father in the hovel, and by Chris Hunter's dangerous, saturnine Oswald. But coming out of this production I was reminded of Wolfit's legendary advice to an actor about to play Lear: 'Watch your Fool.'

Mr Noble renders that advice redundant since, instead of an acting competition, we have the first production I have seen in which Lear and the Fool become as indispensable to each other as Laurel and Hardy, body and soul, ego and id.

*30 June 1982*                                **Michael Billington**


# Mark Arnold-Forster

Mark Arnold-Forster, the *Guardian*'s Diplomatic Editor, has died after a long series of illnesses endured with the greatest fortitude and good humour. He was a splendid journalist and a generous, caring man.

Mark was born in 1920. He went to Gordonstoun and won a place at Trinity Hall, Cambridge, but then came the war.

Before he himself died a few months ago, the *Guardian*'s J. R. L. Anderson remembered Mark's war. 'It is commonly believed,' he wrote, 'that when, in the darkest days, the German battle cruisers *Scharnhorst* and *Gneisenau* slipped out of Brest they proceeded up Channel unimpeded by the Royal Navy.

'That is not strictly true. A small motor torpedo boat which had been on patrol in the Channel was on her way home when suddenly she saw the mighty *Scharnhorst* appear out of the mist. What to do? The MTB was going home, she had no more torpedoes, and her sole effective armament was a .303 rifle.

'Her commander, a young naval officer called Mark Arnold-Forster, had no doubts. "We must try to shoot the captain," he said. A hurried conference indicated that the cook was the best shot on board the MTB, so he left his galley and took post with the rifle while Mark closed on the *Scharnhorst*.

'As soon as they were within range, the cook opened fire, peppering the *Scharnhorst*'s bridge. When the magazine was emptied, Mark decided that it was time for a strategic retreat, and the MTB in turn vanished into the mist.

'This story may be apocryphal in some details, though I hope not, and it doesn't matter, because it illustrates perfectly the courage with a sense of humour that made Mark.

'In war, he was one of a legendary band of small-boat commanders whose exploits put heart into the beleaguered British people. With Peter Scott, R. P. Hitchens, Christopher Dreyer and Eardley Wilmot, and a handful of others whose names became famous in those now almost forgotten days, he showed that the national tradition of Britain as mistress of the seas still had living force. He would have been at home in Nelson's navy, doubtless boarding and capturing cheekily a number of rich prizes.'

Emerging with a DSO, a DSC, and three mentions in despatches, in 1948 Mark approached A. P. Wadsworth, Editor of the *Manchester Guardian*, for a job. 'I should very much like to see how you shape as foreign correspondence,' wrote Wadsworth, suggesting a 'rather unconventional' approach.

'I think you might go out to Germany for a month and put in some solid investigation. You would not need to send messages to the paper. . . .'

The injunction to 'send no messages' clearly and characteristically cut no ice with Mark. Within three weeks, Wadsworth was hailing his views 'with great interest and enjoyment. . . . I had no idea that you had such a light, humorous touch.'

Arnold-Forster was the *Guardian*'s Berlin Correspondent for the Soviet blockade, then United Nations Correspondent, then Labour Correspondent and Deputy London Editor – two jobs he ran in tandem.

Based in the *Guardian*'s old Fleet Street office above the Post Office, Mark was determined the *Guardian* should compete, particularly in his own field of industrial and political news, with an effectiveness which disguised its slender resources. No matter if *The Times* had three labour reporters and the *Telegraph* four; with the aid of one part-time deputy he would keep up and often get ahead.

He had many notable exclusive stories. He gave the world Harold Wilson's description of the Labour Party's organisation as 'a penny-farthing bicycle in an atomic age'. He was also underlining the implications for British politics of the contrast between the German Social Democrats revisionism, enshrined in the Bad Godesberg declaration, and the British Labour Party's continuing adherence to its constitution long before such comment became fashionable.

This appetite for exclusive news lasted throughout his career, even when his principal task had become leader-writing. During Britain's negotiations to enter Europe and afterwards he produced a string of memorable disclosure stories, and did more, and earlier, than any other British journalist to alert the country to the wilder lunacies of the Common Agricultural Policy.

His second quality, unmistakeable in the *Guardian*'s small and understaffed London operation before its move from Manchester, was leadership. In his reporting, he led by example, and faced with the considerable production problems of the London office, he was always determined nothing should prevent Manchester receiving its service from London in time to get it on to the breakfast table next day.

A colleague of those days remembers: 'As a friend and as a boss, he was kind, considerate and had great insight into, and interest in, other people's problems. To know him in peacetime was to understand why he was a great commander in war.'

But the old London days of the *Guardian*, and the branch office in Fleet Street, were perhaps too peaceful, too un-challenging. In 1957 he left the *Guardian* to join ITN in the pioneering days as deputy to the editor, Sir Geoffrey Cox.

From there, he moved to the *Observer*, first as Chief Reporter, later as News Editor and Lobby Correspondent (where he was one of the first, and few, reporters to sense that Sir Alec Douglas-Home would emerge as leader of the Conservative Party).

In 1963, there came a parting of the ways with the *Observer*. Mark approached Alastair Hetherington at the *Guardian*. 'This wanderer hopes very much that he can presently return.'

He returned as Chief Leader Writer to a paper now settled

in Gray's Inn Road and to a role that, in essence, ended the wandering.

Here the breadth of Mark's experience – the contacts, the wisdom and the absorbing interests – began to have full play. If there was a collision in the Channel, he was first to the charts, berating the offending captain for his doziness. He was fascinated by the cross-currents of the Europe he found at first-hand in Berlin. He enjoyed the company and trust of politicians and mandarins.

Through the years that most of us here knew him well, Mark Arnold-Forster was the complete professional journalist, with individual enthusiasms that scored across the surface of professionalism.

No one, thinking coolly, examining the structure as well as the personality of events, was surer to reach original conclusions and set greater historical context.

In his last years on the paper – often in poor health but never in poor spirits – Mark became Diplomatic Editor, based in the Foreign Department, and was able to bring his expertise in international affairs fully to bear.

Much of what he wrote there, even in the last few testing months, is original and profound. We are proud to reprint in today's paper the last of his contributions to the Britain and the World column that he founded.

But words on a printed page do not adequately reflect the loyalty and personal assistance that many on this paper have cause to be grateful for.

Mark Arnold-Foster drew the two parts of his name from an ancestry full of literary and political history – Matthew Arnold and E. M. Forster are both in the family trees. His marriage to Val Mitchison (as we noted at the time) established a new branch where a kinswoman of the author of the Haldane reforms (which created the Territorial Army and the office of the Chief of the Imperial General Staff) was joined by a kinsman of H. O. Arnold-Forster, a Tory Secretary of State for War.

Mark wrote several books, one of which, *The World At War*, became an international bestseller, somewhat to his surprise. His home in London, filled with children, was also open house to countless friends, and to what seemed a perennial flow of refugees, people who needed help in political storms.

He was a slight, wiry man who came at the end – despite his wanderings – to seem the bridge between the old *Guardian* and the new. He will be much mourned and sadly missed.

*28 December 1981*                                      **Peter Preston**


# The Great Brazilian Ant War

Father's business was telegrams, and my early teachers had trouble in persuading me not to write everything out in capitals, including punctuation. There were other consequences, serious only to me, chief of which was that I spent my childhood in Brazil, moving up and down the coast from one cable station to another, between sojourns at different schools.

The style of the telegram was well suited to Father's temperament and laconic utterance. The few letters he wrote to me at school were code telegrams reporting household events with the curt urgency of agency messages. As:

TORPEDOED BENSUSAN FAMILY ASHORE HERE FOLLOWING FORTNIGHT OPEN BOAT STOP SON BIMBO COMPANY FOR YOU STOP COOK SACKED DRUNK MIDDAY STOP RUMOURED YOU PUBLIC FISTICUFFS CONFIRM OR DENY STOP YOUR BED CONSUMED BY TERMITES REPLACEMENT IN HAND STOP GUAVAS RIPENING HENS EXCEEDING QUOTA MOTHER SENDS ABRAZOS THIS STATION FINGERS CROSSED ACCEPTABLE DAD.

It wouldn't have upset me to have stayed at school for the holidays, since school at that moment was a house tucked between skyscrapers a forty-yard dash from Copacabana beach. However, this was as close to euphoric as any communication I'd ever received from Father. I decoded 'fingers-crossed acceptable' as Paradise. It was actually the port of

Victoria, capital of the state of Espirito Santo, and about 300 miles north of Rio.

And indeed, the only disappointment was Bimbo. I'd always been passionately fond of the sea, and liked nothing so much as trips to the small offshore islands. Bimbo, to my amazement, had been soured by his experience in an open boat, and never wanted to go near the sea again. When I eagerly sought details of the torpedoing, and showed myself willing to admire any part he might have played in the subsequent journey, he only said bleakly, 'You'd better ask my mother. She's been torpedoed twice.'

Between two good dazzling beaches, the cable station itself was mounted on a granite headland, whence the cables passed through a fissure in the rocks to splay out, via the guts of Atlantis and relay centres like St Helena and Ascension, to Africa, on some point of which my uncle Arthur managed a station for the *Eastern Telegraph*. (It was always said in the family that, to keep the peace between my father and his brother, they had to work on separate continents.)

At some unimaginable distance these cables stretched also to Britain, home to father, but not to me. On this subject there was some tension between us. Any extravagant dress, conduct or speech of mine that he disliked, he disparaged with the tense comment, 'Brazzy!'

Near the 'works', joined to the residential quarters to make a long rectangle supported on rock at one end by pillars, a small conical structure stood apart in the compound. It was the incinerator, exclusively for burning thousands of miles of paper tape, pitted all its length by Morse perforations. A lot of this stuff escaped and fluttered in streamers from the cactus and sisal all around. This annoyed Father as a blight on the landscape almost as much as the orchids did, which he regarded as parasites. He would conscientiously collect it all.

What did dead telegrams matter? I asked. 'They're confidential,' he'd say. But who could read these holes in the paper? Surely not the milkman, the fellows who stole the fruit, the guy with the bullock cart who brought the carboys of acid?

'I can read them,' he said. He could too, as easily as if it were print. He ran them along his fingertips, alternately smiling, frowning, pursing his lips. I asked for a sample, but he shook his head. I provoked him by saying I didn't believe they made any sense.

Then he relented, and read a long irritated complaint about delays in iron ore shipments. Boring, I said. 'Yes, I chose a boring one,' he replied. 'They're not all boring. One must be careful of espionage.' I said I wasn't a spy. 'No,' he agreed. 'If you were you could read Morse.'

This was irrefutable. I thought I'd swot up some Morse and read the tantalising secrets for myself.

Many hours of private deciphering revealed that a Dr Amaral would be arriving at Santos on a Friday six months ago, and that Clara was ecstatic at the birth of a child to Maria. A third made no sense to me because below the Morse lay a further code, to which the key was in Father's safe. I decided he was too finicky about espionage.

Regularly, Father told us that it behoved us to be ambassadors for Britain. We should take note of the Brazilian satire of Yankee bragging, and try to be factual and restrained about our successes. We must foster good relations with the neighbours. These aims were periodically at risk in Victoria because of our abundant crop of fruit.

From the enclosed veranda that went all round our long box of a bungalow on stilts, one could, at the back, look down at the rock disappearing into a sandy compound. This was a mass of cashew, guava, mango and banana trees, with a high wall at the perimeter that seemed to be scaled by every Brazilian youth who ever looked at it.

This fretted the wife of Father's colleague, the manager. She was a tall angular woman who lived in jodhpurs, and tried to teach me to split sugar cane with her throwing knife at twenty paces. She let herself become paranoid about the invasions of the fruit stealers. 'Nothing ever ripens on these trees but young men,' she would snort.

Goaded at last beyond patience by the sight of their mocking, agile forms, she saddled up her horse, and, together with a pair of bloodhounds, she launched a one-woman cavalry charge. As she went, she blazed away with a revolver, but kept the knife for close quarters.

For one long moment after the shots the world took pause for breath. Inert with shock, a score of youths dangled in the foliage as if they were indeed the fruit of the trees.

Then a concert of outrage swelled up. Monkeys gibbered, cockatoos screamed. The vultures, from being a shimmering turbulent black lake against the bone-white sand, exploded upwards like clusters of flapping rags. Then from all angles a barrage of squashy fruit came pelting down on the lone horsewoman. It proved, as it drenched her in juice and pulp, that she'd been wrong in saying it never ripened.

Father felt she'd deserved every pip of her rout, and said it was lucky the coconuts grew on the other side of the house. He blamed her in part for the sad sequel, when some of the boys came back by night, and poisoned the dogs. To restore the *modus vivendi*, he had all the fruit gathered and heaped in mounds beyond the wall as an offering, like Danegeld.

It had the contrary effect, though. Not one was touched. It was all left to rot. By the following year he had a name for being a good man, and it did his heart good to see the trees full of thieves again. It meant we were forgiven.

But in the case of the Great Ant War, which accidentally made an awkward dent in the good-neighbour policy, Father was the aggressor.

He could live with snakes and spiders and mosquitoes; he liked bats and lizards; he made positive pets of the geckos, contemplating them motionless for minutes on end as they throbbed on the wall. He did not care individually for the vultures, which roamed free range the way some people had chickens, but he approved of them as representing a form of order, being protected by the law as scavengers. Ants, however, much as he admired their discipline, were foe.

He viewed them as a sort of insect *Wehrmacht*. One night they marched in column through his lovingly tended vegetable garden, leaving a blank shallow depression where his best produce had been.

An urgent indent went out for formicide. When it came, it was a lorryload. An extra nought must have been cabled.

Father mustered his full strength: including Natalia the maid and Margarida the cook, the two gardeners, the man who happened to be with Natalia, introduced as her brother, myself, and even Mother's knitting circle, who fanned out looking puzzled, a dozen Brazilian matrons with half-made cablestitch sweaters clasped to their busts like shields.

We set up iron tripods which soon glowed red hot as we pumped the burning powder down the burrows, driven on by bellows. In a radius of about a hundred yards from the main orifice, gouts of opaque, catarrhal smoke clotted the air. As C-in-C, Father sported his peaked cable-ship cap and a red neckerchief, and stood with legs apart and binoculars ready on the apex of a rock megaphoning orders.

The first auburn trickles of refugees soon were followed by seething writhing cascades, as the earth vomited up ants in their thousands, their millions. It was appalling, a kind of Armageddon.

The gardeners, a young Negro and an old man of Indian stock, hopped about frenziedly in bare feet as they shovelled earth and the fuzz of ants back down the holes, tamped them down, and struck wildly at ants that pincered their flesh.

After we'd sealed the last of a dozen exits, when the smoke was dispersing and Father was saying the job was done, the phone began ringing.

It was the first of several neighbours with similar messages. Smoke and ants had emerged at a great distance. They didn't want our ants, they said. They'd thank us to keep them, and would we kindly stop choking people with our poisons.

Ridiculous disputes about the ownership of ants went on for weeks. A lot of rude words were spoken, and threats of reprisal. I dreamed of ants converging on us from the whole estate, ants like thumbs, marshalled by Rommel. 'Limited theatre wars are impractical,' Father would say thereafter. 'All local wars tend to become general.'

Discussing this point with Father twenty-five years later, as we walked the platform of a little English country station, waiting for the train that would take me back to London from a visit to him in his retirement, I asked if he remembered the failure of our blitzkrieg on the ants. He halted, and said,

'You were a dervish that day. Ten out of ten. It was a bad business with the neighbours though. They were very slack. The climate, you know. Even Dr Pombal, who came for tennis, was a disappointment. They gave the ants asylum, you see. And in the end they came back. Bound too. Like everything in Brazil, you couldn't get on top of it for long enough. Every effort we made was an absolute wash-out.'

To cheer him, I sang a few lines of a Carnival ditty of that time:

*Tem galinha no bonde,*
*Tem, tem, que eu vi!*

'There are hens on the tram. There are, there are, I saw them.'

Father glanced at me suspiciously. He'd always bracketed Carnival with malaria, as a malign disruptive fever, likely to recur. Then he said abruptly, with a shy smile, '*O loucomotivo*'. My train wasn't due. In both directions the track curved away vacant into the still, quilted English countryside. What locomotive? Then I twigged – it was our old pun, '*O loucomotivo*'. It was forged in an episode that had enormously embarrassed him, but in Victoria it had underlined him as a man bent on being a good neighbour.

Our connecting link between the cable station and the town spread round the inner harbour had been the tramway. Trams in Brazil had been called *bondes* ever since the British who built the lines had floated an issue of bonds. In Victoria the trams were open on both sides, with running boards giving access to a row of lateral wooden benches.

As these often sagged with the weight of men riding them, who sometimes climbed on the roof as well, the conductor had to get off and on again at each stop to collect the fares. It was a sweaty, congested and, as the song observed, often a chicken-infested journey.

The first time he made it, Father achieved some sort of record by being turned off. He had transgressed the by-law that said he must wear a jacket. Now Father, meticulous in every way, was a dapper dresser. Every morning as he dressed, at the point where he stood with his hair brushed back, in his shirt and tie and socks, and fastened his suspenders, he called out 'Five!' to Mother in the kitchen, to let her know the number of minutes before she should place his breakfast on the table.

He was mortified by this public rebuff. Most of the men on board the *bonde* were bare legged, in swimming costume. But they complied with the decency rules by wearing pyjama tops. In his immaculate linen, Father was made to walk.

But this was a relatively slight chagrin, compared with the misadventure in which he starred as a hapless central figure some moons later.

On a latter stage of its trip out of town, the *bonde* crossed a tidal marsh, in which ancient shawled women with sacks and sharp stakes probed the tangle of scrub for giant crabs. There were no stops, after one day a crab and a cockerel had fought to the death.

There was one driver who found this untrammelled stretch irresistibly exhilarating. As soon as the salt air entered his nostrils, he imagined himself a speed king on the measured mile. He'd take the *bonde* over the causeway as fast as it would go, his foot all the while banging up and down to clang the bell, at the rate of a needle in a sewing machine. For this he was widely celebrated as *Pedro o Louco* – Pedro the Madman.

When Father boarded, one late afternoon, to come home in the usual way, he was innocent of any idea that he'd become an important figure in Pedro's private life. As soon as Pedro saw him, it later transpired, he decided to mark his feelings by giving him the ride of his life.

When the surge across the causeway began, neither Father, cocooned as always from the crowd by his newspaper, nor anybody else among the 150 or so passengers, was aware of any change from the norm of screaming wheels, hammering bell and agitated poultry. The first intimation of a special event came when Pedro took the curve at the end without decelerating, and the starboard complement of travellers on the running board was ejected by centrifugal force into the mud, together with the conductor.

The next turn stripped the vehicle of outriders on the port

side. Amid a cacophony of grinding iron, the insistent bell, babbled protests of vendors and shrieking chicken-and-crab-women, Pedro pursued his headlong course. Like a bemused bull, the swaying tram went belting on, gathering a swarm of excited pariah dogs in its wake, ignoring all stops and other traffic. Until, that is, it reached the gates of the cable station, where Pedro abruptly switched off.

Father habitually sat on the one bench facing backwards, with his 'wallet to the engine.' Extricating himself from the embrace of a stout person who'd been pitched into his lap, he alighted to find Pedro already on the ground, waiting to greet him.

Pedro straightened his peaked cap – and saluted. 'Not as quick as your submarine cable, *Senhor*,' he said, 'but I hope you enjoyed your Express home to the bosom of your family, to whom long life and happiness.'

A circle of outraged passengers rapidly formed around them. Much as he loathed being the centre of attention, Father hoped that by humouring Pedro he could make a dignified exit. He thanked him for his special attention, but stressed the engineering skill that had made this lightning trip possible. Machinery must nevertheless be treated with respect, or deaths may be the result.

Pedro nodded genially, then rounded on his audience, and ordered them to make clear passage for the distinguished engineer. He shouted down the loudest and called them dogs, whom he, as Captain of the tram, was entitled to refuse conveyance at any time. The row increased as Father made his escape into the compound.

From hints and whispers we pieced together the explanation. It seemed that Pedro had fathered the child of Natalia, the young cable-station kitchen-maid. Both had expected her to be dismissed, so when he had the news that she was to be kept on, he'd expressed his joy in his own exuberant way.

She would certainly have gone if my own role in the matter had been known, which was to act as a runner between Natalia and Pedro. I liked Pedro. He showered me with *balas futebol* – sweets wrapped in pictures of footballers. I often waited for his tram purely for the pleasure of the dash across the causeway.

But I kept quiet about the fact that I also carried the overtures of other men to Natalia, and arranged assignations. If Pedro had got mad with me, even being Father's son might not have helped. I imagined him driving his tram through my bedroom.

After coining the pun, *O Loucomotivo*, to describe Pedro and his *bonde*, Father never liked to mention the incident. For some time, though, it was hard for him to forget. People waiting for a tram would point at him, and say it would be better to wait for him to be gone, in case his driver was in the mood to compete with the urgency of a telegram.

*28 November 1981*                    **Alex Hamilton**

# Index